IMAGES
of Aviation

Alaska's Bush Pilots

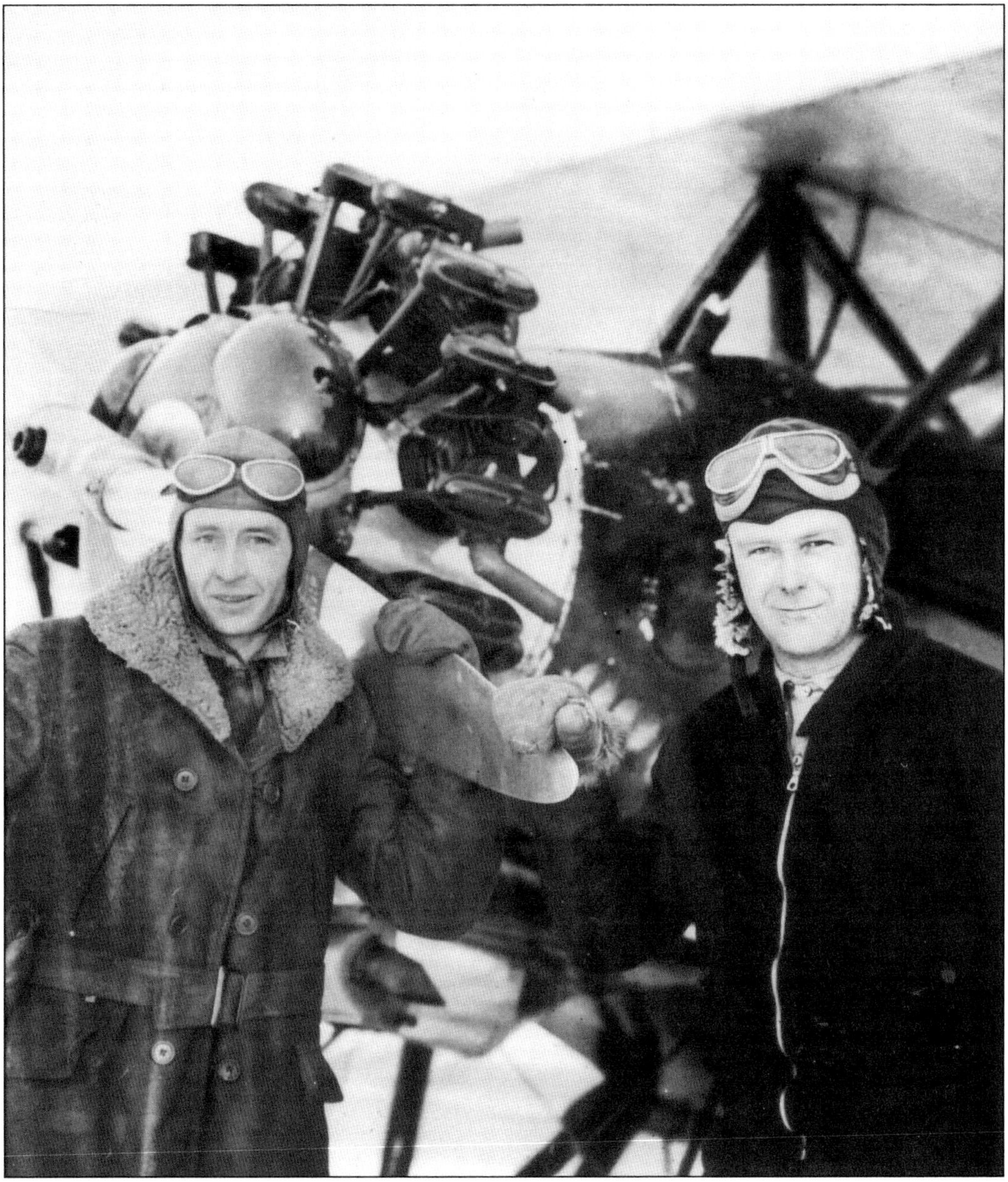

Percy Hubbard (left) and Ralph Wien pose in front of a Laird-Swallow (NC2774). This photograph was taken while Hubbard was learning to fly in December 1929. Ralph Wien, Noel Wien's older brother, was cofounder of Wien Alaska Airways in Nome. Noel and two Catholic priests died in a crash of a Bellanca at Kotzebue on October 13, 1930. The Kotzebue airport in northwest Alaska is named Ralph Wien Memorial Airport. (Courtesy of the Alaska Aviation Museum.)

On the Cover: After the gold rush of the early 1900s in the Seward Peninsula, fur coats and clothing became popular means to ward off frigid temperatures. Later pilots donned fur seal pants and fur coats trimmed with polar bear or wolverine fur. This unidentified passenger is prepared for the cold, wearing a beaver hat and a coat made from mink pelts. (Courtesy of the Alaska Aviation Museum.)

IMAGES
of Aviation

ALASKA'S BUSH PILOTS

Rob Stapleton with
the Alaska Aviation Museum

ARCADIA
PUBLISHING

ISBN 978-1-4671-3183-4

Published by Arcadia Publishing
Charleston, South Carolina

Printed in the United States of America

Library of Congress Control Number: 2014932918

For all general information, please contact Arcadia Publishing:
Telephone 843-853-2070
Fax 843-853-0044
E-mail sales@arcadiapublishing.com
For customer service and orders:
Toll-Free 1-888-313-2665

Visit us on the Internet at www.arcadiapublishing.com

To all the pilots who have navigated their way in the skies over Alaska and forged aviation history while doing so.

"There are old pilots and bold pilots but no old bold pilots . . . except in Alaska! Alaska's full of them."

—Shari Hart

Contents

Acknowledgments

Any publication effort requires the cooperation of many people during the process. The Alaska Aviation Museum has opened up its files, archives, publications, and collections for the production of this historic volume.

Thanks go to Shari Hart, executive director of the Alaska Aviation Museum, for allowing me to sort through the photographic collections and work with the museum staff. Inspiration and knowledge are important, and several members of the museum's board of directors provided that. Former board chairman and founder of Peninsula Airways Orin Seybert provided background and contacts for attaining additional information on specific aircraft and pilots.

Board member Chuck Miller and the Centennial Celebration group and its main sponsor, the Alaska Airshow Association, provided funding and publicity for the flights to rural and urban areas in Alaska. This celebration was especially important, as it provided a platform to illustrate the influence and impact that the military has had on aviation in Alaska. Miller and Jane Dale's presentations during the Centennial Celebration flights included those on the Black Wolf Squadron and the Douglas World Cruiser, adding perspective to this book.

Following the stages of the renovation of the 1931 Fairchild Pilgrim in the museum's restoration hangar made me feel like I was in the early 1930s. Researching the history and talking to master woodworker Mitch Mitchell and George Dorman, Al Fleener, and Dick Benner, who were some of the team members on the renovation, gave much insight into the building and subsequent uses of this aircraft. When the Pilgrim was completed, Terry Holliday piloted the lumbering tail-wheel aircraft and explained its flight characteristics and added information underlining the Pilgrim's historic importance.

Thanks are also due to Arcadia Publishing, especially to Jeff Ruetsche, whose guidance and patience were necessary to complete this book.

The support given for this project by the Alaska Aviation Museum staff, its board, and its members underscores the commitment to meet its mission: "Preserve, Display, Educate and Honor the History of Aviation."

—Rob Stapleton

Introduction

The history of aviation in Alaska is a fascinating story that, as told by all the different players, may be more entertaining than factual. All that is left of the days gone by are some mementoes, letters, and stories told by others. The one aspect of the past that does exist plentifully are photographs. Many of the photographs in the Alaska Aviation Museum's collection exist elsewhere, but the museum houses several collections from private individuals that helped illustrate this volume.

This book is intended to trace the timeline of aviation in Alaska from the first flight through the hallmarks of influential aviation activities. Within those activities are not only the lives of aviation pioneers but also the development of aircraft to meet the demands of the land and eventually the expansion of commerce before Alaska became the nation's 49th state. Many images show the style, places, and types of aircraft for eras gone by.

The images in *Alaska's Bush Pilots* tell the story of a different lifestyle, quiet and serene sometimes and frigid, blustery, and tough at other times. Whether flying over stretches of frozen sea, navigating between towering walls of granite, or landing on glaciers, rivers, and gravel bars, these pilots operated a fine line between fear and luck.

The people in the early era of Alaskan aviation were tough. Where possible, their colorful stories have been added. Because of them, the aircraft that they flew were pushed farther and faster into the Circumpolar North. Among these aircraft were de Havilland, JN-4 Jenny, Hisso Standard, Fokker F.III, Fairchild, Ford Tri-Motor, Stearman, Stinson, Hamilton Metalplane, Bellanca, Travel Air, Noorduyn Norseman, Boeing, Beechcraft, Cessna, Curtiss, Douglas, Lockheed, Pilatus Porter, Short Skyvan, and Waco.

The pilots who flew these planes for hire included the following: Toivo Aho, Frank Barr, Vernon Bookwalter, Estol Call, Jack Carr, Chris Christensen, Joe Crosson, Roy Dickson, Jim Dodson, Carl Ben Eielson, Bob Ellis, Archie Ferguson, Harold Gillam, Percy Hubbard, Jack and Ruth Jefford, Mack McGee, Russ Merrill, Owen Meals, Hans Mirow, Jack Peck, Ray Petersen, Frank Pollack, Bob Reeve, Charley Ruttan, Murrell Sasseen, Scotty Scott, Mudhole Smith, Slim Walters, Noel, Ralph, and Sig Wien, Oscar Winchell, and Art Woodley.

From Alaska aviation's beginning in 1913 to the present, many events inspired the use of aircraft. Among the milestones are the following: the Douglas World Flyers; the Black Wolf Squadron; the search for Carl Ben Eielson; the crash involving Will Rogers and Wiley Post; World War II; the consolidation of air services that made up the Wien dynasty; and the Cold War, from 1959 to perestroika and the eventual fall of the Soviet Union. Along with those events was the formation of air services and their sales, which led to the eventual formation of Alaska Airlines. These are all turning points in Alaska aviation history.

This book highlights the men and women who loved aviation and realized its potential and many who died doing what inspired them—flying. While developing this book, the centennial celebration of aviation in Alaska took place. The first flight of a manned aircraft in Alaska took place on July 3–5, 1913. One hundred years later, it is fitting that World War II–era aircraft graced the skies of Alaska from May to July 2013, flying into locations still not on a road system in Alaska.

These aircraft and pilots presented the history of Alaska aviation to local communities along their route from Anchorage to Valdez, Kenai, Homer, Iliamna, Dillingham, Bethel, Aniak, McGrath, Galena, Nome, Kotzebue, Bettles, Fairbanks, and Wasilla. This was done with the help and planning of many of the Alaska Aviation Museum's board members and the Alaska Airshow Association and its supporters, not to mention the use of the museum's Fairchild Pilgrim and a Japanese Mitsubishi Zero.

Military aviation in the past and to this day has had a huge influence on the lives of Alaskans. With bases in Fairbanks and Anchorage, the skies are daily filled with the sounds of jets and helicopters training in defense of our nation.

The Alaska Aviation Museum, through its exhibits, honors many of the bush pilots who greatly deserve recognition, ensuring that they are not forgotten. In reading the biographies of Alaska's bush pilots, the reader will find that they experienced difficulties and challenges. And those struggles are not forgotten, having been preserved in each photograph. In many ways, this book could also have been titled *Alaska's Bush Pilots: Flying the Hard Way.*

One

THE EARLY YEARS

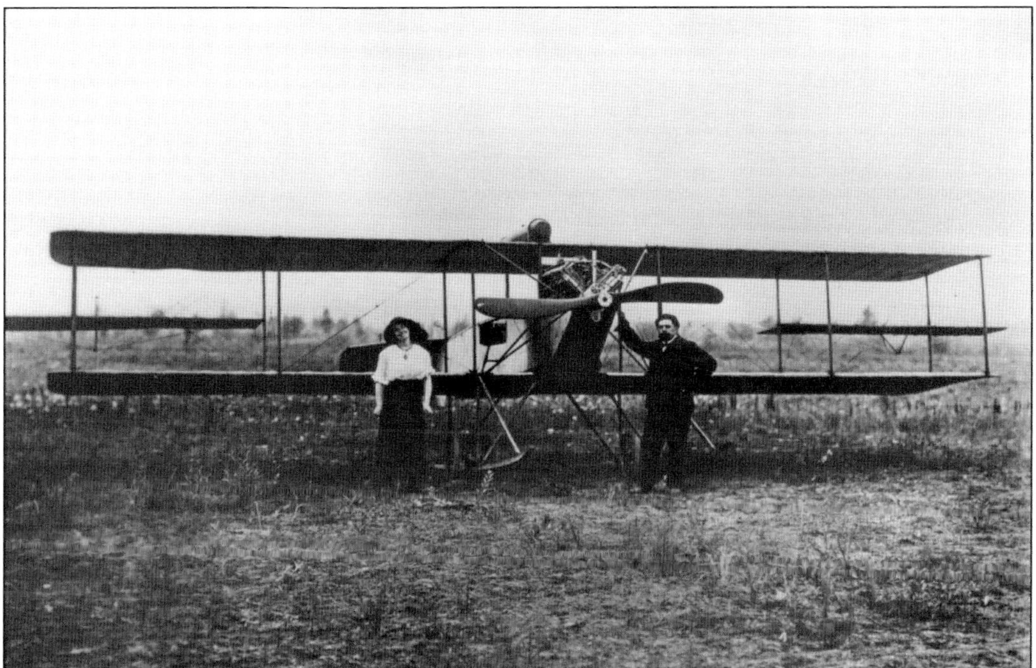

The first aircraft to fly in Alaska was the Gage-Martin tractor airplane, designed by James V. Martin. He and his wife, Lily, were hired by a Fairbanks businessman to put on an aerial exhibition in 1913. The Martins packed up their aircraft, left San Francisco, and headed north to Fairbanks. According to reports by the Fairbanks newspaper, the Martins gave five performances in early July. Fairbanks residents, eager to see the aircraft fly, sat on rooftops to see the Gage-Martin rather than purchase tickets for bleacher seating at Exposition Park. The event involved the first Alaskan aircraft flight, but it was a money-losing venture. The flights, held on July 3, 4, and 5, were plagued by poor fuel that would not allow the aircraft to gain much altitude. The flights were thus much shorter than planned. (Courtesy of the Alaska Aviation Museum.)

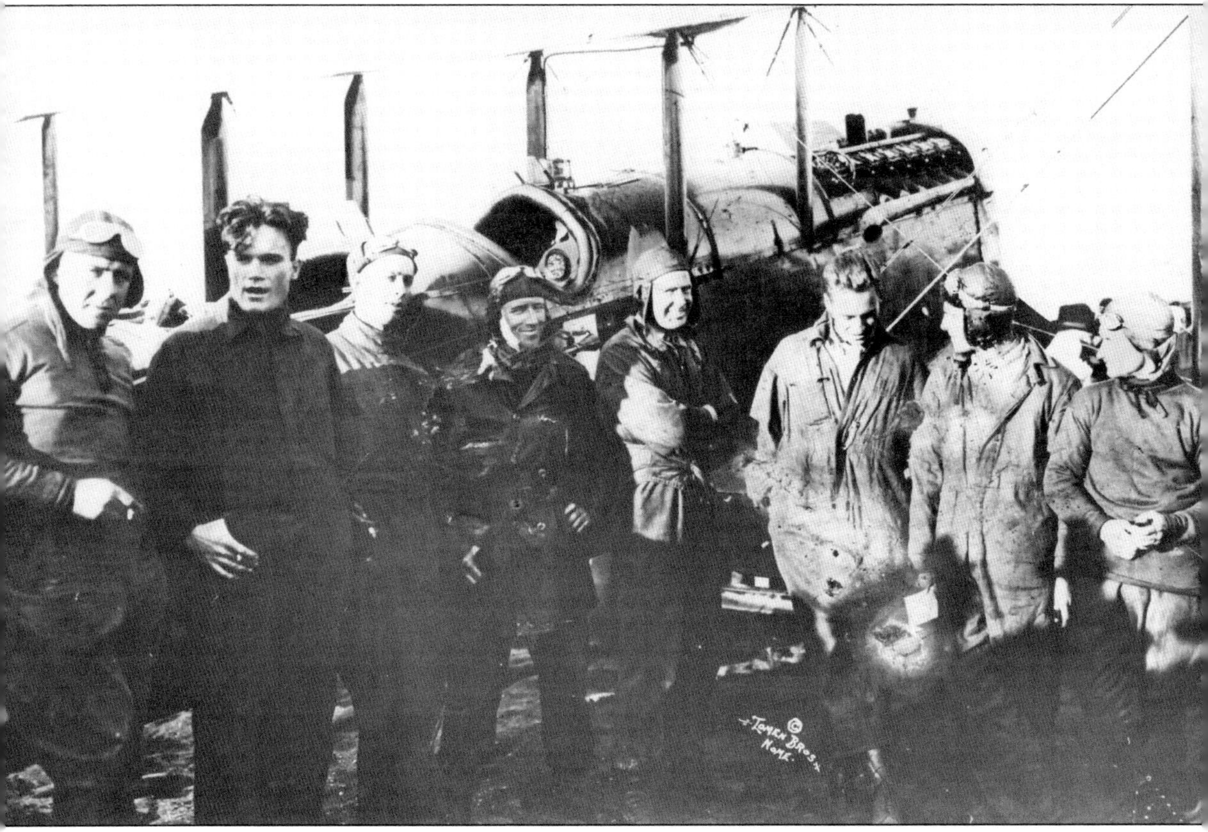

Members of the Black Wolf Squadron, four de Havilland DH-4Bs and eight crewmembers flew from New York to Nome, Alaska. Departing New York on July 15, 1920, the squadron reached Nome on August 23, covering 4,500 miles in 55 hours of flying time. They are shown shortly after they arrived in Nome, Alaska. (Courtesy of the Alaska Aviation Museum.)

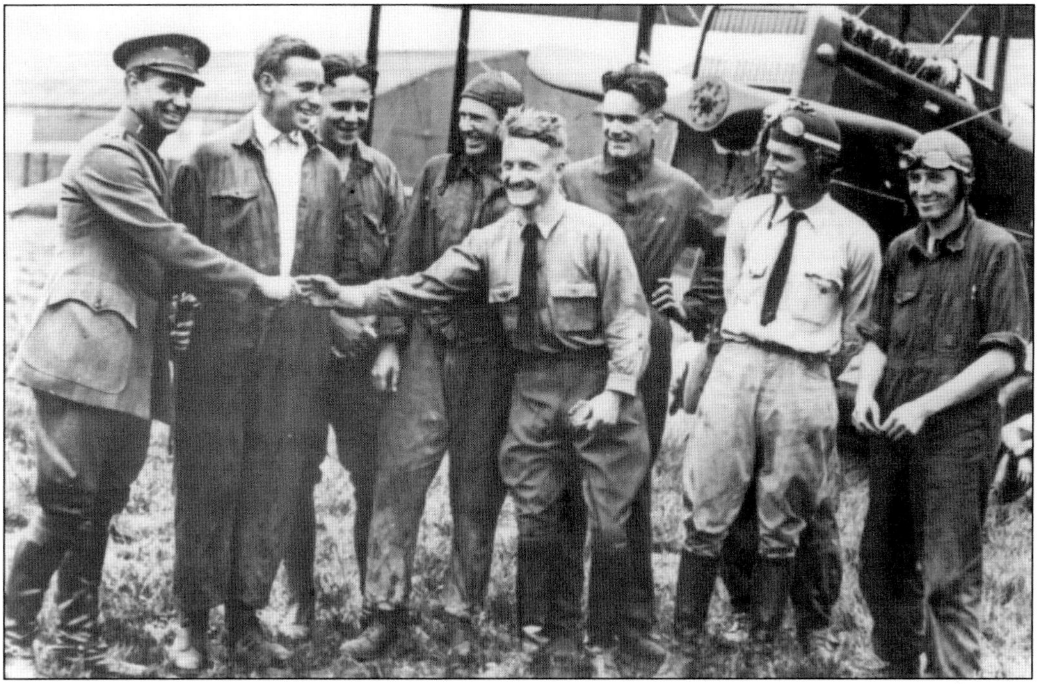

Billy Mitchell (center) shakes hands with Capt. St. Clair Street after the Black Wolf Squadron landed in Nome in 1920. Aviation events such as this left a strong impression on those in Alaska who realized its vast expanses and lack of transportation options. (Courtesy of the Alaska Aviation Museum.)

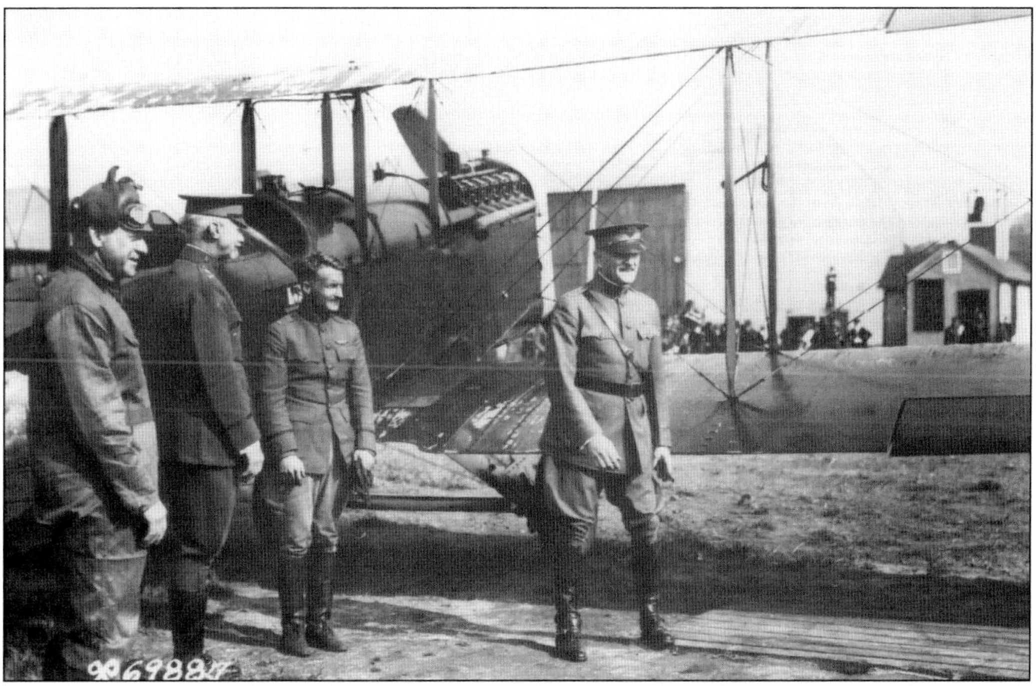

Gen. John Pershing (right) addresses the Black Wolf Squadron at Bolling Field in Washington, DC, in 1920. (Courtesy of the Alaska Aviation Museum.)

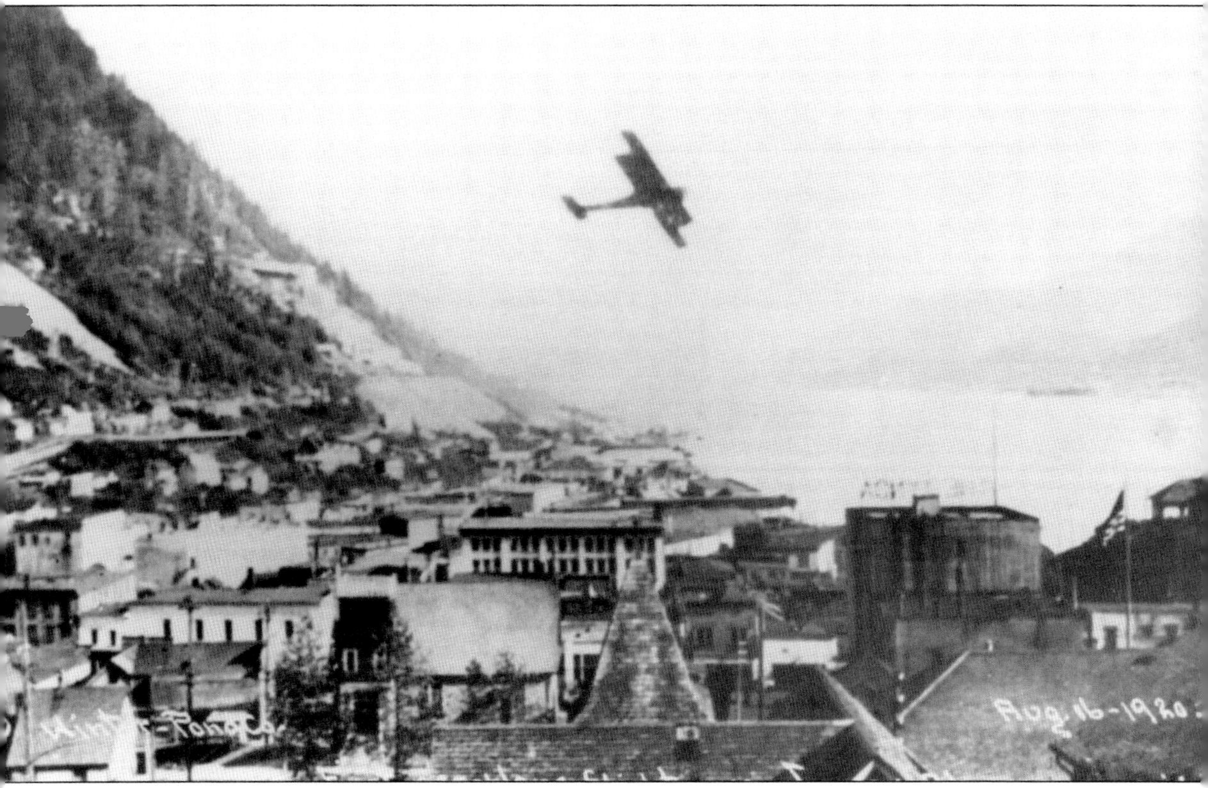

This Winter & Pond photograph of a Black Wolf Squadron aircraft, taken on August 16, 1920, shows the first aircraft to be flown over Juneau. Also visible are the city rooftops, the Treadwell Mine, the Gastineau Channel, and Douglas Island. It was seven years after the Martin-Gage aircraft was built and flown in Alaska that airplanes and flying returned to the territory. Known as the Black Wolf Squadron, four de Havilland DH-4Bs and eight crewmembers departed New York on July 15, 1920, and reached Nome on August 23, covering 4,500 miles in 55 hours of flying time. The group began its return trip two days later, arriving back on October 20, 1920. The Black Wolf Squadron was sent by Brig. Gen. William "Billy" Mitchell to demonstrate that there could be a link between the US East Coast and the Russian Far East via Alaska. (Courtesy of the Alaska Aviation Museum.)

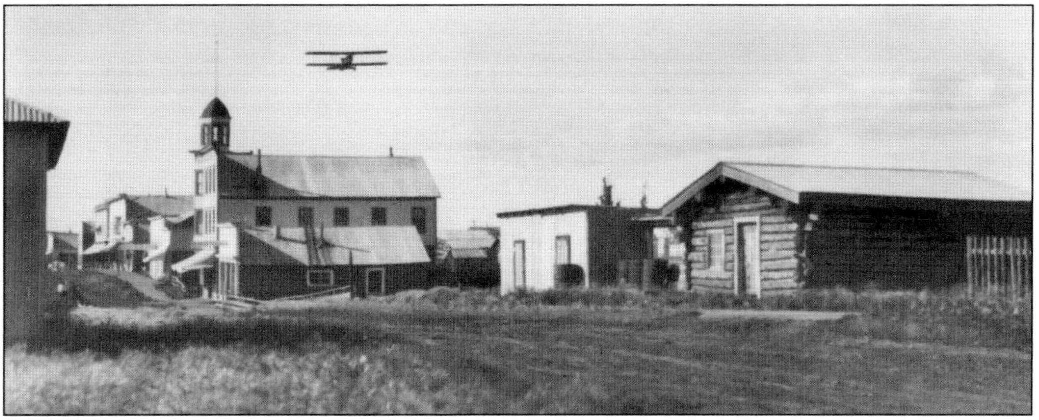

A DH-4 from the Black Wolf Squadron, on its way to Nome, flies over the village of Tanana in 1920. (Courtesy of the Alaska Aviation Museum.)

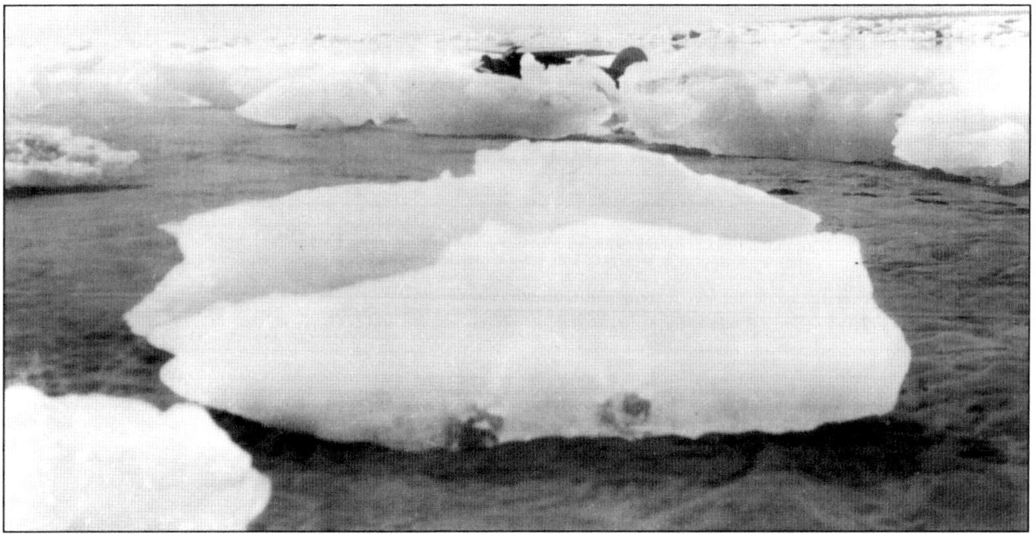

The Lockheed Vega *Taku* (NC102W) is shown sitting between ice chunks in Icy Bay, Alaska, on July 13, 1930. Bob Ellis, flying for Alaska Washington Airways, landed the plane and water taxied between the grounded ice to pick up Clayton Scott and John Selby after they were forced down in their Boeing flying boat "Nugget" (NC115E) on July 10, 1930. (Courtesy of the Alaska Aviation Museum.)

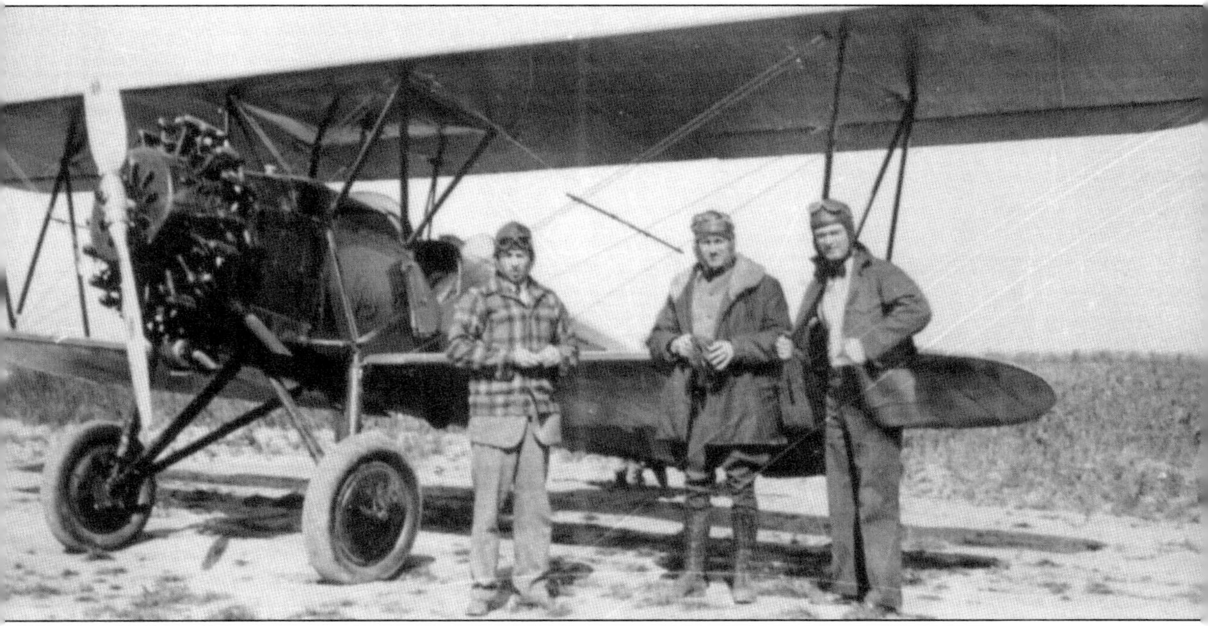

The Stearman C2B, associated with Alaska's most illustrious aviation pioneers, is considered the most historic aircraft in the collection of the Alaska Aviation Museum. Originally owned by Noel Wien, who acquired the aircraft as a wreck in 1928, the Stearman is considered one of the most valuable pioneer aircraft in the world. The plane was sold to Ben Eielson in 1929 and used for service on Alaskan Airways. When Eielson and mechanic Earl Borland disappeared in Siberia in November 1929, Harold Gillam flew the Stearman to Siberia to conduct the search for Eielson. This aircraft, piloted by Jerry Jones in 1932, is also credited with being the first to land on Mount McKinley's Muldrow Glacier, to rescue a sick mountain climber. The Stearman flew throughout Alaska, from Barrow to Juneau, with Pacific Alaska Airways until it was sold to Merle "Mudhole" Smith and Cordova Air Service in the mid- to late 1930s. (Courtesy of the Alaska Aviation Museum.)

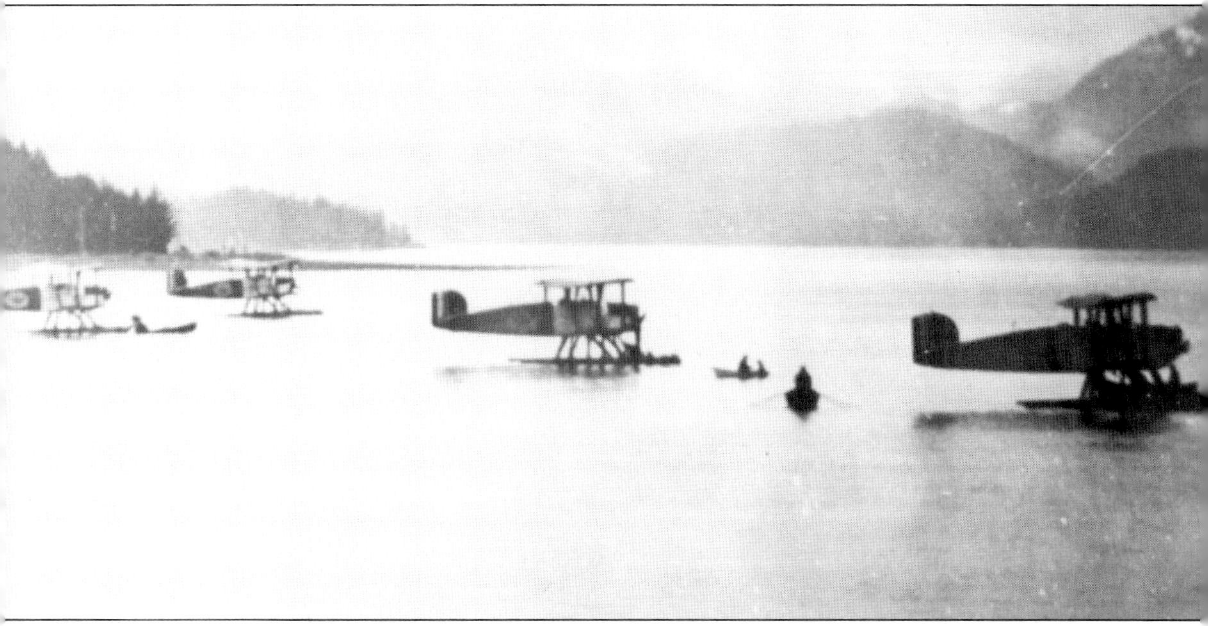

One of the greatest feats in early aviation history began on April 6, 1924, when four US Army Air Service Douglas World Cruisers took off to circumnavigate the globe. Named after the cities of Boston, Chicago, New Orleans, and Seattle, the aircraft departed Sandpoint, Washington, and headed north to Alaska. Setting up camps in Seward, Dutch Harbor, and Attu, Alaska, for aircraft maintenance and logistics made the expedition of great interest to local Alaskans. One of the aircraft, the *Seattle*, crashed at Dutch Harbor on April 30, 1924. The engine and parts of the *Seattle* are on display in the Alaska Aviation Museum today. The other three Douglas World Cruisers continued on, but they required continual maintenance, engine changes, rebuilds, and patching and endured adventurous scrapes. The three aircraft returned to Seattle on September 28 after 175 days of circumnavigation. (Courtesy of the Alaska Aviation Museum.)

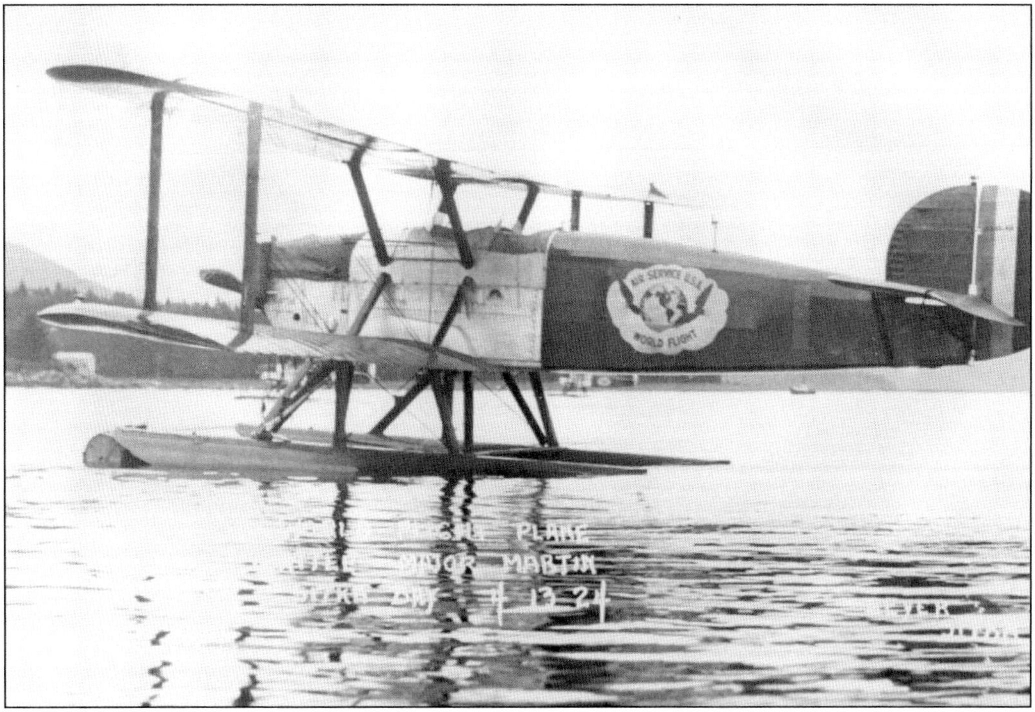

The Douglas World Cruiser flown by Maj. Frederick Martin (pilot and flight commander) is shown sitting in Sitka Bay on April 13, 1924. (Courtesy of the Alaska Aviation Museum.)

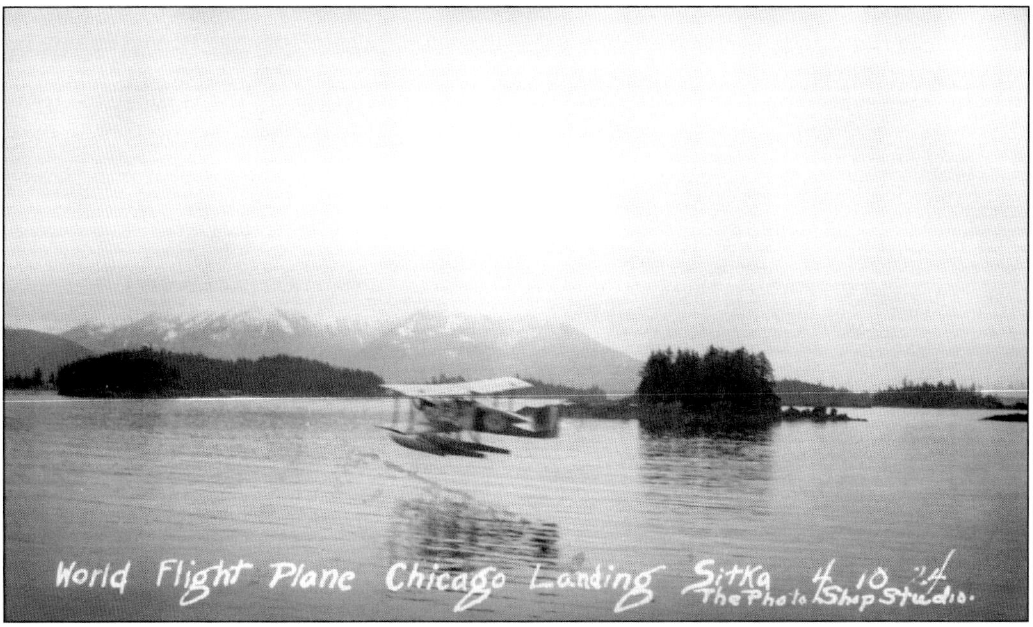

The Douglas World Cruiser *Chicago* lands in Sitka Harbor on April 10, 1924. The flights fascinated those interested in aviation. Of special interest were the distances covered by the floatplanes. The flights of the Black Wolf Squadron and the Douglas World Cruisers influenced entrepreneurs, who invested in aircraft that eventually opened up the far north. (Courtesy of the Alaska Aviation Museum.)

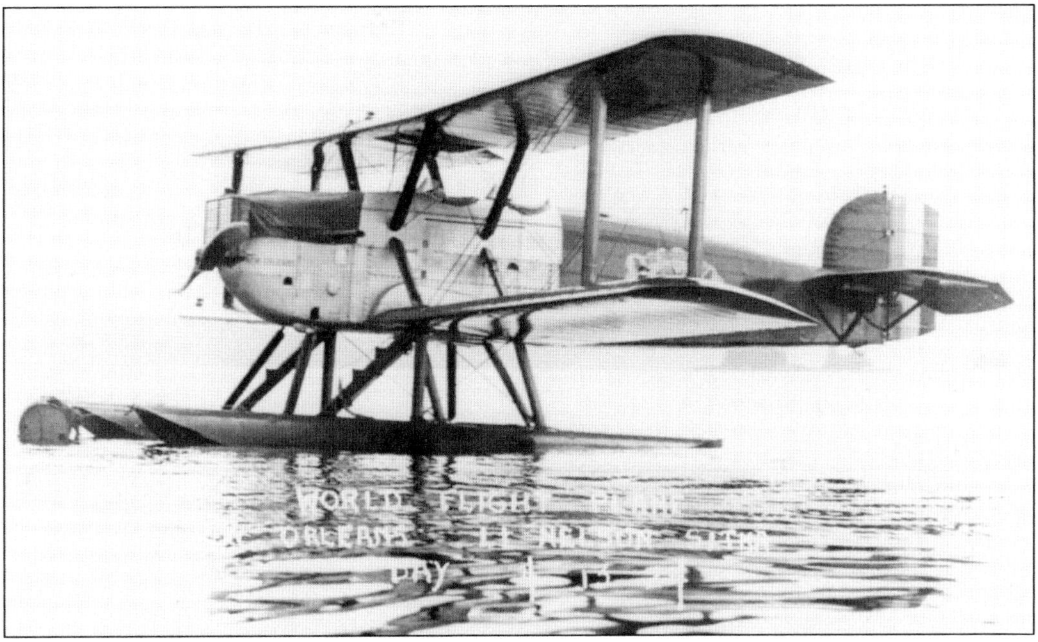

The Douglas World Cruiser *New Orleans*, pictured in Sitka Harbor, was one of the two original aircraft that completed the world circumnavigation. (Courtesy of the Alaska Aviation Museum.)

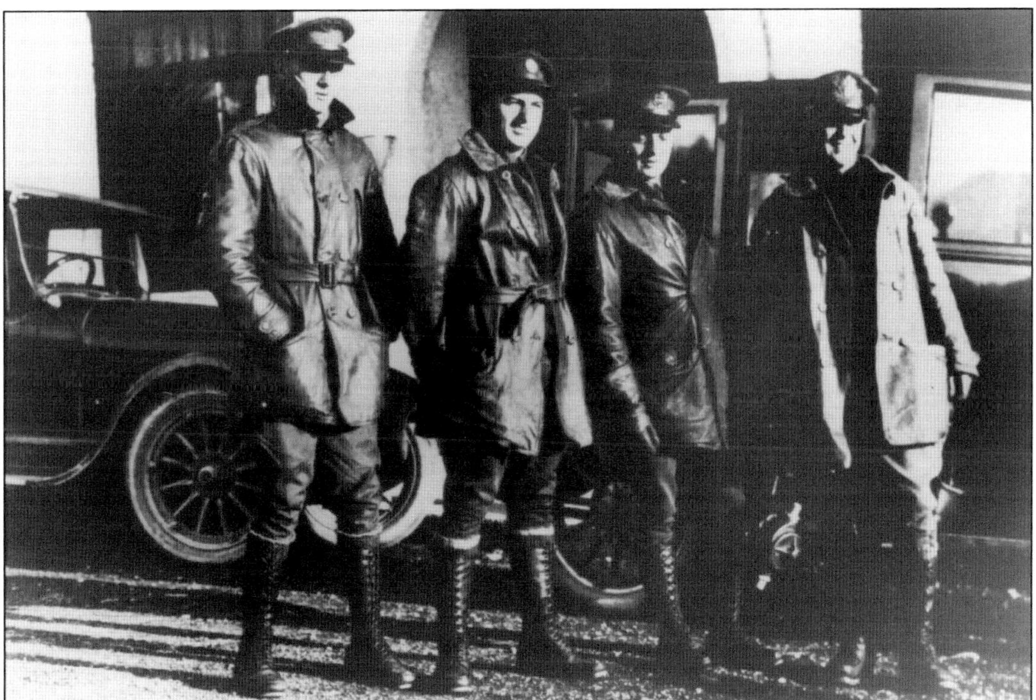

Mechanics for the Douglas World Cruisers are shown in Seward while on one of their mechanical stops during the circumnavigation flight in 1924. (Courtesy of the Alaska Aviation Museum.)

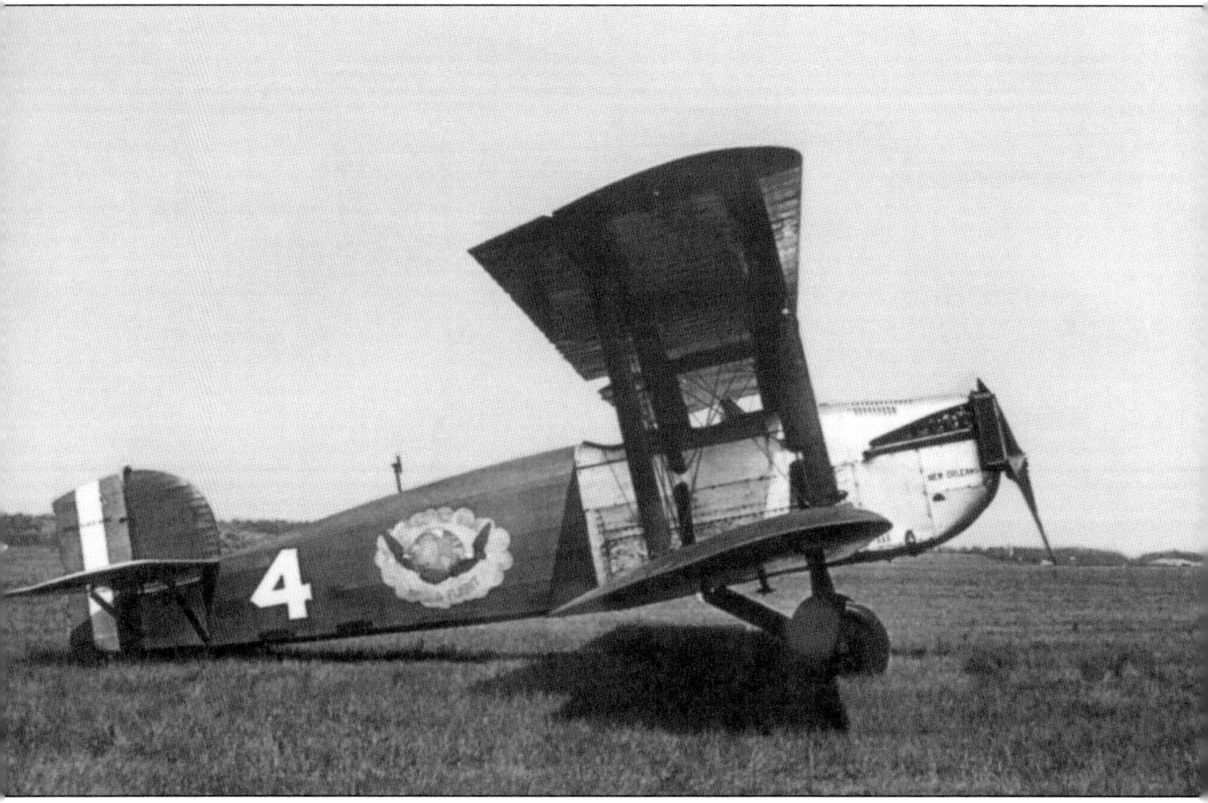

While most of the Douglas World Cruiser flight was done over water, three of the aircraft were eventually put on wheels for the return flight to Seattle. During the circumnavigation, the time in flight was 371 hours, 11 minutes, and the average speed was 70 miles per hour. (Courtesy of the Alaska Aviation Museum.)

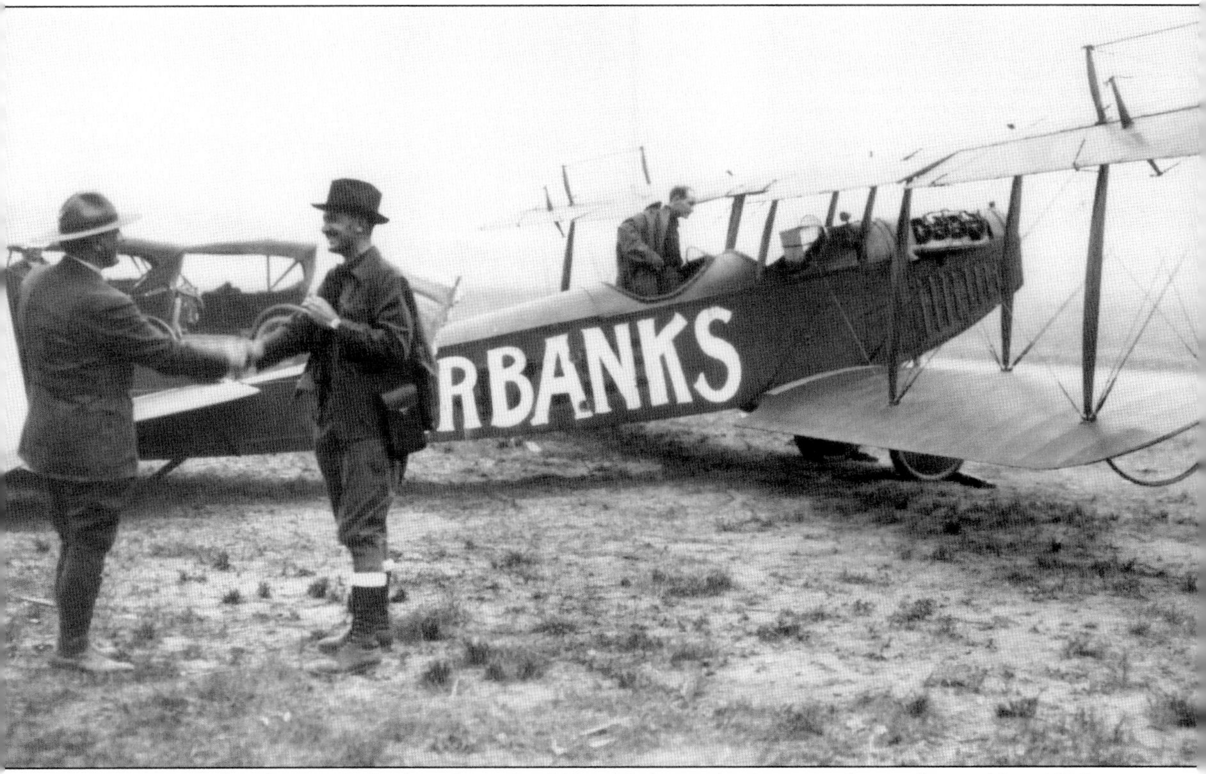

Here, two Fairbanksans shake hands as Carl Ben Eielson climbs into the cockpit of his 1923 JN-4D Jenny to prepare for a flight. Eielson was a schoolteacher in Fairbanks when he began demonstrating the potential of the surplus trainer. This aircraft is now hanging in the passenger terminal at Fairbanks International Airport. (Courtesy of the Alaska Aviation Museum.)

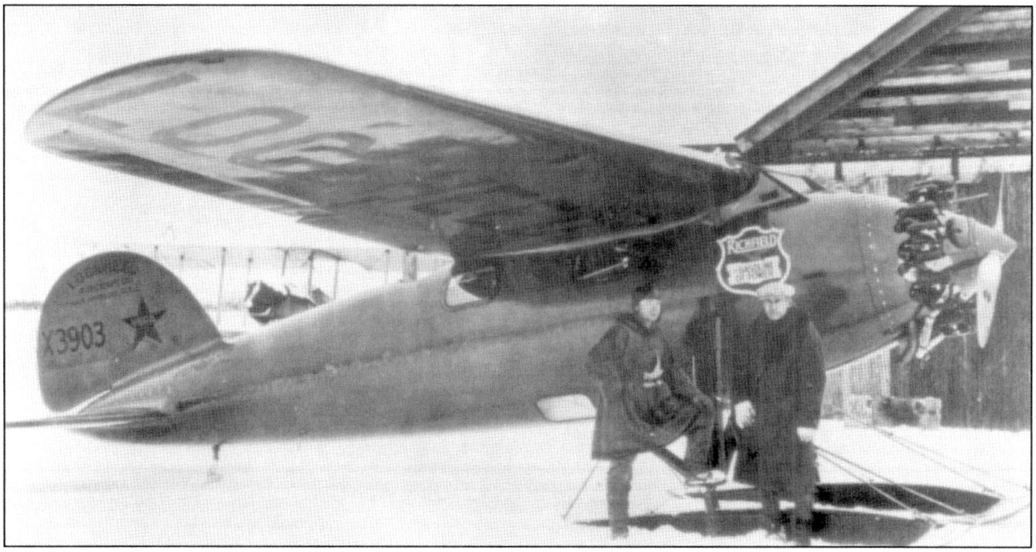

Carl Ben Eielson (left) and Capt. Hubert Wilkins pose in front of the Lockheed Vega X3903, which was flown over the North Pole. This photograph was taken at Rickerts Field, in front of the Fairbanks Aircraft Corporation hangar, in March 1928. (Courtesy of the Alaska Aviation Museum.)

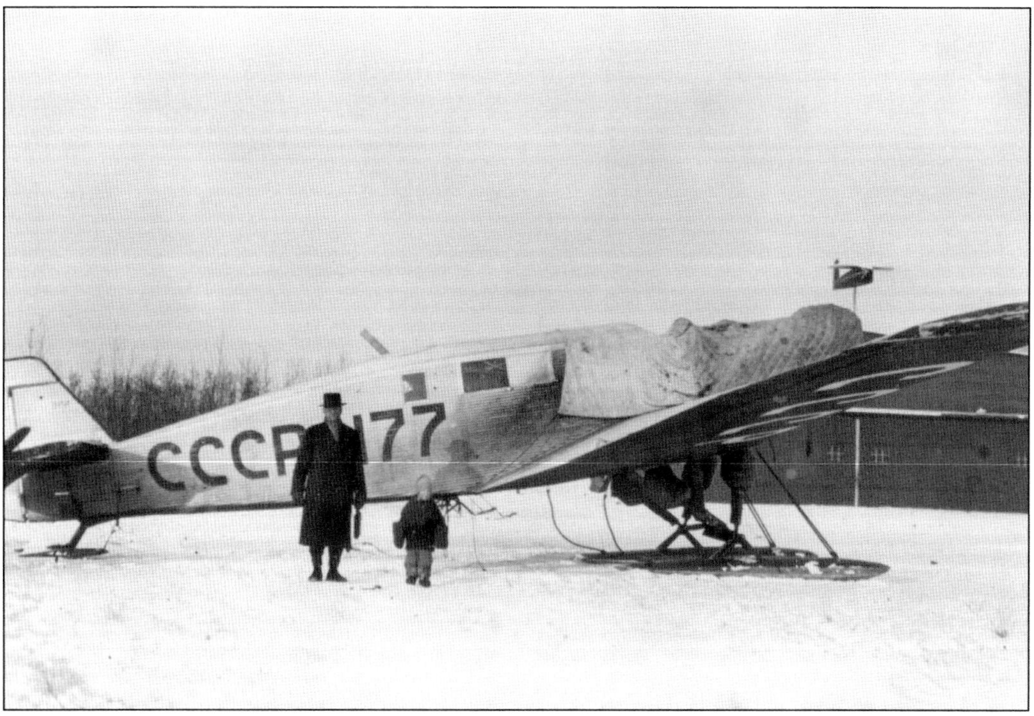

An unidentified man and child stand in front of a Russian Junkers F-13 aircraft at Weeks Field in Fairbanks. In the background is the Alaskan Airways hangar. The F-13 returned the body of Carl Ben Eielson to Fairbanks from the Northeast Cape of Chukotka, Russia. (Courtesy of the Alaska Aviation Museum.)

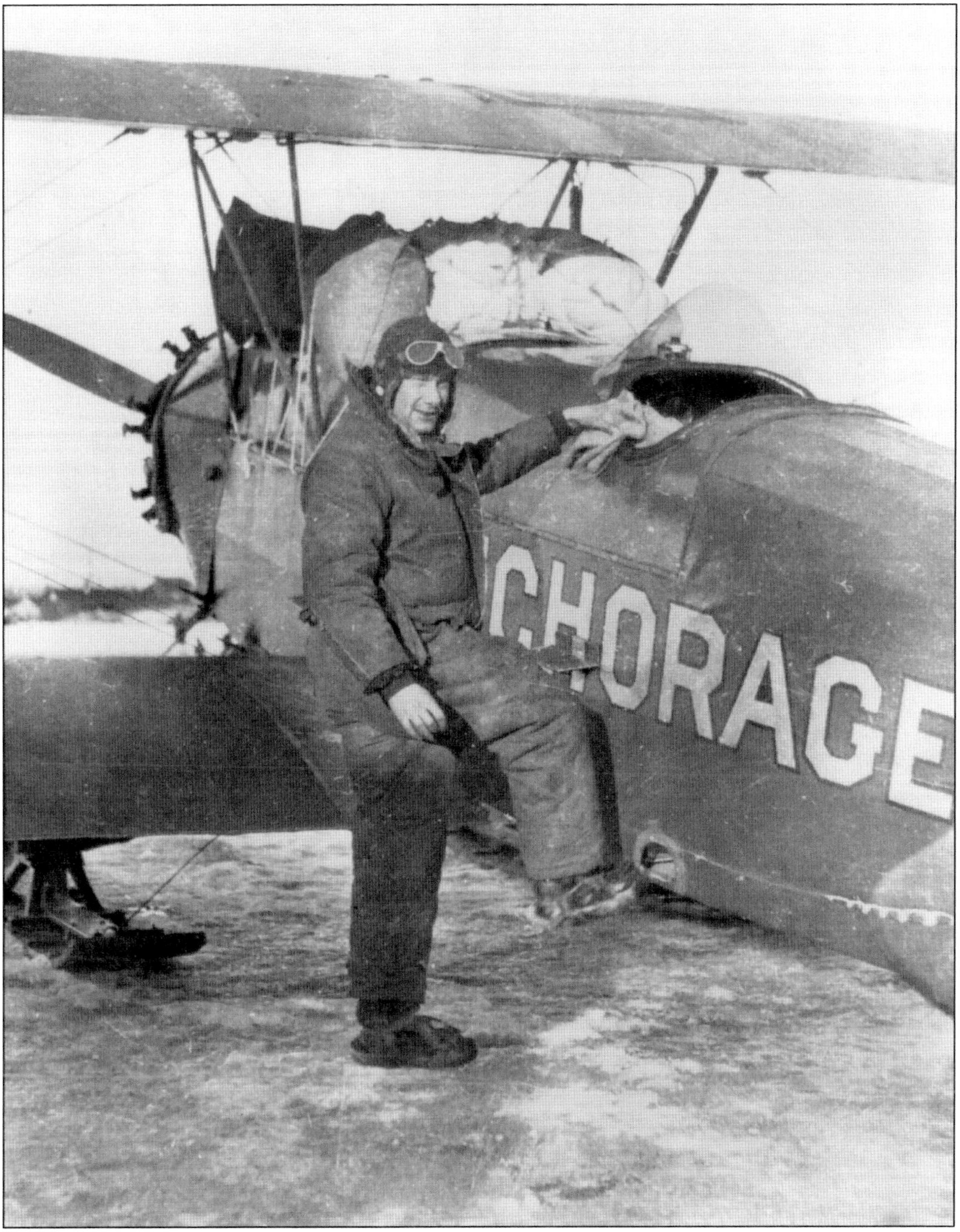

Russel Merrill climbs into the Anchorage No. 1, a cabin Travel Air, with sacks of furs strapped to the struts and fuselage. Merrill disappeared on a flight on September 16, 1929, and was never seen again. Merrill Field in Anchorage is named after the pioneer bush pilot, who is remembered with a plaque at the base of the tower: Russel Hyde Merrill, "whose life's aim was the development of aviation in Alaska." (Courtesy of the Alaska Aviation Museum.)

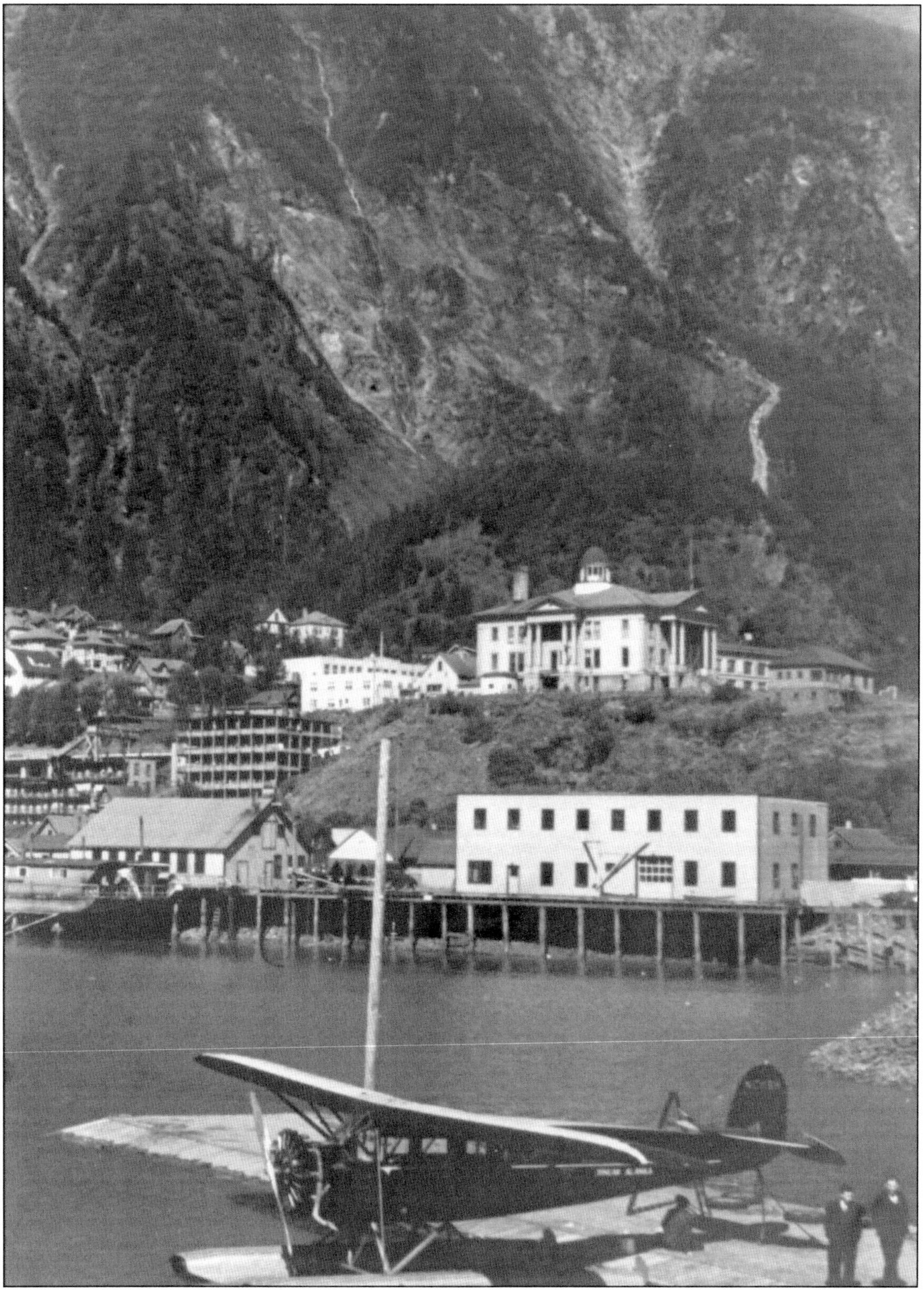

A Fairchild 71 sits moored to the dock in the capital city of Juneau, Alaska. The capitol building can be seen on the hill above the wharf. (Courtesy of the Alaska Aviation Museum.)

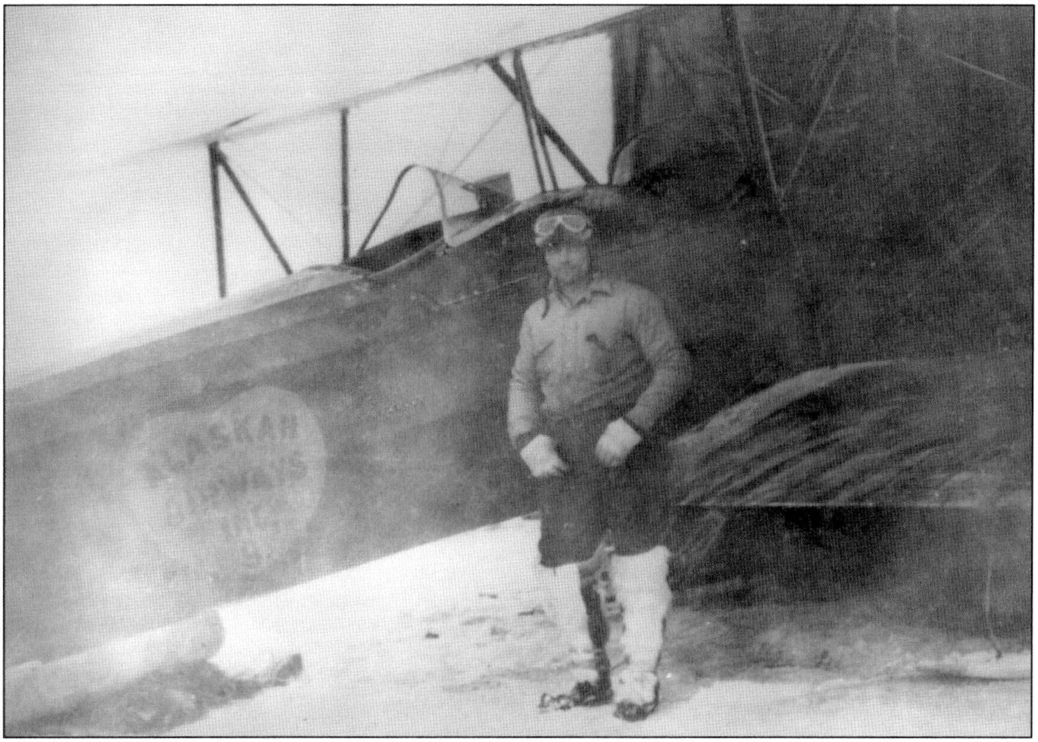

Harold Gillam stands next to his Stearman C2B before searching for Carl Ben Eielson and Earl Borland. The men and their all-metal Hamilton Standard were lost in the area of the North Cape of Chukotka, Russia, in 1929. (Courtesy of the Alaska Aviation Museum.)

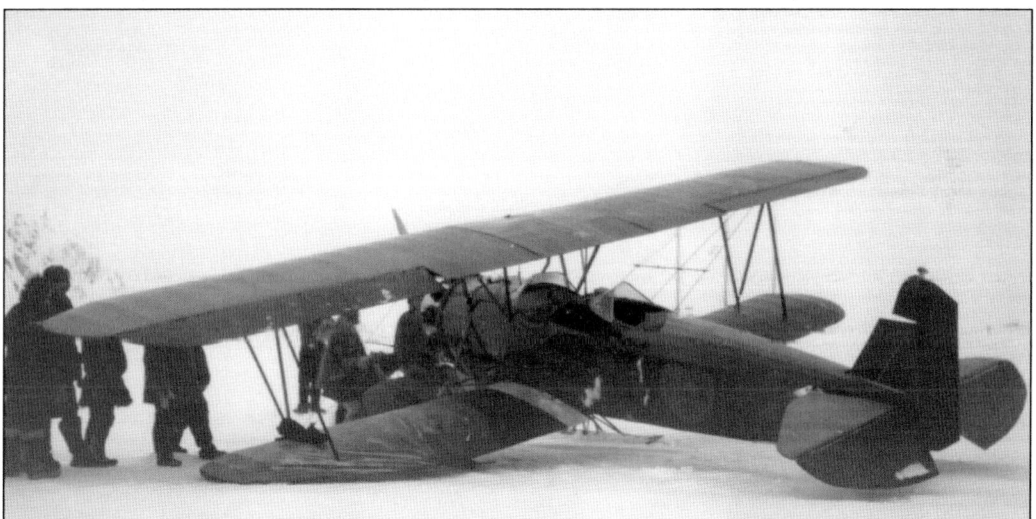

Harold Gillam ground-damaged this Stearman C2B (NC5415) after an engine failure on takeoff, forcing him to land on rough Bering Sea ice. Gillam and passenger Demetri Miroshnishshenko were not injured in the forced landing. The plane was launched as part of a search for Eielson and his all-metal Hamilton Standard aircraft, lost near the North Cape of Chukotka in December 1929. The Alaskan Airways aircraft, repaired by Gillam with the help of Russian engineers, was able to fly three weeks later. (Courtesy of the Alaska Aviation Museum.)

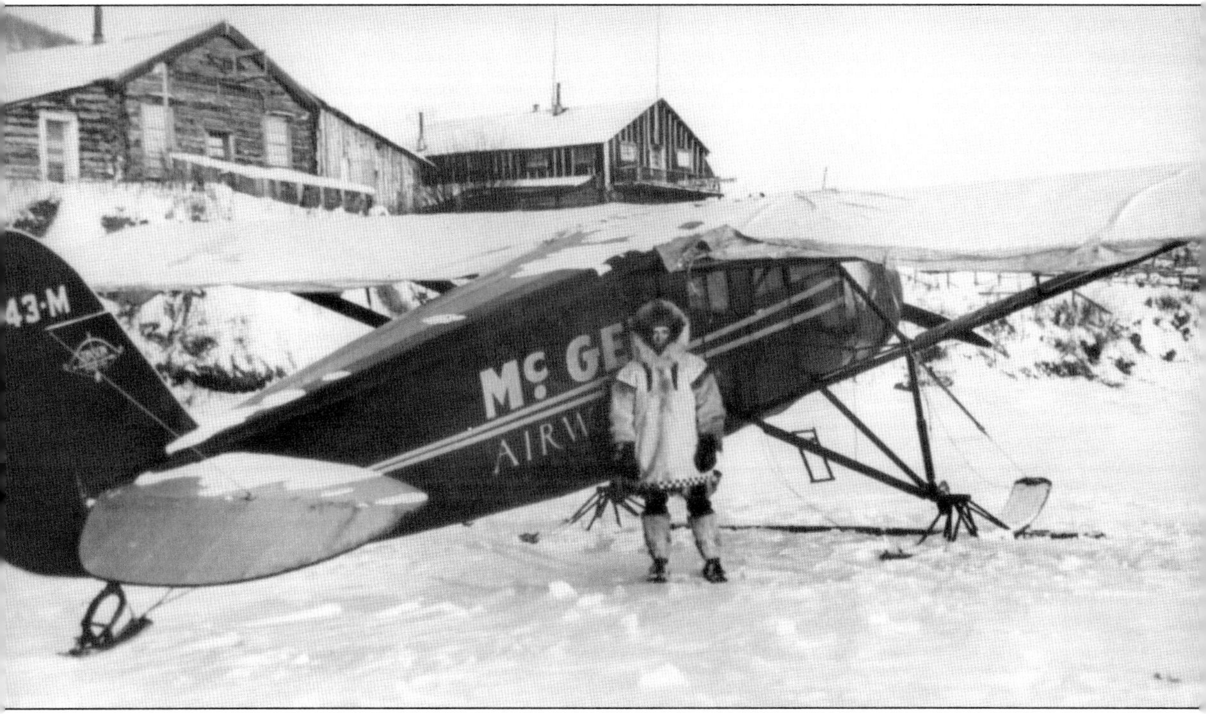

In this c. 1932 photograph, McGee Airways pilot Estol Call stands next to the Stinson SM8A NC-443-M on the Yukon River. He is dressed for the cold in an Alaska Native parka and mukluks. (Courtesy of the Alaska Aviation Museum.)

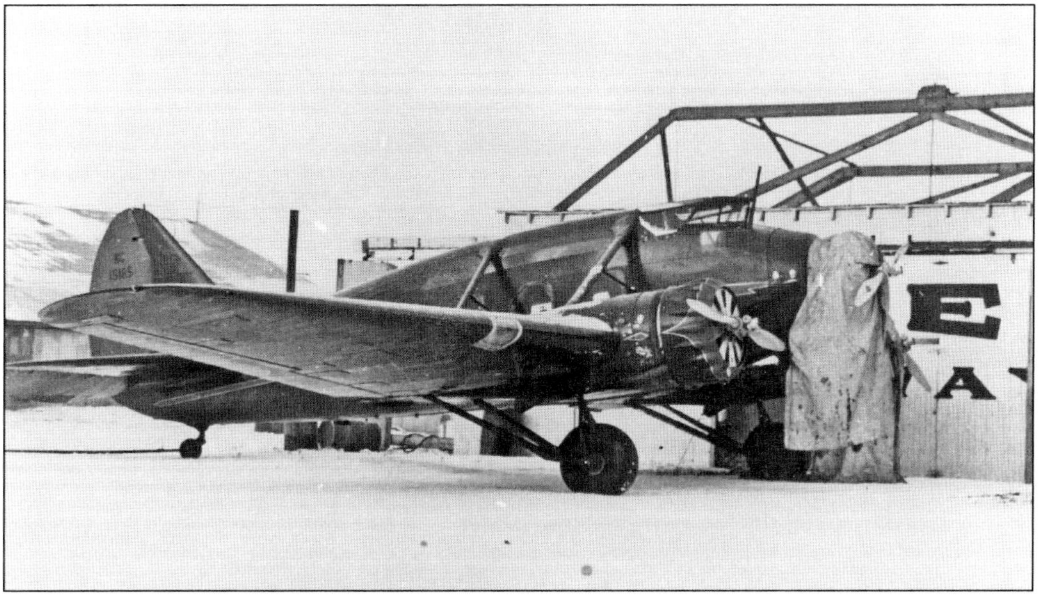

A Stinson Tri Motor (NC-15165) gets its front engine warmed up before a winter flight. The Stinson Tri Motor contributed to the advancement of rural Alaska's transportation infrastructure. (Courtesy of the Alaska Aviation Museum.)

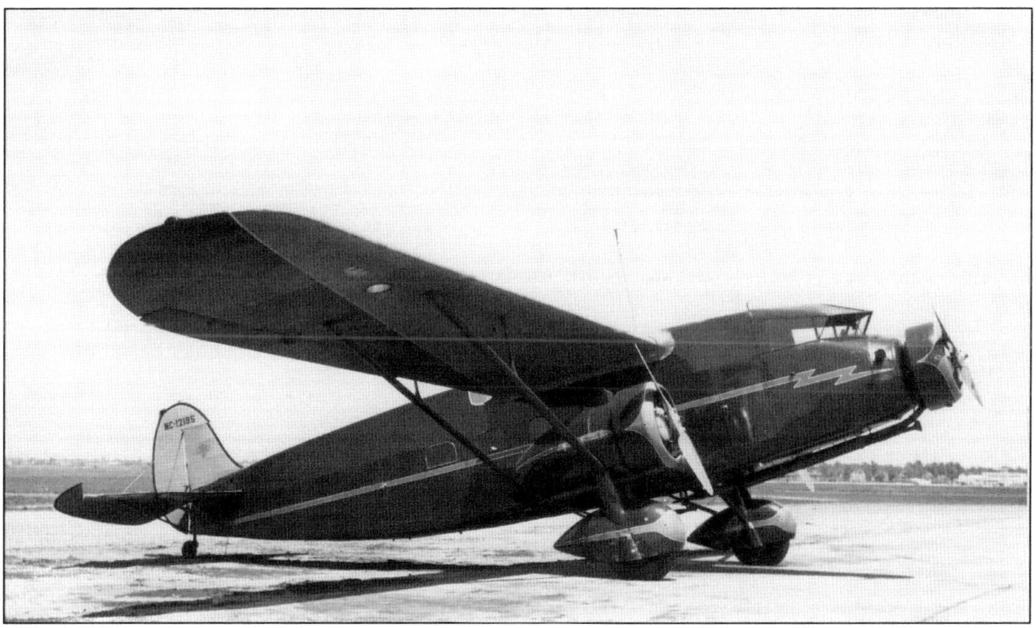

This is a rare photograph of a Stinson Tri Motor "Airliner," used by Harold Gillam for air service in Alaska on the north gulf coast and in south central Alaska. (Courtesy of the Alaska Aviation Museum.)

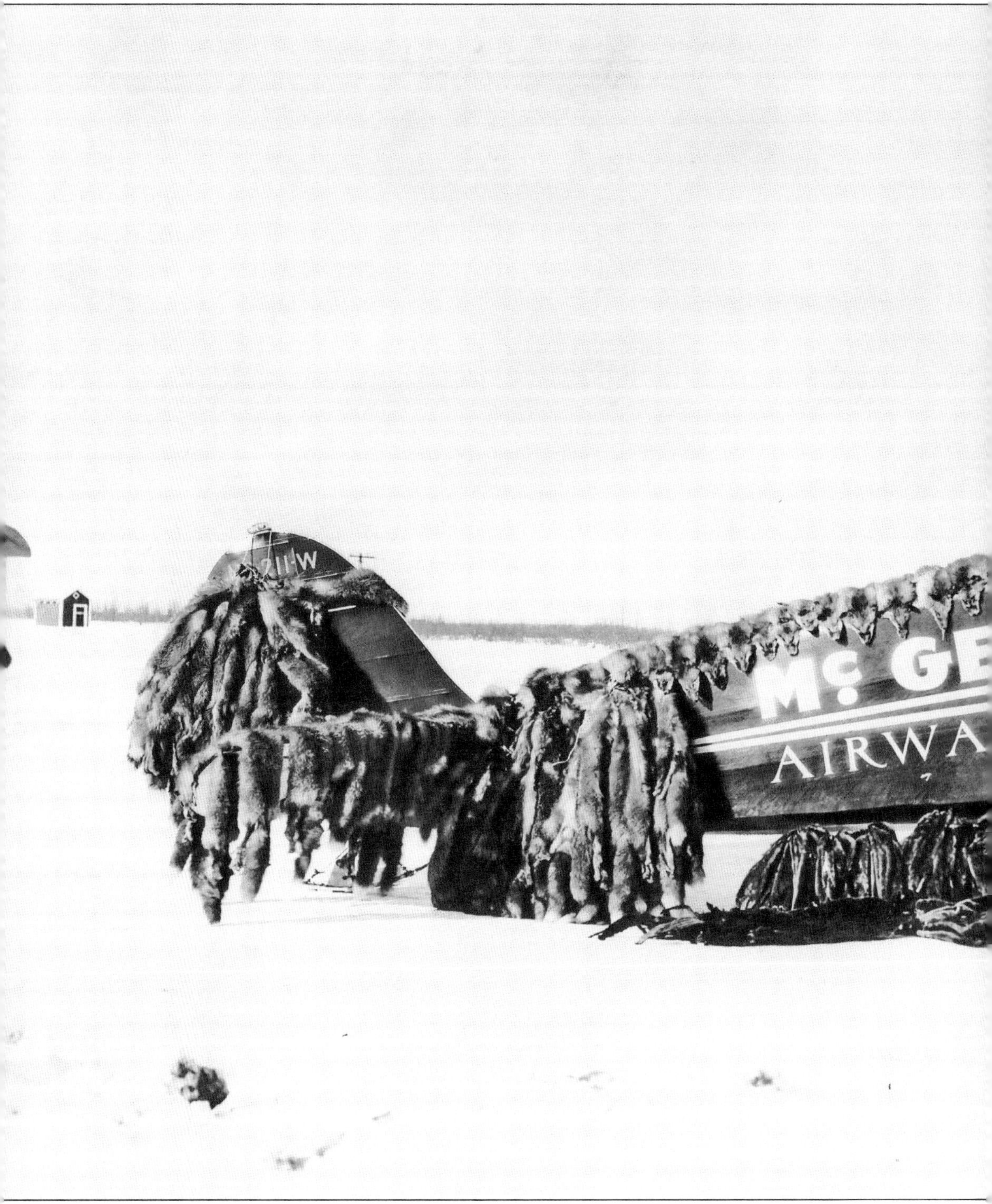

A miner and trapper, Linious "Mac" McGee had earned enough wealth in fur trading to fund an airline, as illustrated in this photograph from 1932. An Indiana native, the unemployed McGee had stowed away on a steamship bound for Alaska during the Great Depression. He partnered with

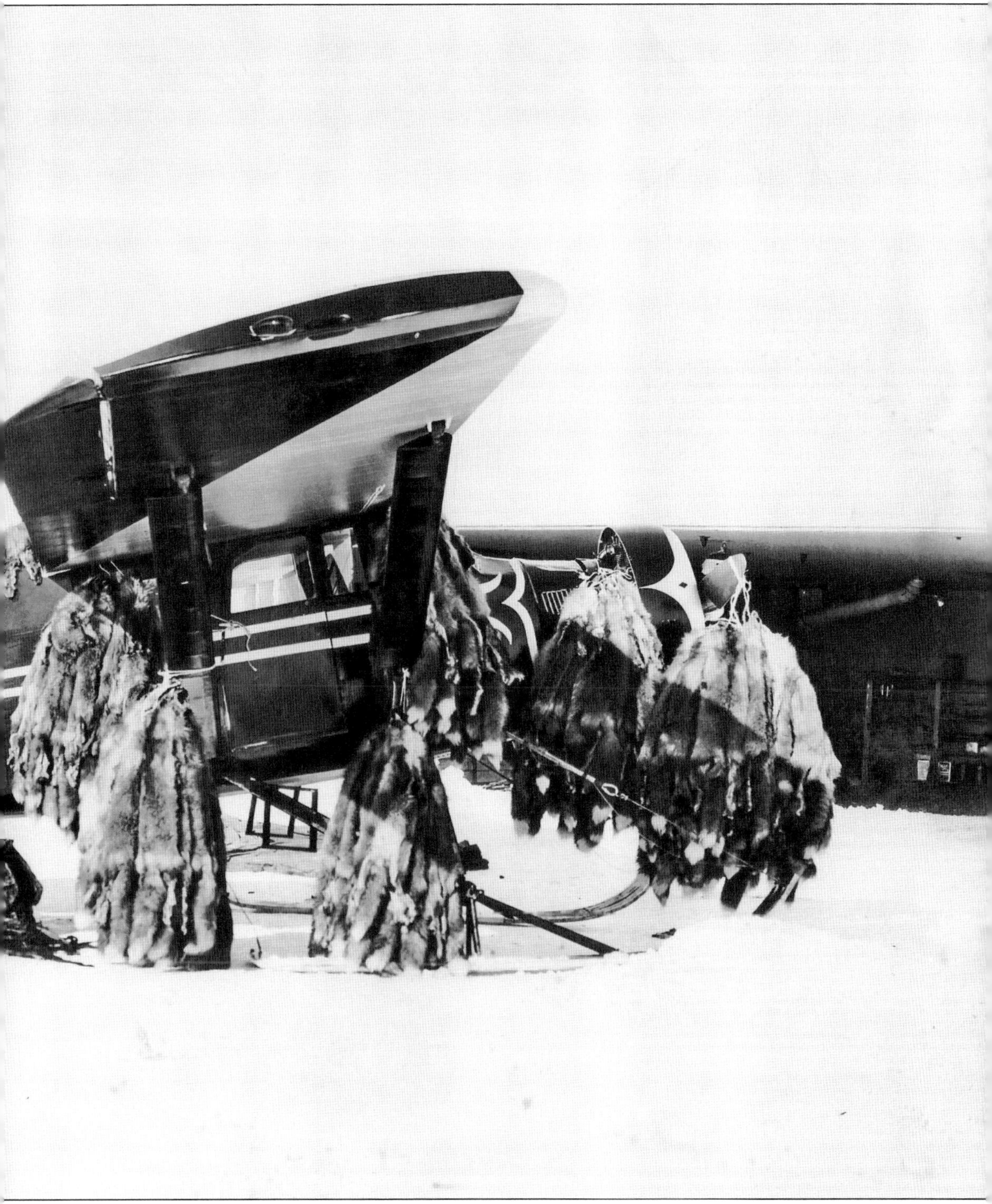

fellow aviator Harvey Barnhill to found McGee Airways in 1931. Their first plan was a Stinson three-seater purchased for $5,000, offering service flights from Anchorage and Bristol Bay. This would eventually become Alaska Airlines. (Courtesy of the Alaska Aviation Museum.)

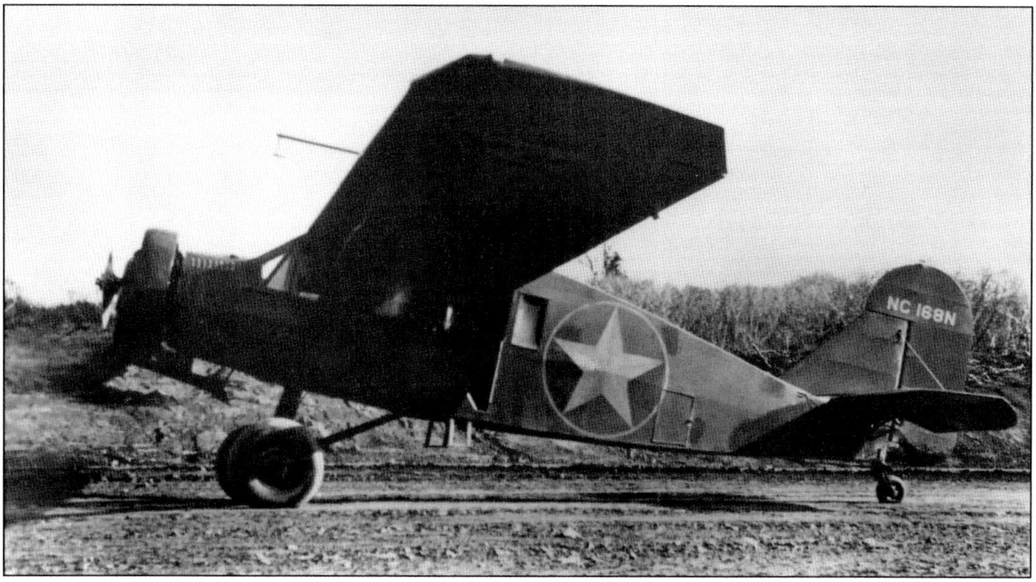

The Bellanca Pacemaker was used on wheels (above) and on skis (below) extensively throughout Alaska. Built in 1929, the Pacemaker above came to Alaska in 1934. The aircraft is credited with having flown from the Anchorage Park Strip and later Merrill Field for Star Airways. The Bellanca crashed in Rainy Pass, northwest of Anchorage, in the Alaska Range in October 1946. The wreckage was retrieved by a gold miner and taken to Nevada. (Both, courtesy of the Alaska Aviation Museum.)

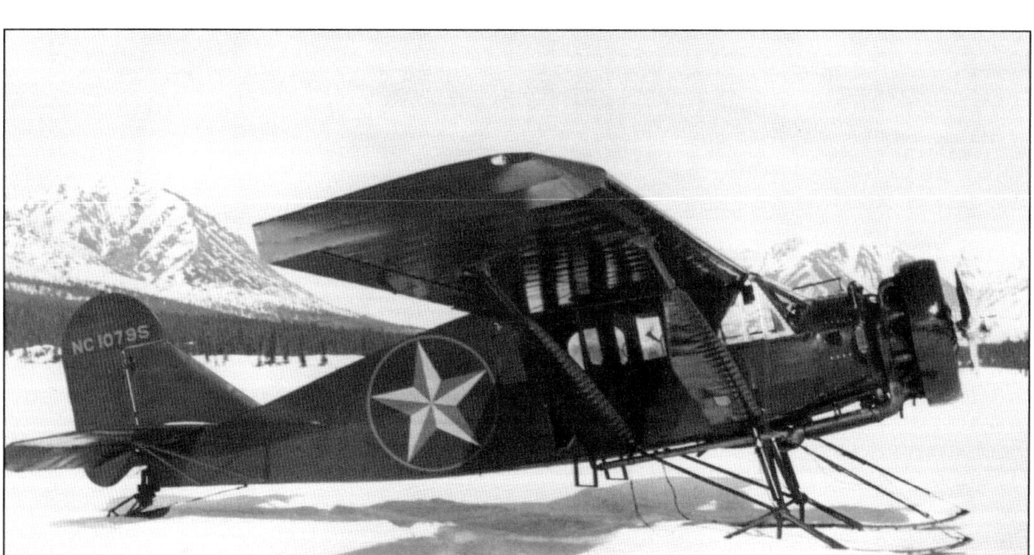

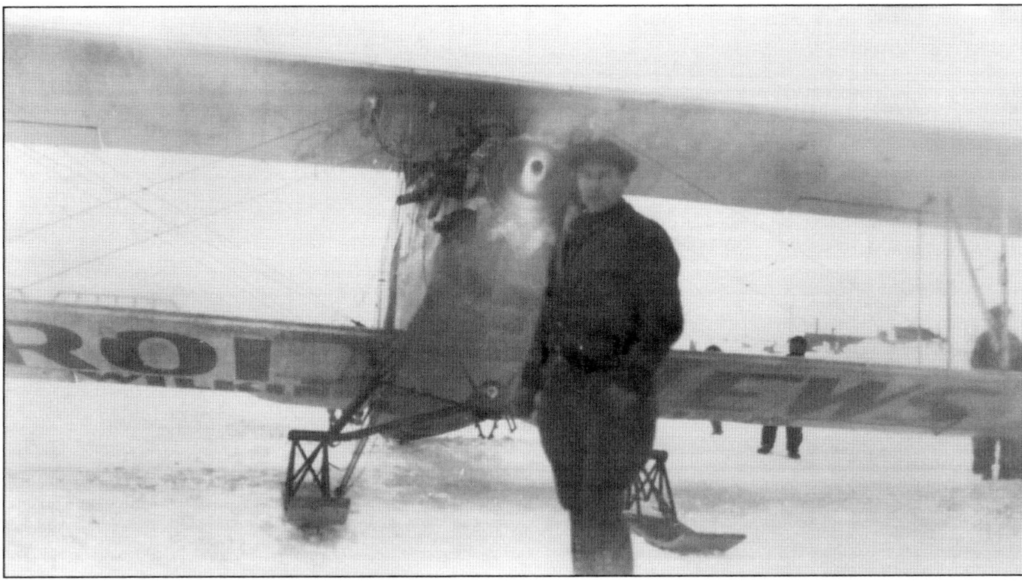

Noel Wien stands in front of a Stinson Detroiter in the late 1920s. Wien, the founder of one of the country's first airlines, was the first man to fly nonstop from Anchorage to Fairbanks. Wien was inducted into the National Aviation Hall of Fame in 2010. (Courtesy of the Alaska Aviation Museum.)

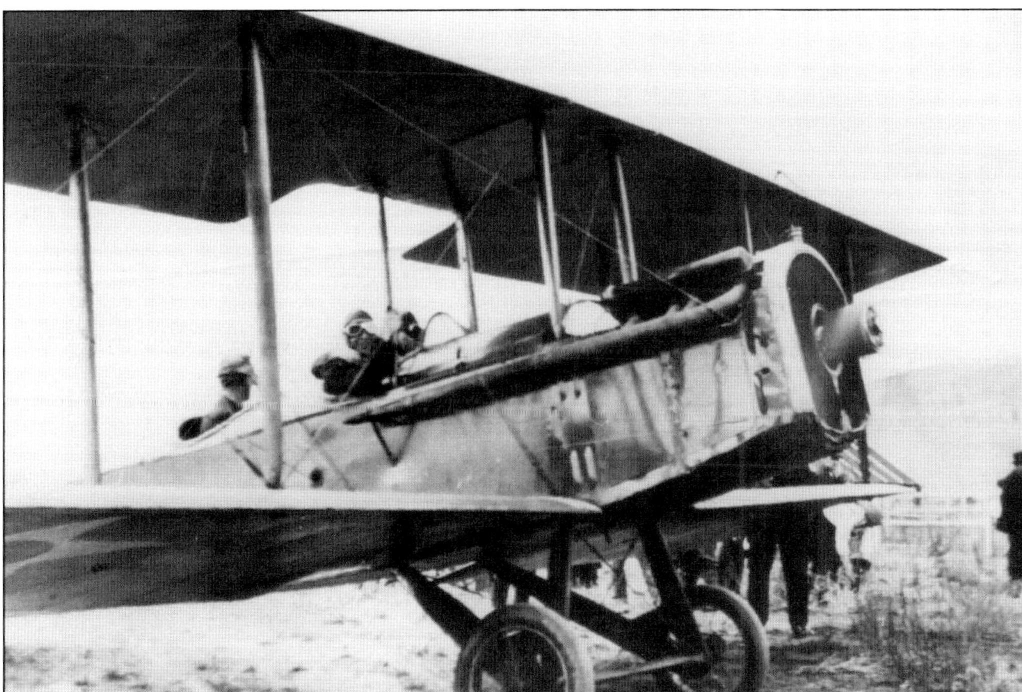

Noel Wien readies for takeoff from Fairbanks, Alaska, in a Hisso Standard. The plane is also carrying two passengers. (Courtesy of the Alaska Aviation Museum.)

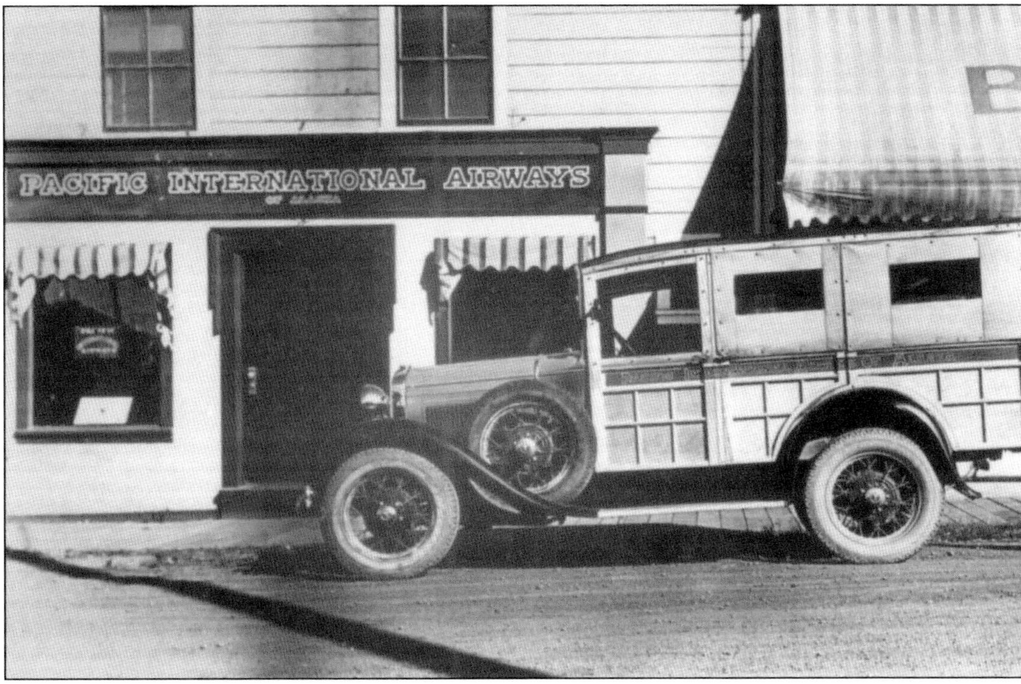

This vehicle was used for transporting cargo and passengers to the airport from the downtown Fairbanks offices of Pacific International Airways of Alaska. (Courtesy of the Alaska Aviation Museum.)

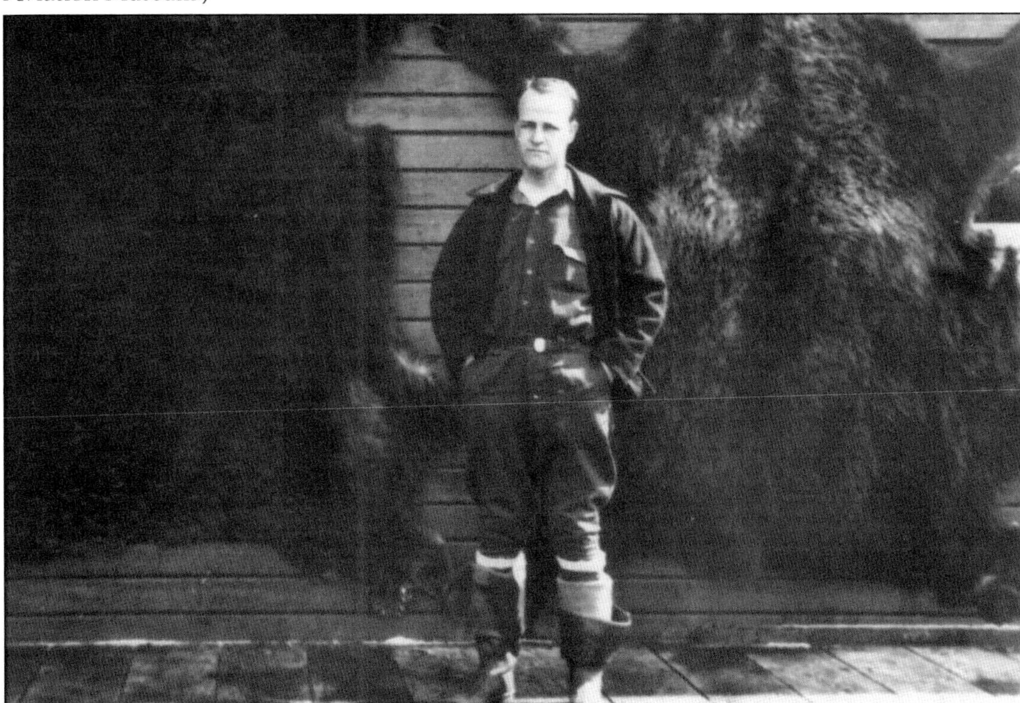

Art Woodley stands in front of brown bear hides at Lake Spenard near Anchorage in this 1935 photograph. (Courtesy of the Alaska Aviation Museum.)

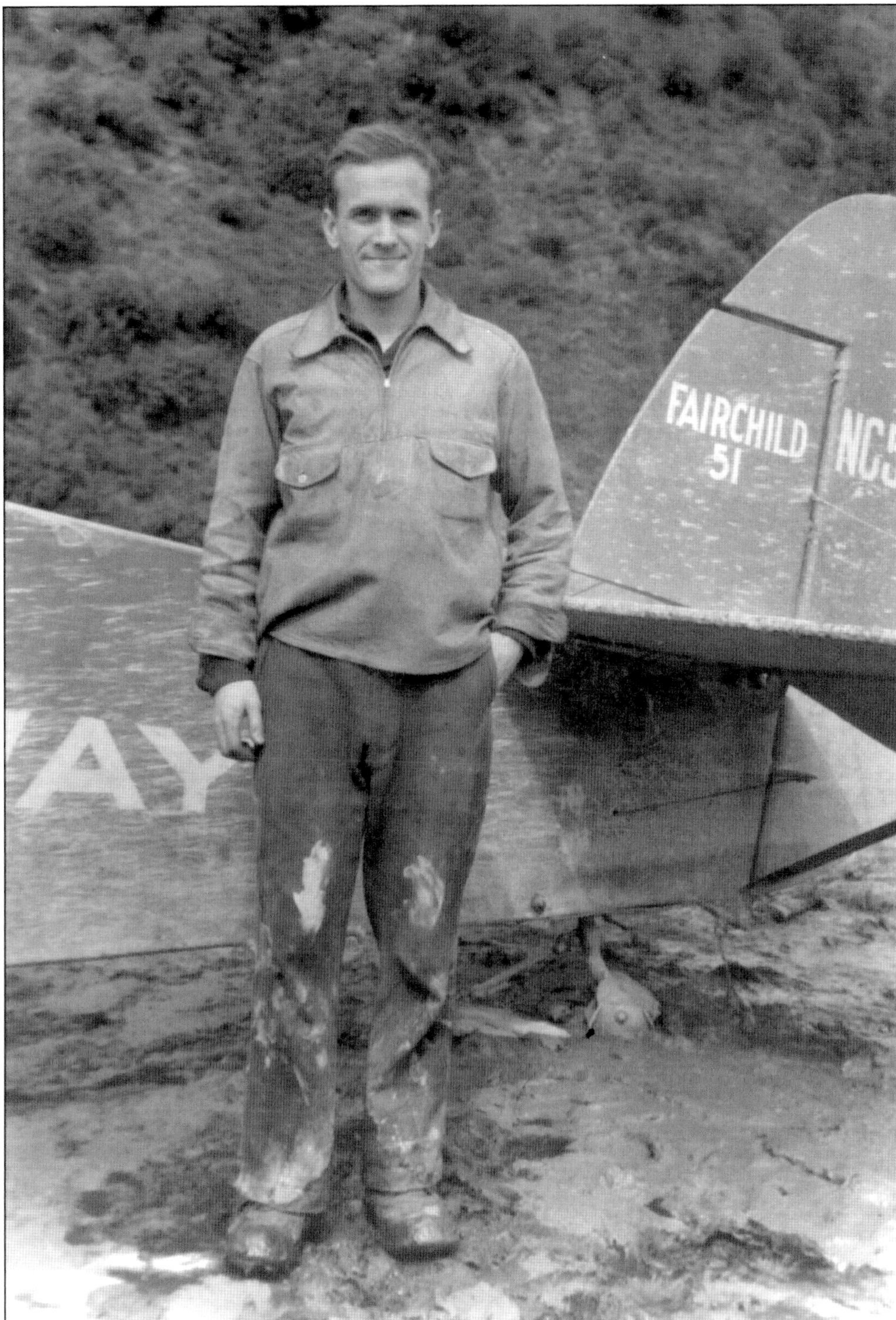

Famous photographer and mountaineer Brad Washburn stands in front of a Reeve Airways Fairchild 51 in Valdez. Washburn used Reeve for many aerial reconnaissance flights in Alaska. (Courtesy of the Alaska Aviation Museum.)

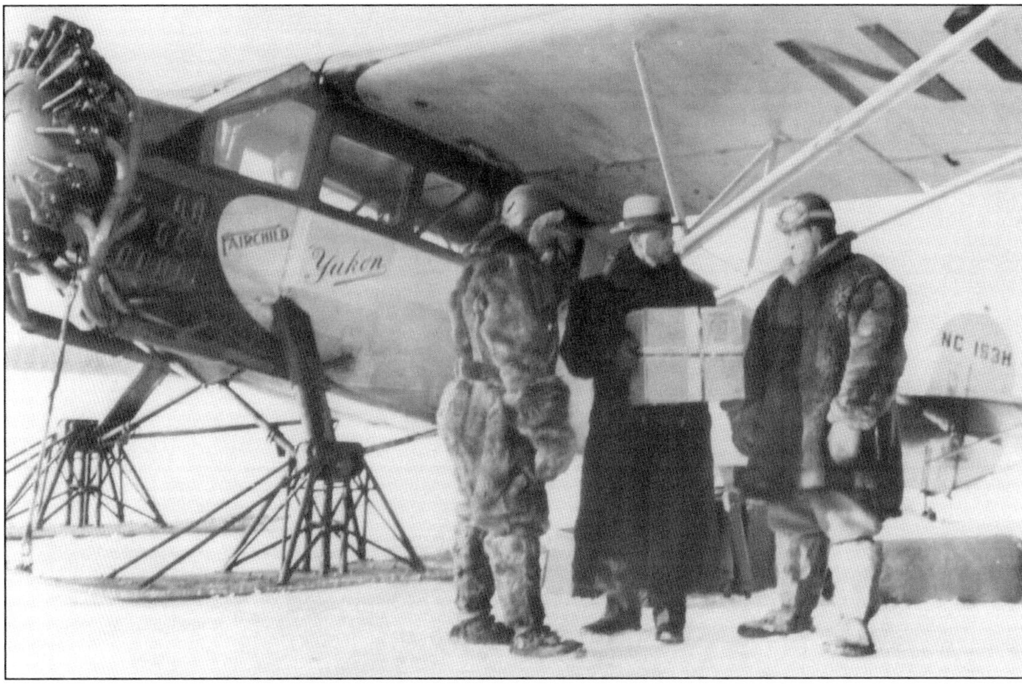

Bush pilot Joe Crosson (right) receives a box of diphtheria serum from Mayor Ed White (center). They are standing under the wing of a Fairchild named *Yukon*. (Courtesy of the Alaska Aviation Museum.)

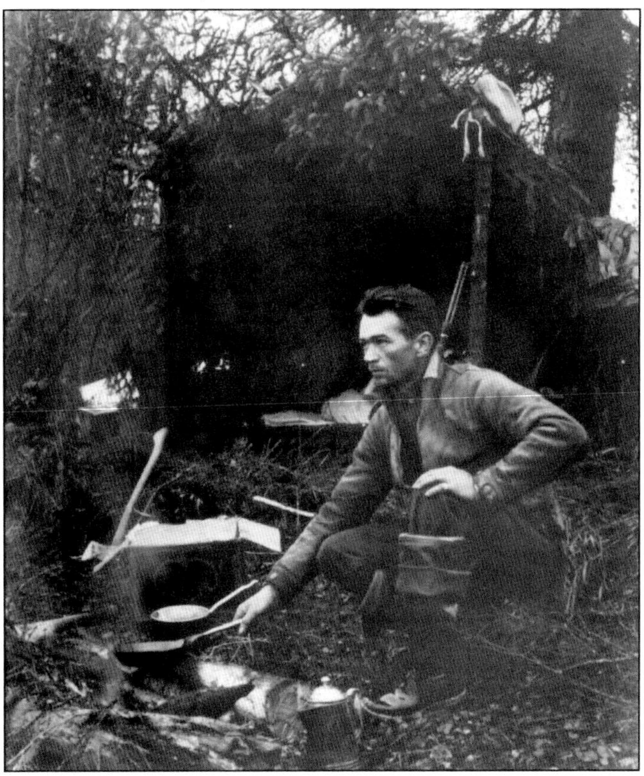

Estol Call prepares a meal in one of his outdoor camps, referred to as "Siwash" camps, in 1930. Call was well known for his ability to rough it in the wilds of Alaska. (Courtesy of the Alaska Aviation Museum.)

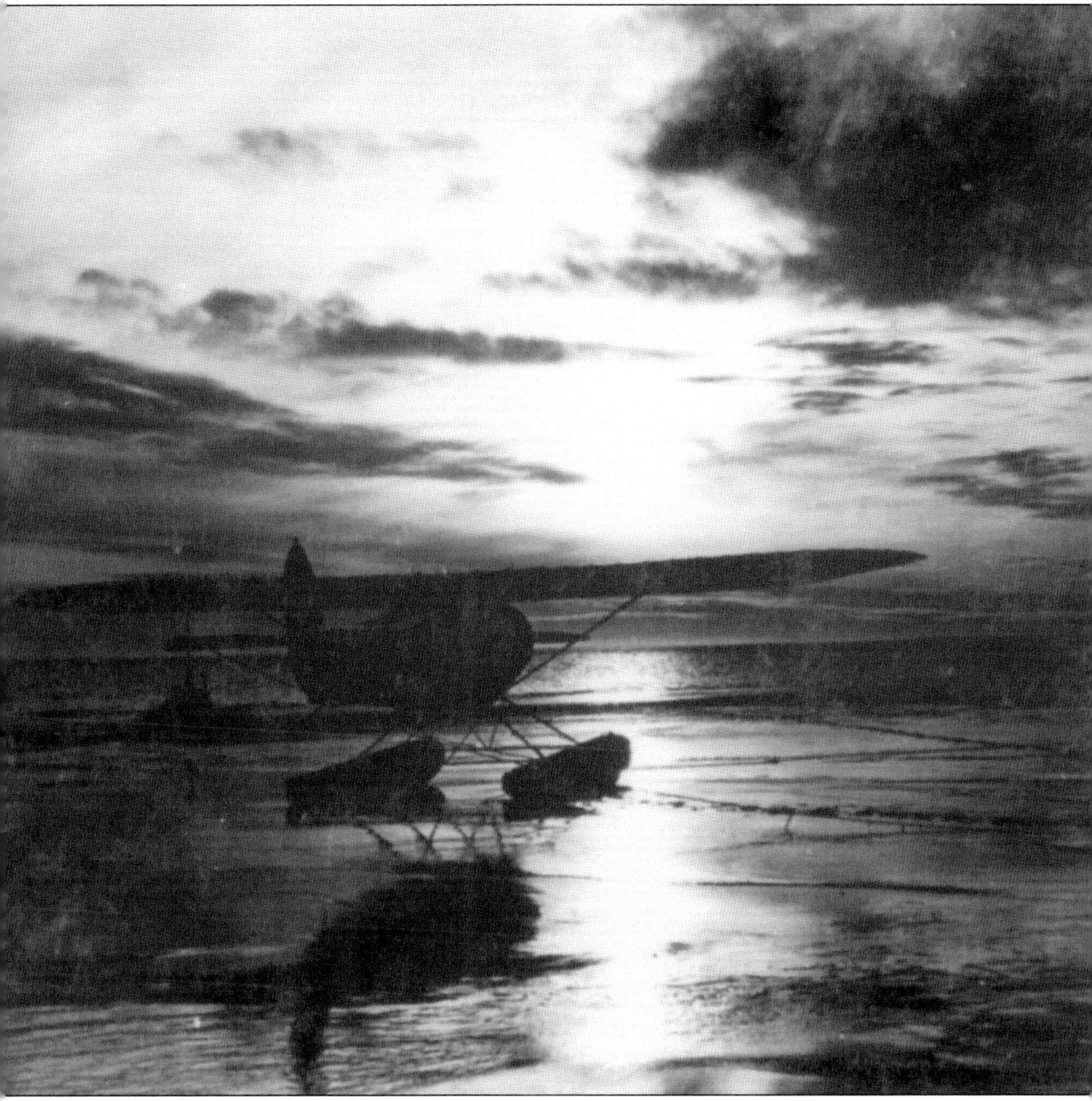

This photograph of a Pacific International Airways (PIA) Fairchild 71 at sundown on the Bering Sea was taken near Nome, Alaska, in 1935. (Courtesy of the Alaska Aviation Museum.)

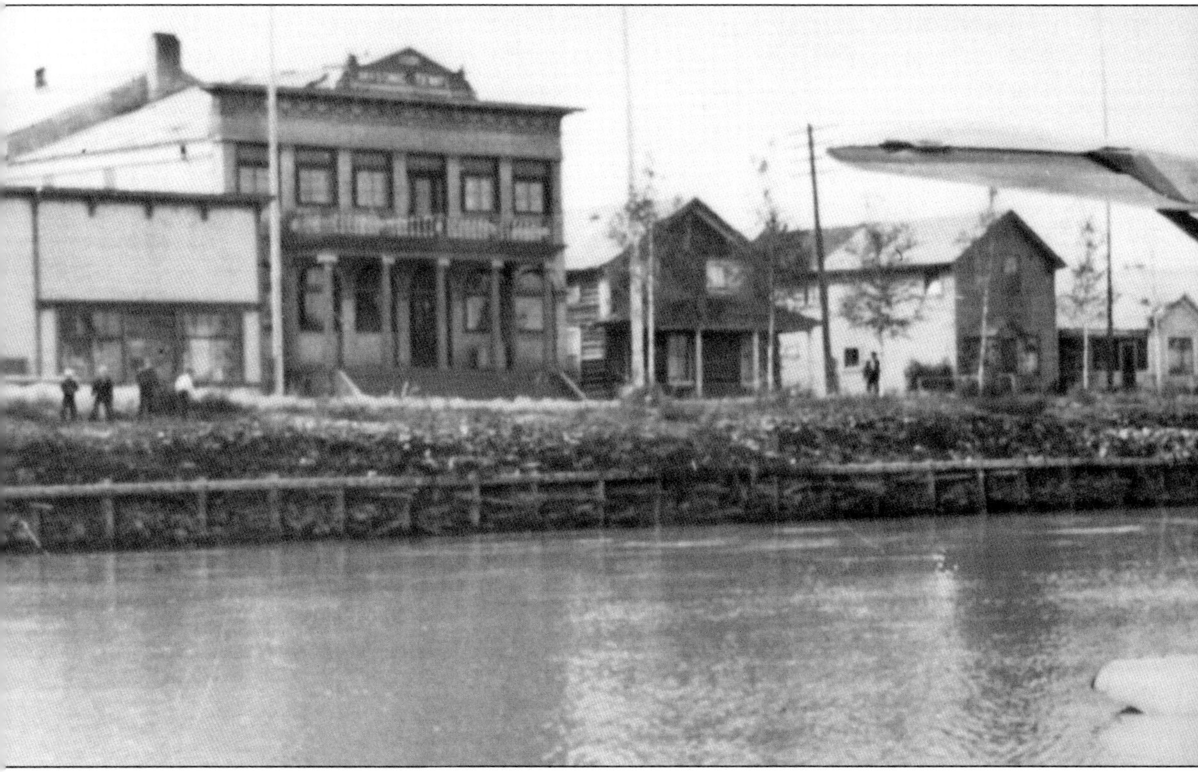

A McGee Airways Stinson is sitting tied down on the shore of the Chena River in downtown

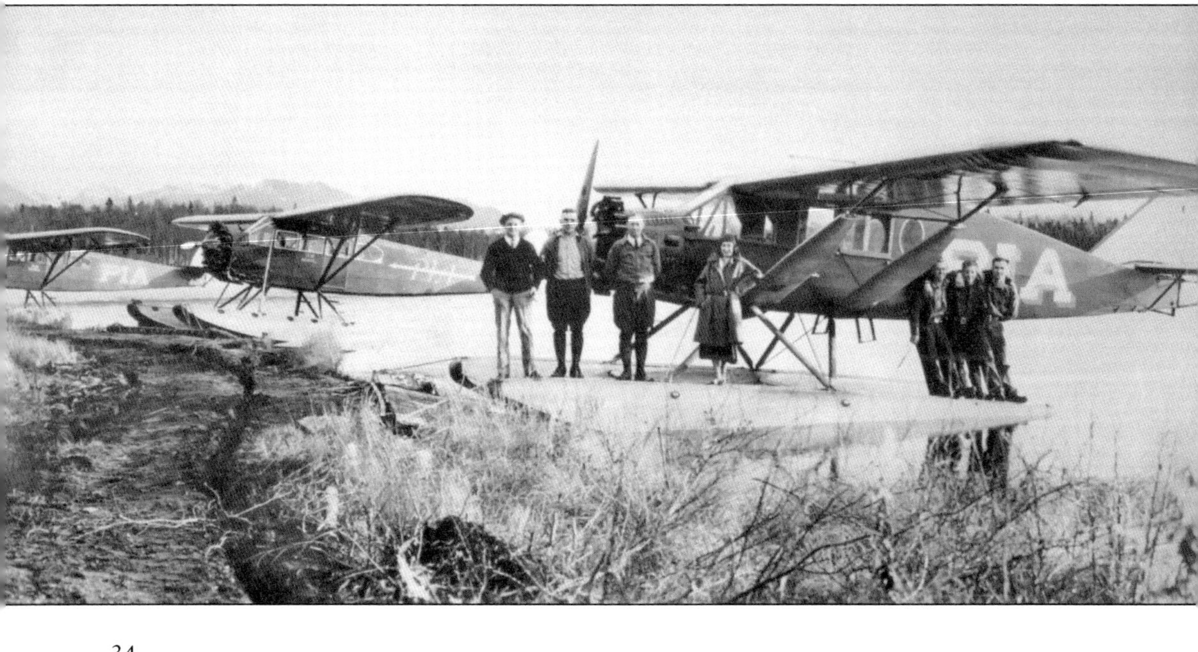

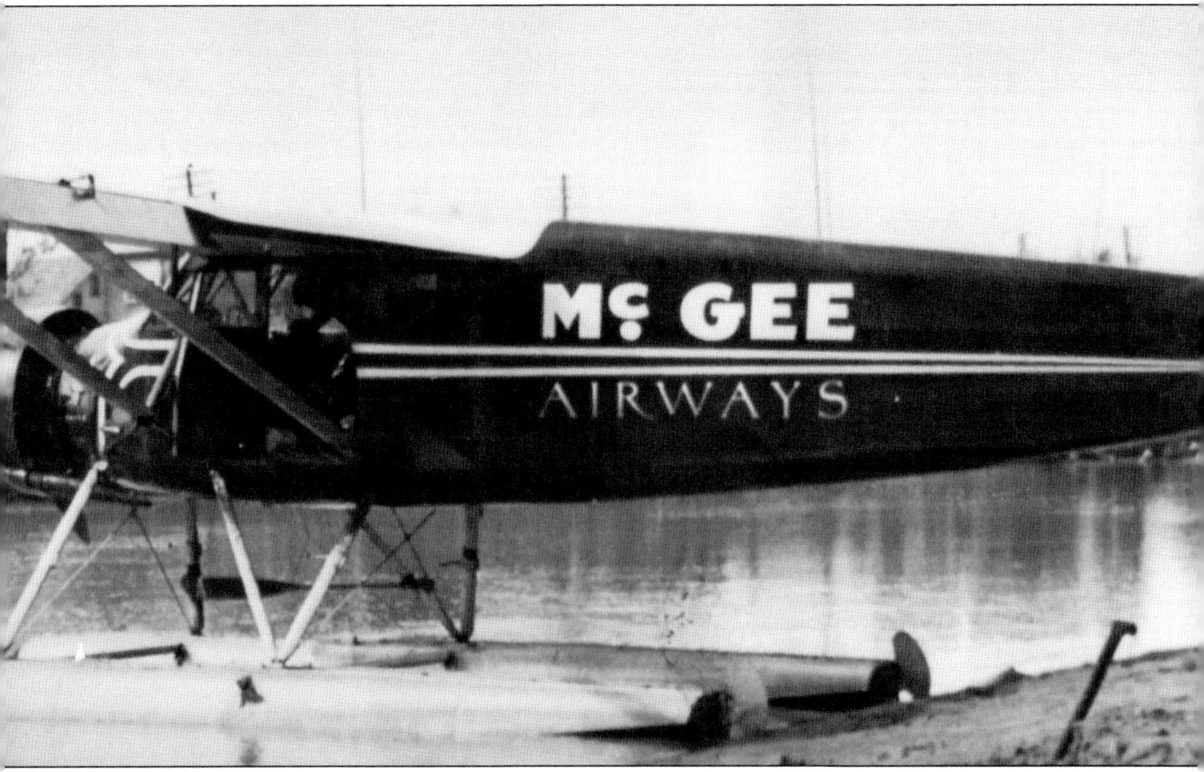

Fairbanks in 1933. (Courtesy of the Alaska Aviation Museum.)

Opposite: Employees of PIA of Alaska stand on the floats of a Bellanca that is tied down with other PIA aircraft at Spenard Lake near Anchorage around 1934. Lake Spenard, now joined with Lake Hood, is home to Lake Hood Seaplane Base, the busiest seaplane base in the world. It is located at Ted Stevens Anchorage International Airport. (Courtesy of the Alaska Aviation Museum.)

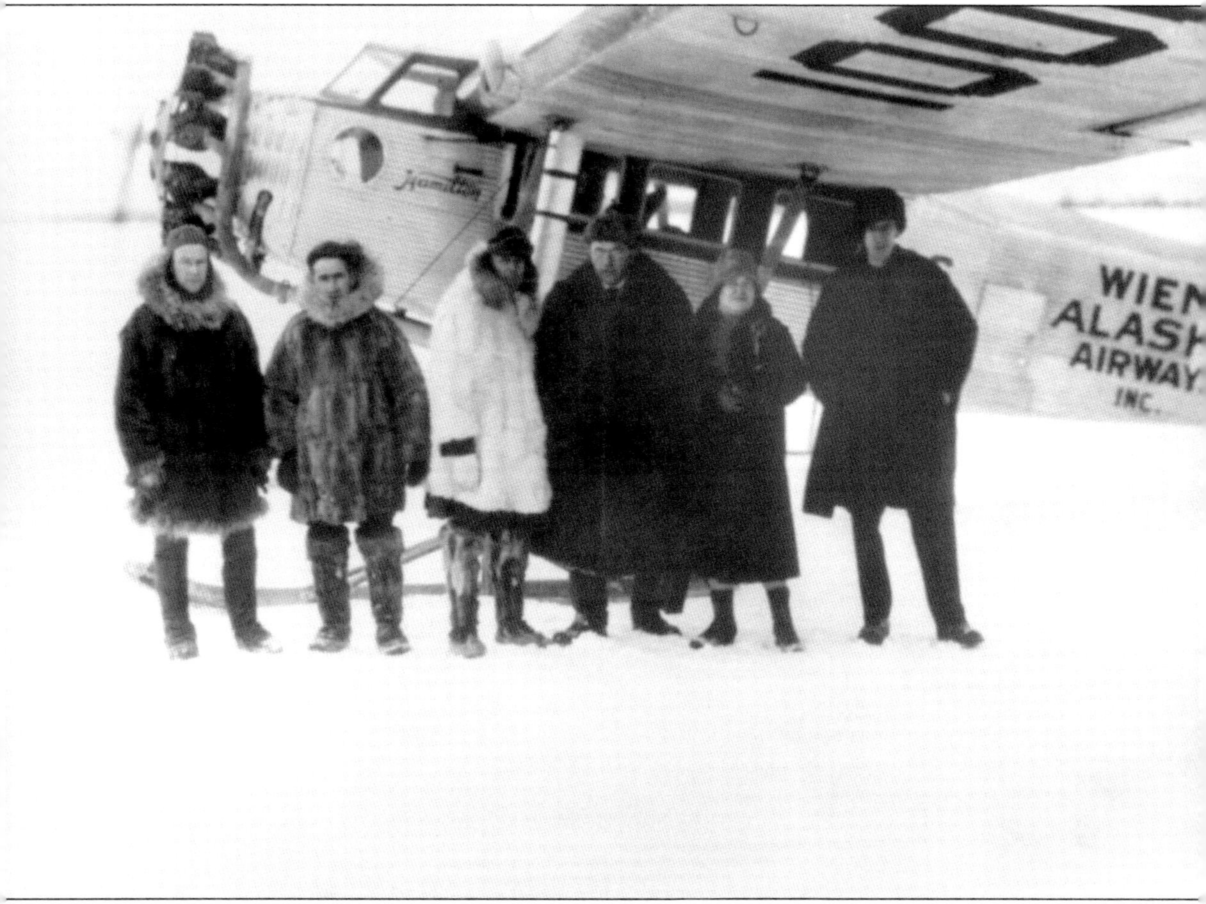

A group of passengers stands under the wing of a Hamilton Standard metal plane operated by Wien Alaska Airways in the 1930s. The company was located in Nome, Alaska. (Courtesy of the Alaska Aviation Museum.)

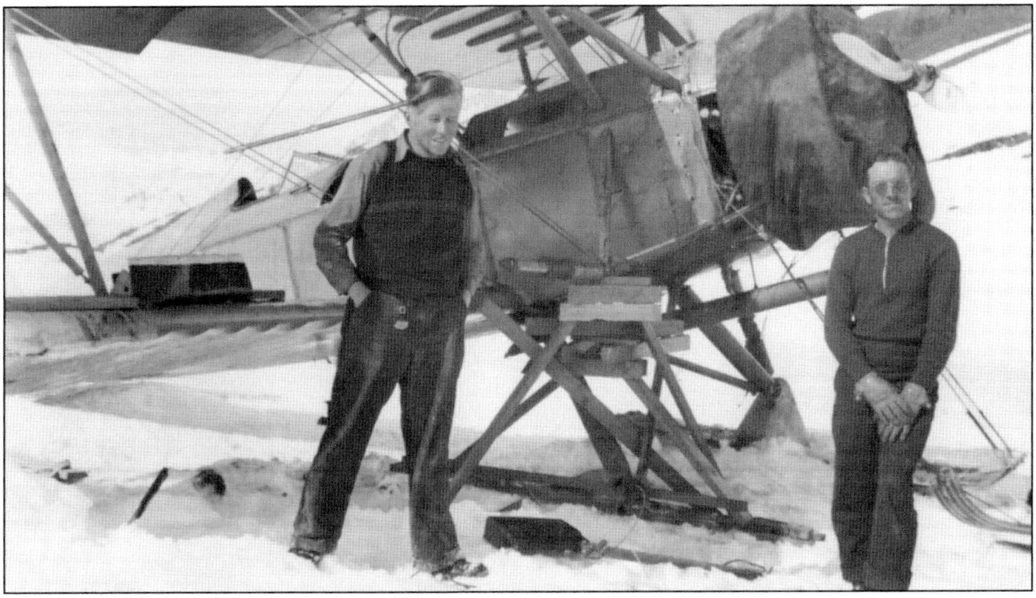

Pilot Jack Peck (left) and an unidentified mechanic conduct on-the-spot repairs to replace a ski on one of his planes at Valdez. (Courtesy of the Alaska Aviation Museum.)

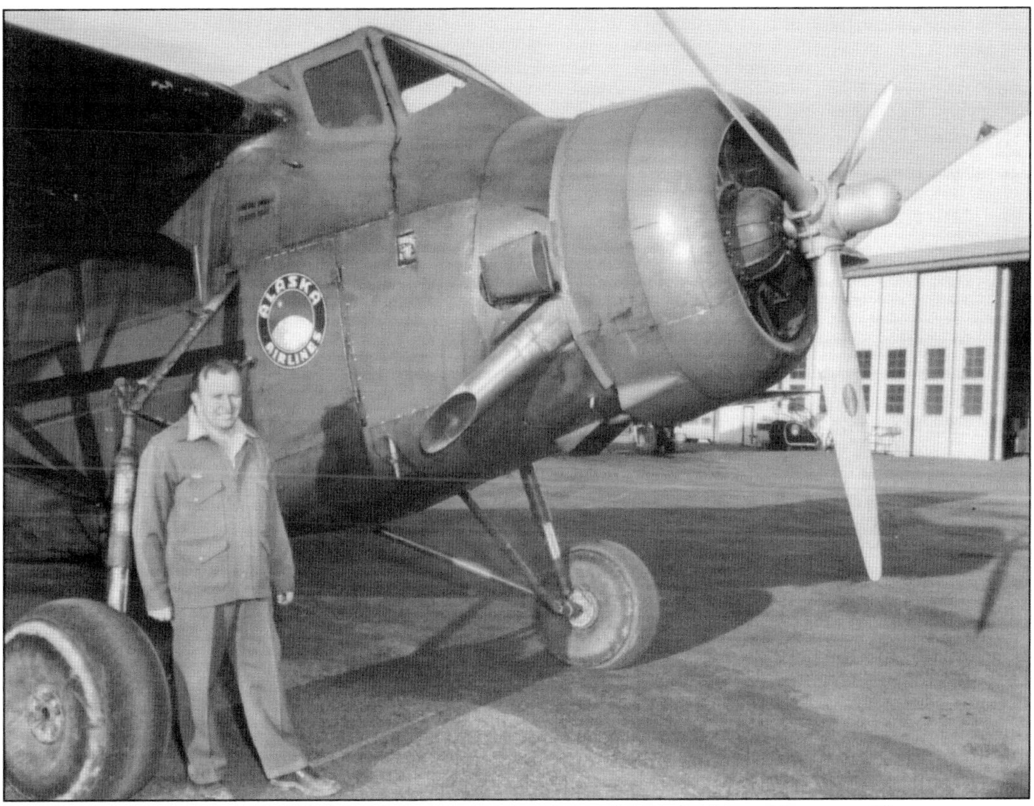

Jack Peck poses with a Fairchild Pilgrim in the 1970s at his Lake Hood hangar. The site is now the location of the Alaska Aviation Museum. (Courtesy of the Alaska Aviation Museum.)

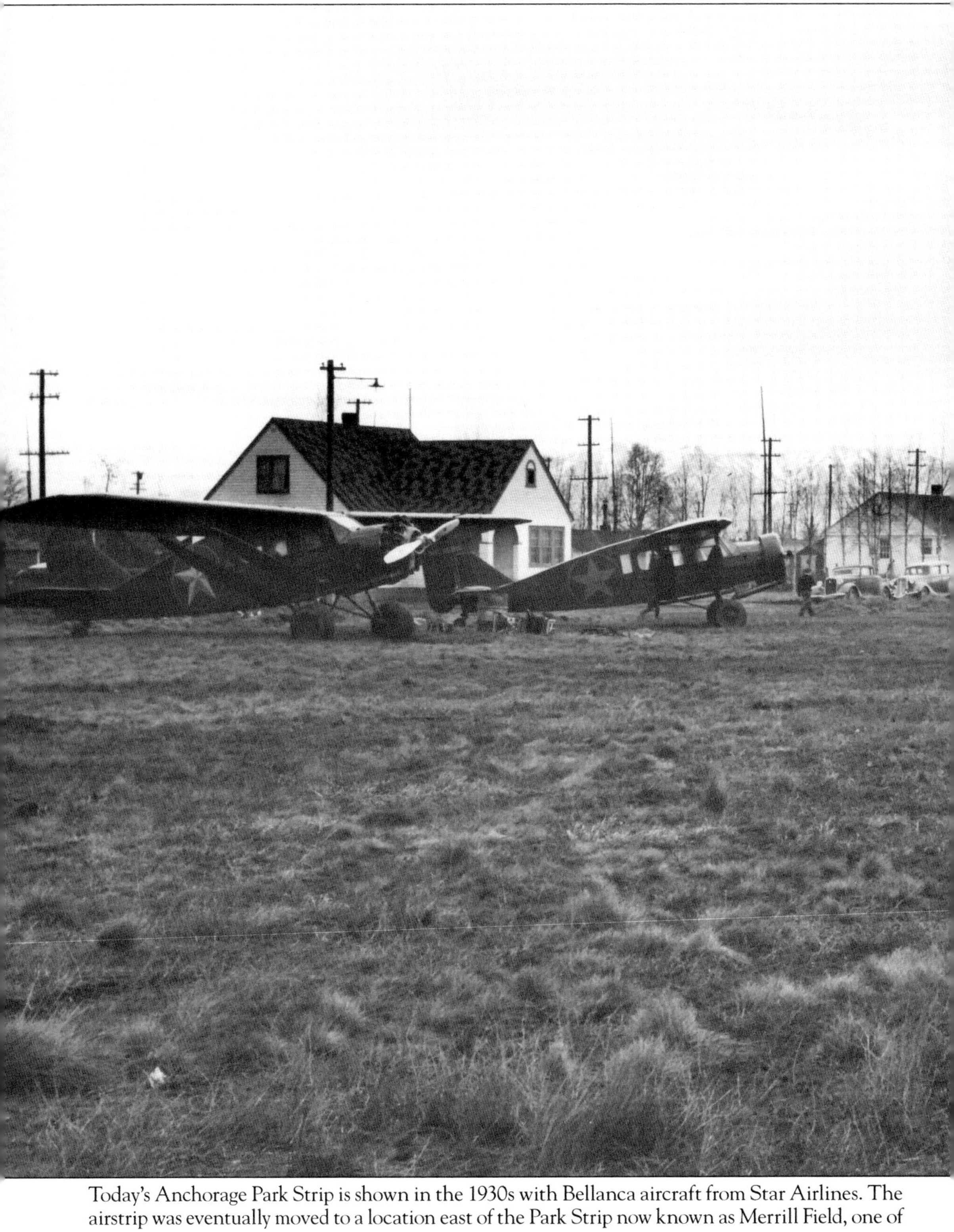

Today's Anchorage Park Strip is shown in the 1930s with Bellanca aircraft from Star Airlines. The airstrip was eventually moved to a location east of the Park Strip now known as Merrill Field, one of

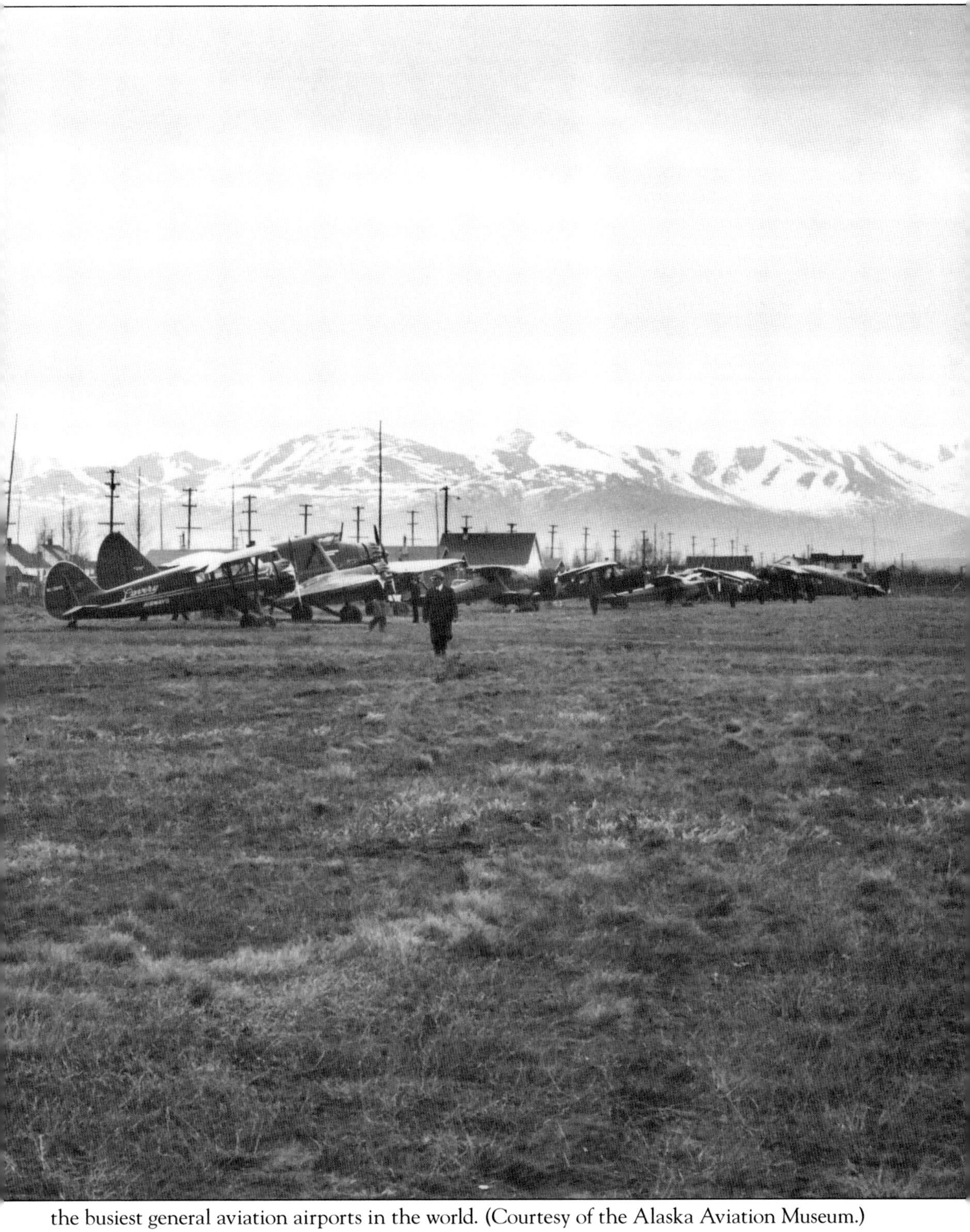

the busiest general aviation airports in the world. (Courtesy of the Alaska Aviation Museum.)

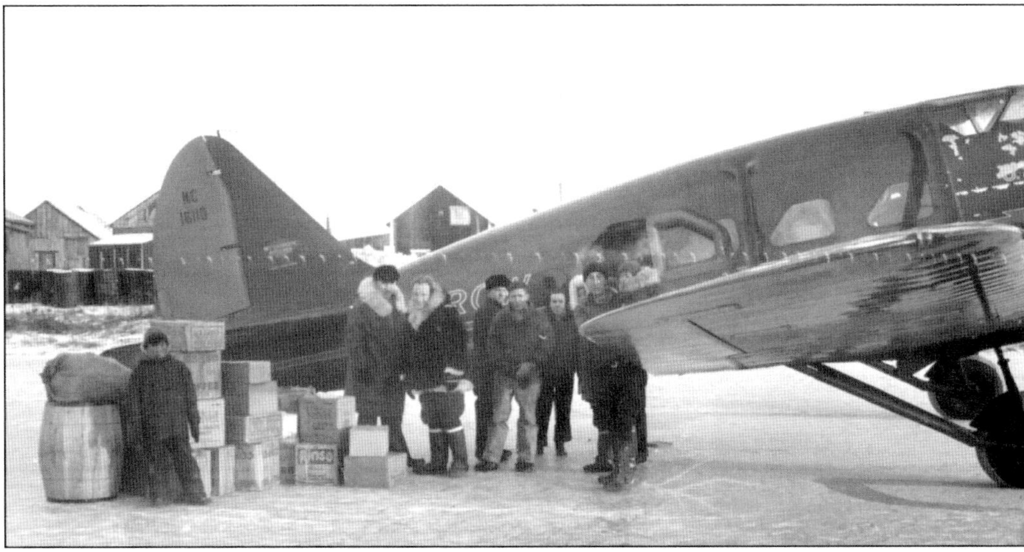

Passengers and cargo are offloaded at a village. The Stinson Tri Motor aircraft was used extensively in rural Alaska in the 1930s. (Courtesy of the Alaska Aviation Museum.)

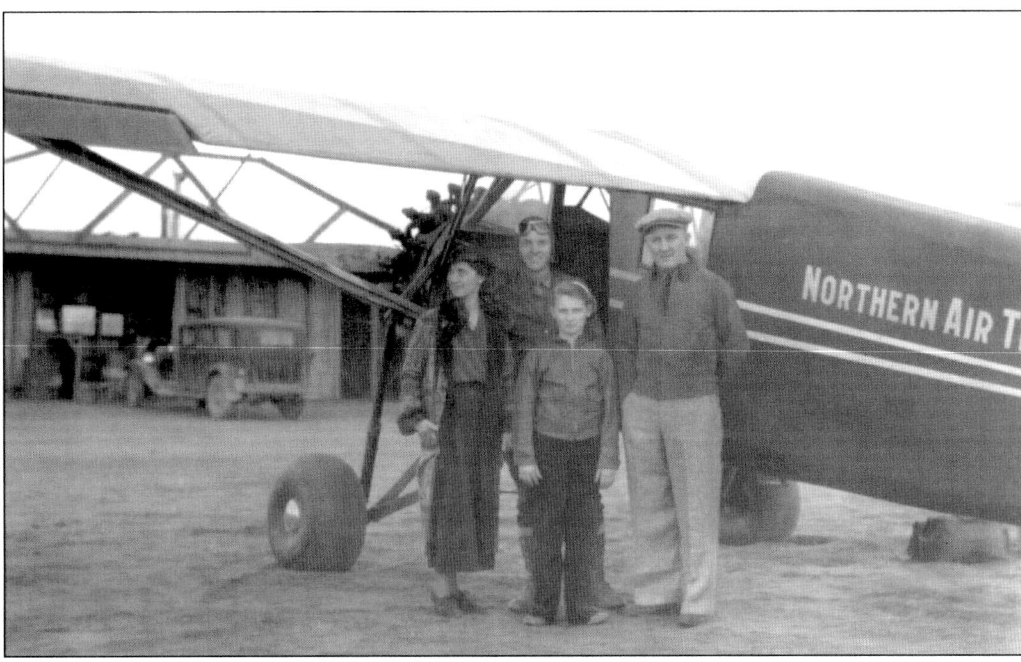

John Lee (rear), a pilot for the Northern Air Transport, poses for a photograph with passengers from a flight from Fairbanks. (Courtesy of the Alaska Aviation Museum.)

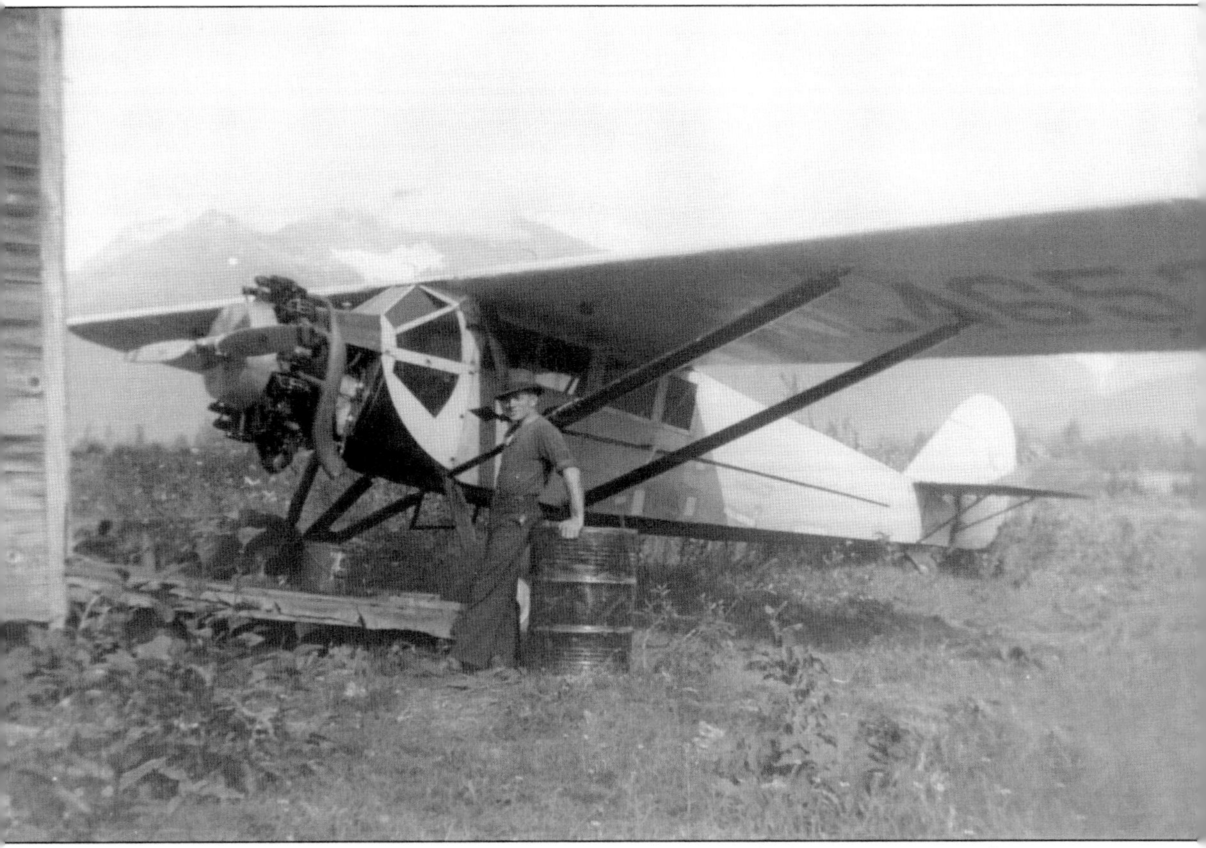

Jack Peck stands next to a Ryan monoplane in Valdez, Alaska, in the late 1920 or 1930s. (Courtesy of the Alaska Aviation Museum.)

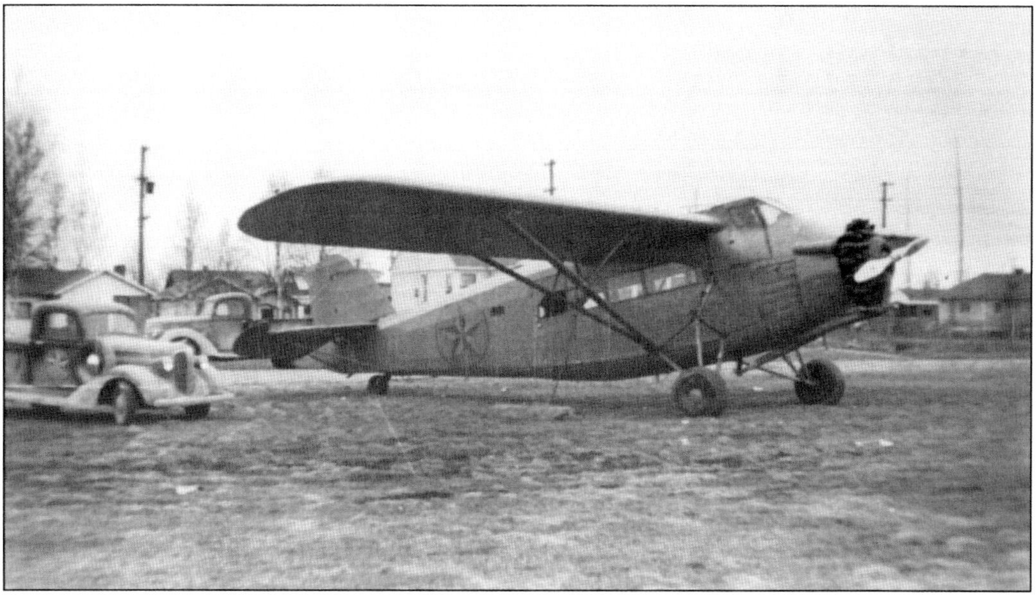

The Fairchild Pilgrim was a well-used plane. This Pilgrim, with Star Airlines markings, is seen on the Anchorage Park Strip in the 1930s. (Courtesy of the Alaska Aviation Museum.)

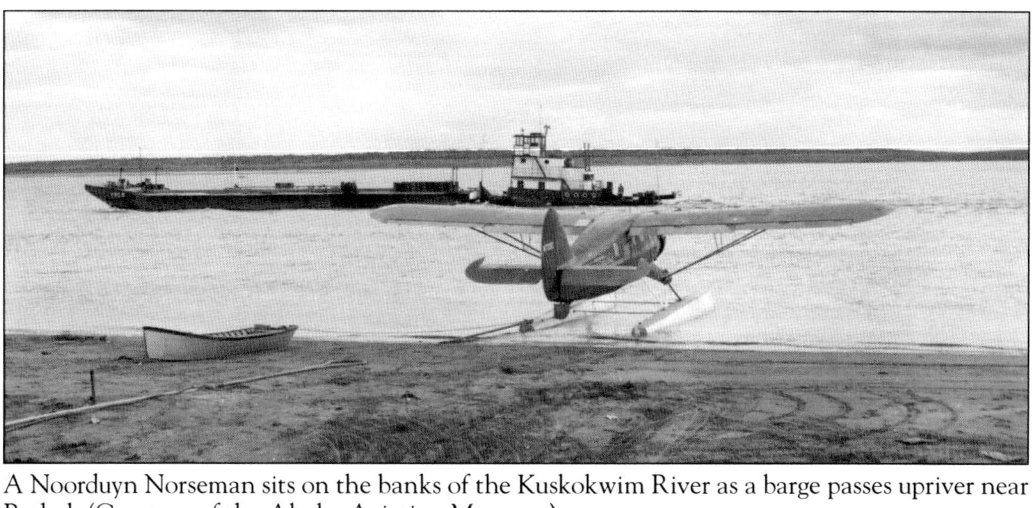

A Noorduyn Norseman sits on the banks of the Kuskokwim River as a barge passes upriver near Bethel. (Courtesy of the Alaska Aviation Museum.)

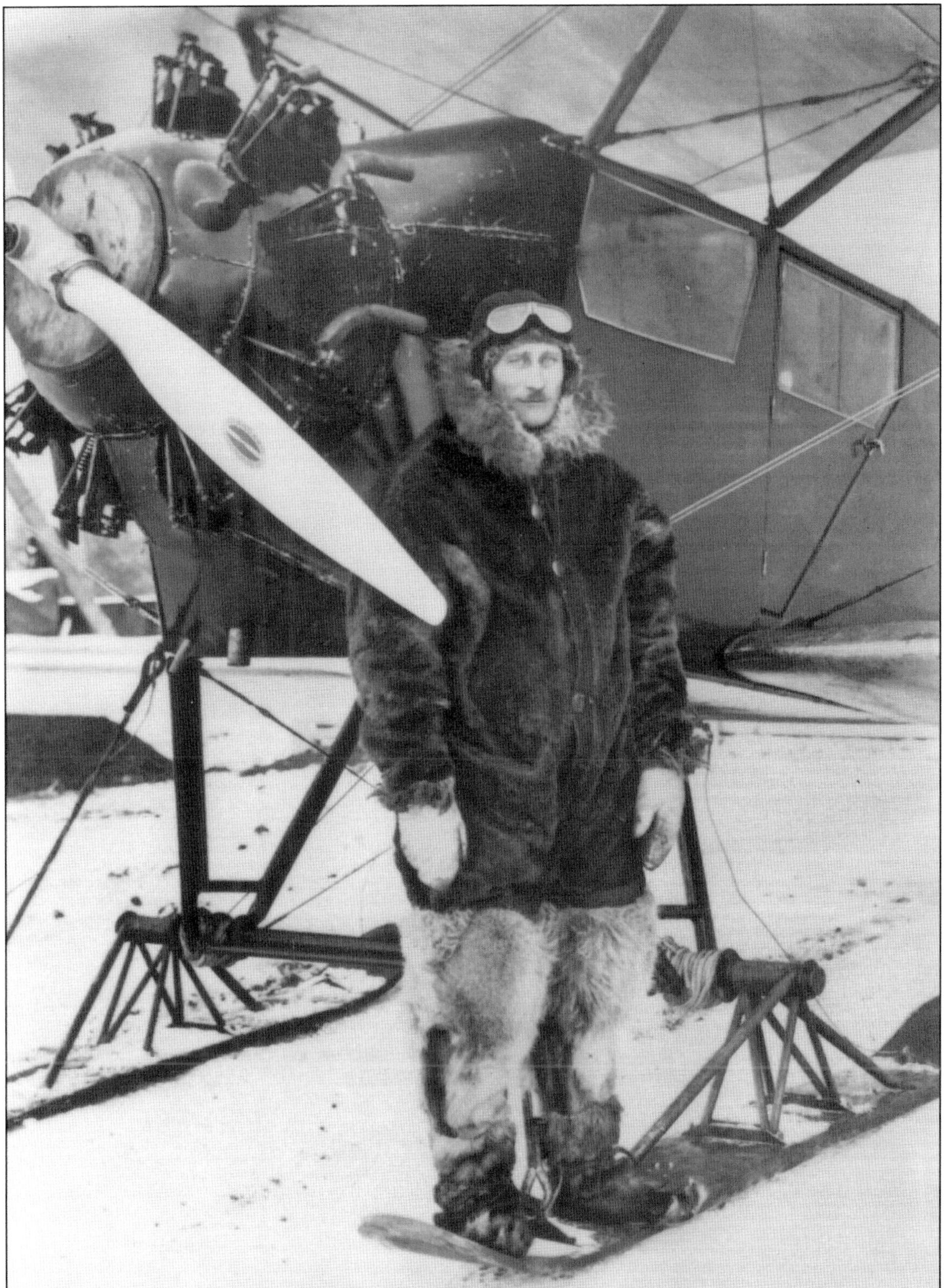

Born in 1888 in Oregon, Elmer "A.A." Bennett came to Alaska in the mid-1920s. Bennett is believed to be the first pilot to land on the Kuskokwim River ice at Bethel, Alaska. He was the flying partner of Bennett-Rodebaugh Company in Fairbanks. Bennett left the territory of Alaska for Idaho in 1930 and later lived in Las Vegas, Nevada. (Courtesy of the Alaska Aviation Museum.)

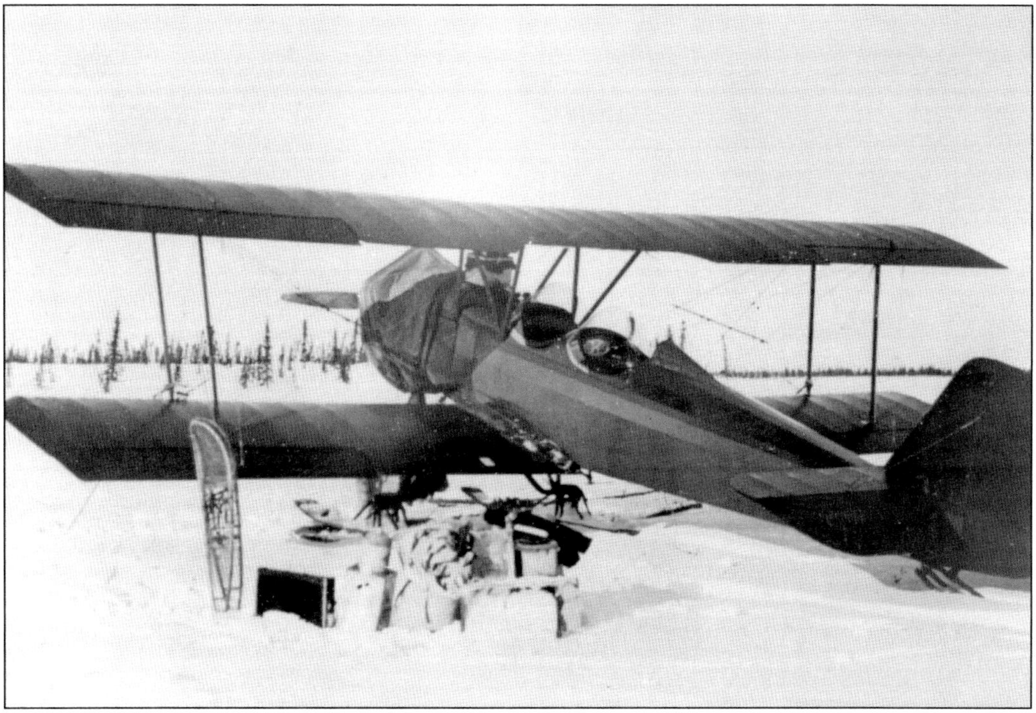

This Stearman C2B sits with a typical load of gear for a wintertime trip into the Alaska bush. (Courtesy of the Alaska Aviation Museum.)

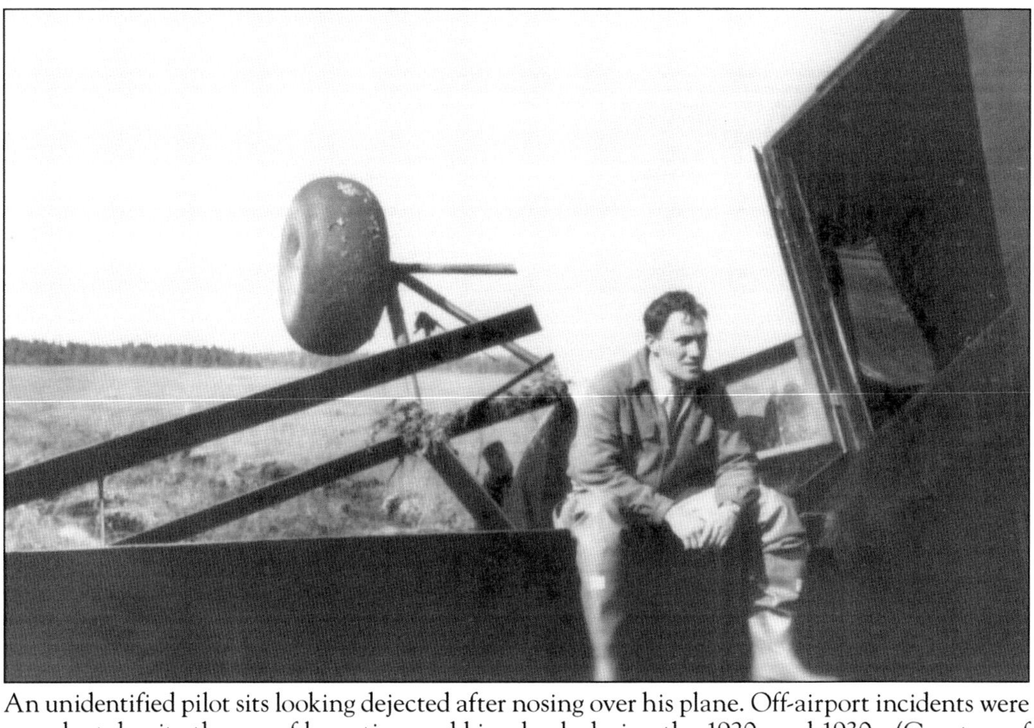

An unidentified pilot sits looking dejected after nosing over his plane. Off-airport incidents were prevalent despite the use of large tires and big wheels during the 1920s and 1930s. (Courtesy of the Alaska Aviation Museum.)

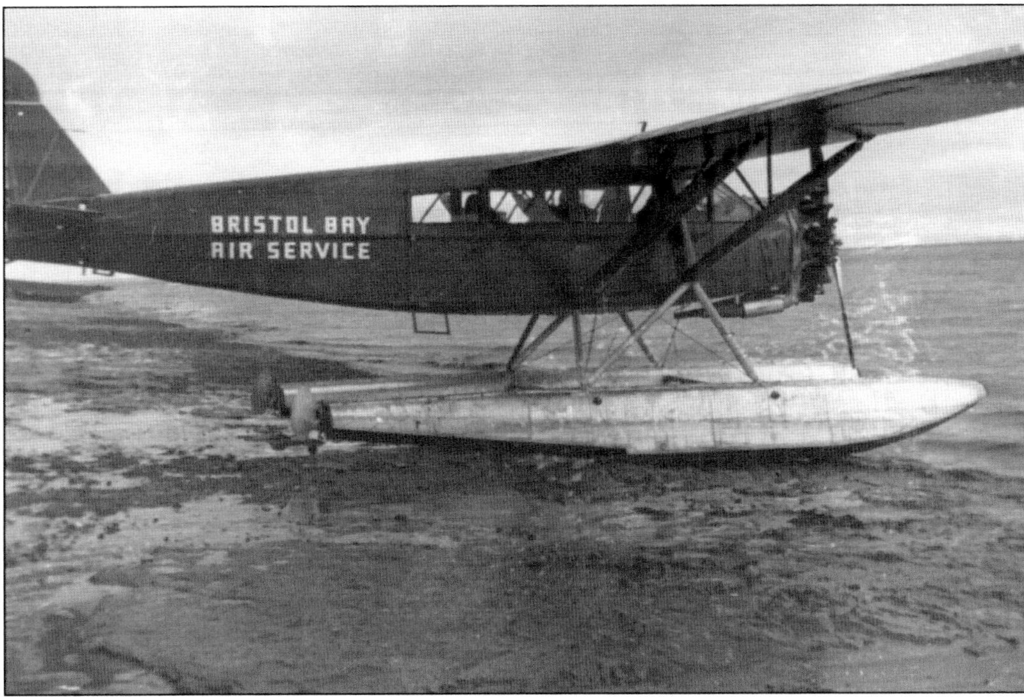

A Bristol Bay Air Service Travel Air is shown on the water. The airline was founded by Frank Pollack in 1933. He eventually sold the air service to Alaska Star in 1942, and it later became Alaska Airlines. (Courtesy of the Alaska Aviation Museum.)

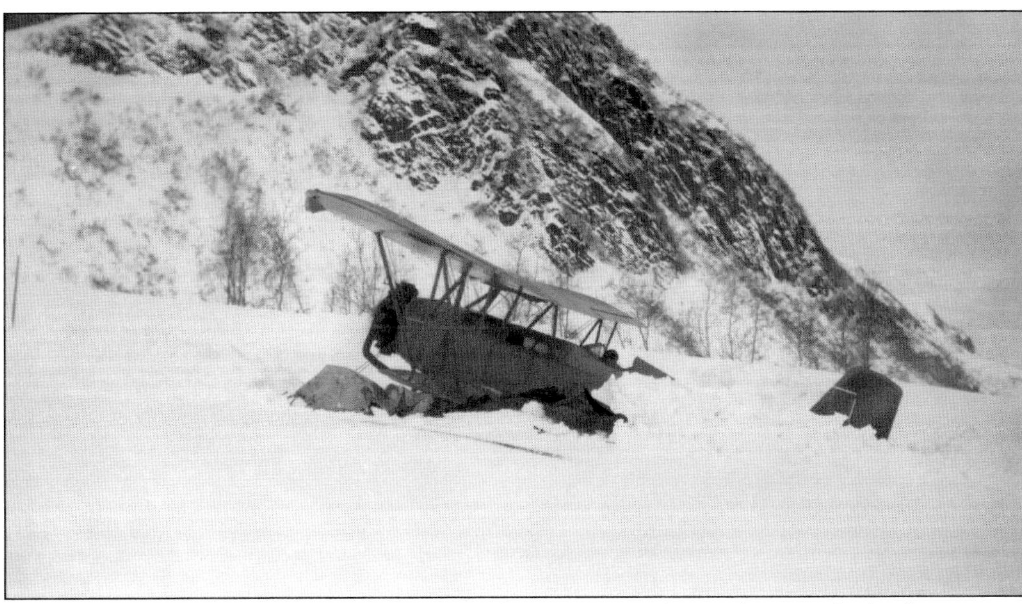

A Boeing 40 on skis is shown at a camp in the snow. Note how pilots roughed it by camping under the wing. (Courtesy of the Alaska Aviation Museum.)

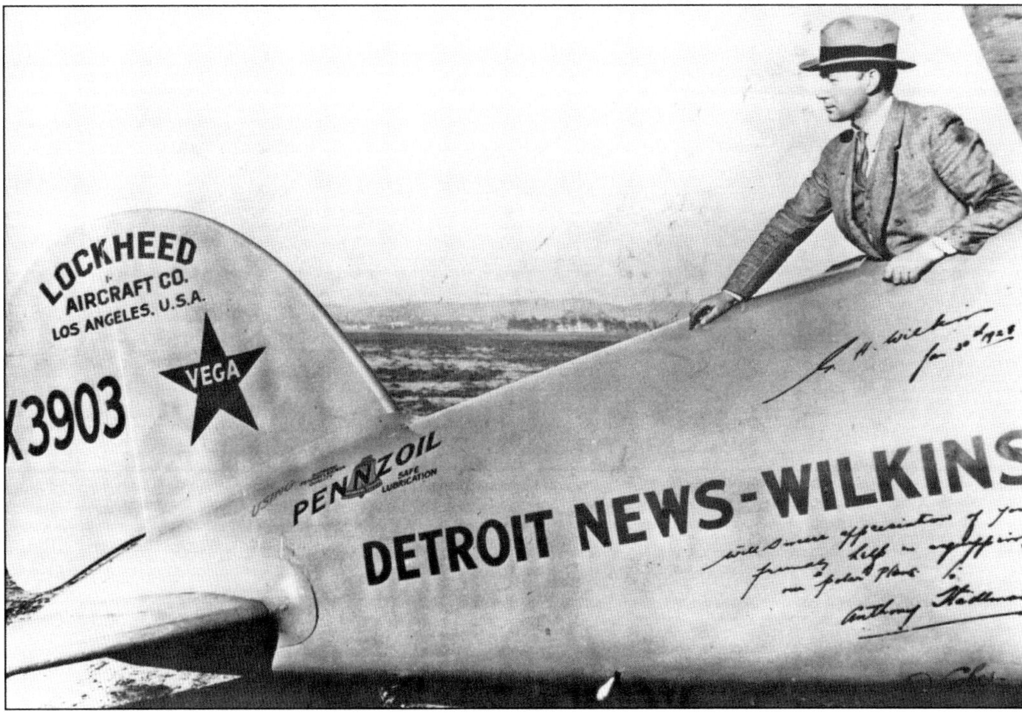

After returning to Australia in 1917 from the Arctic, George Hubert Wilkins joined the Australian Flying Corps. Commissioned in May 1917 as a lieutenant, he was sent to France as an aerial photographer. He quickly developed a reputation for top-notch work, taking many excellent photographs of Australians fighting on the Western Front. (Courtesy of the Alaska Aviation Museum.)

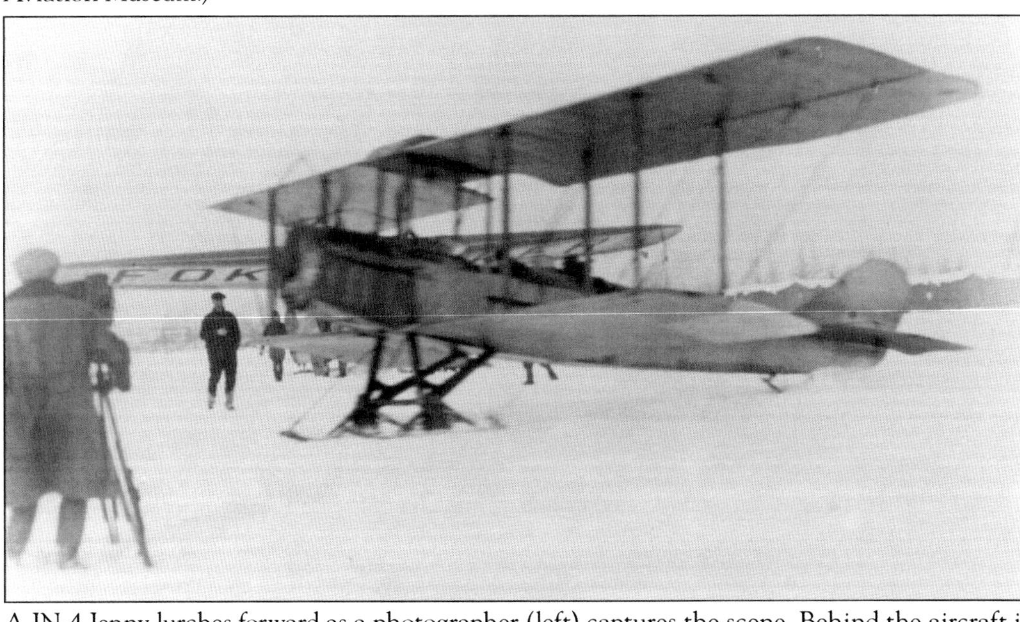

A JN-4 Jenny lurches forward as a photographer (left) captures the scene. Behind the aircraft is the Fokker flown on the Detroit Arctic Expedition headed by George Hubert Wilkins in 1926. (Courtesy of the Alaska Aviation Museum.)

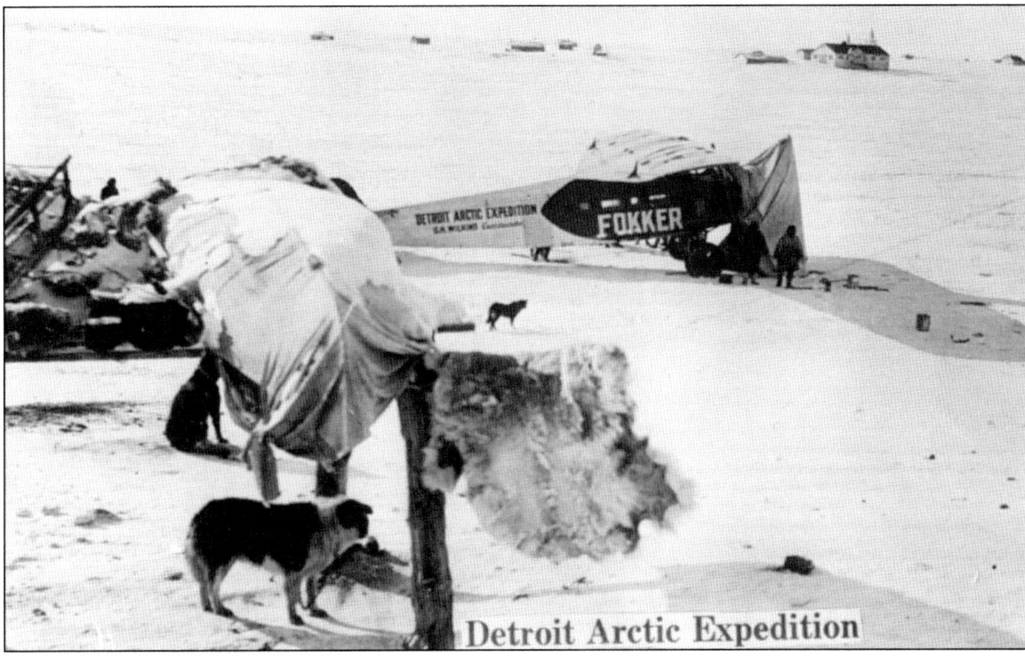

Wilkins (below at left on ski) was the only Australian official photographer to be decorated for bravery. He was awarded the Military Cross in 1917 and a bar in 1918. After World War I, he became famous as an Arctic and Antarctic explorer. In 1928, he purchased a Lockheed Vega and, with pilot Carl Ben Eielson, flew from Barrow in Alaska to Spitsbergen in Norway. It was the first flight to be made across the Arctic Sea. Both men became celebrities. Wilkins was knighted and chose to be known as Sir Hubert Wilkins. He died on November 30, 1958, and his ashes were scattered at the North Pole by a US Navy submarine. (Both, courtesy of the Alaska Aviation Museum.)

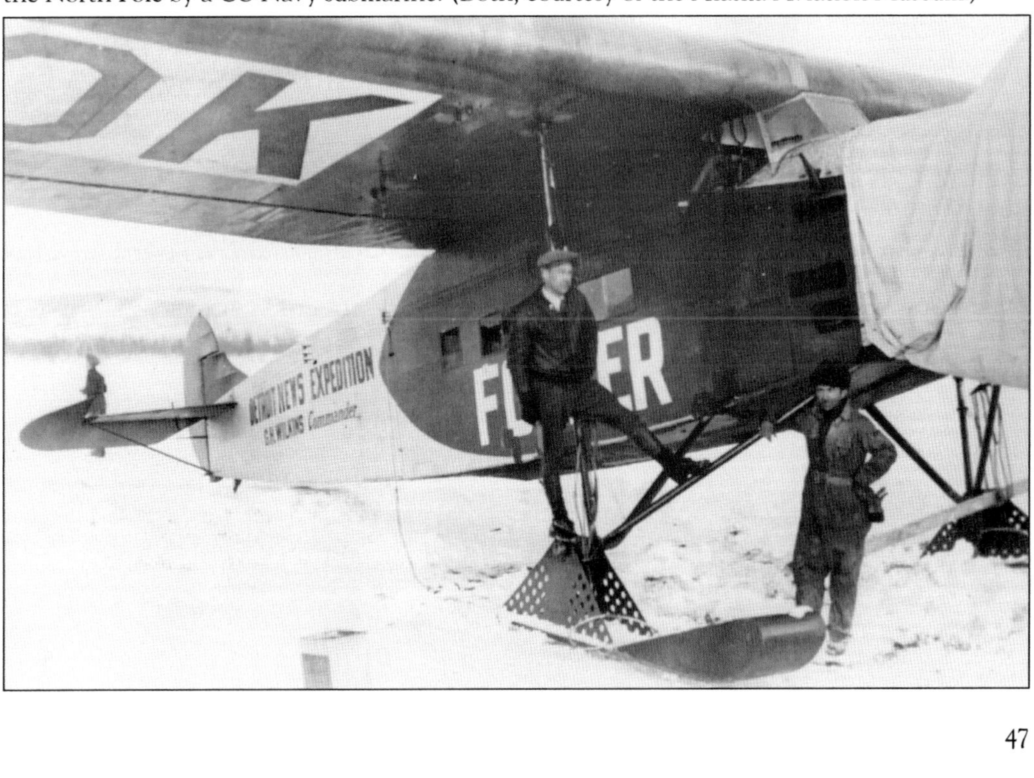

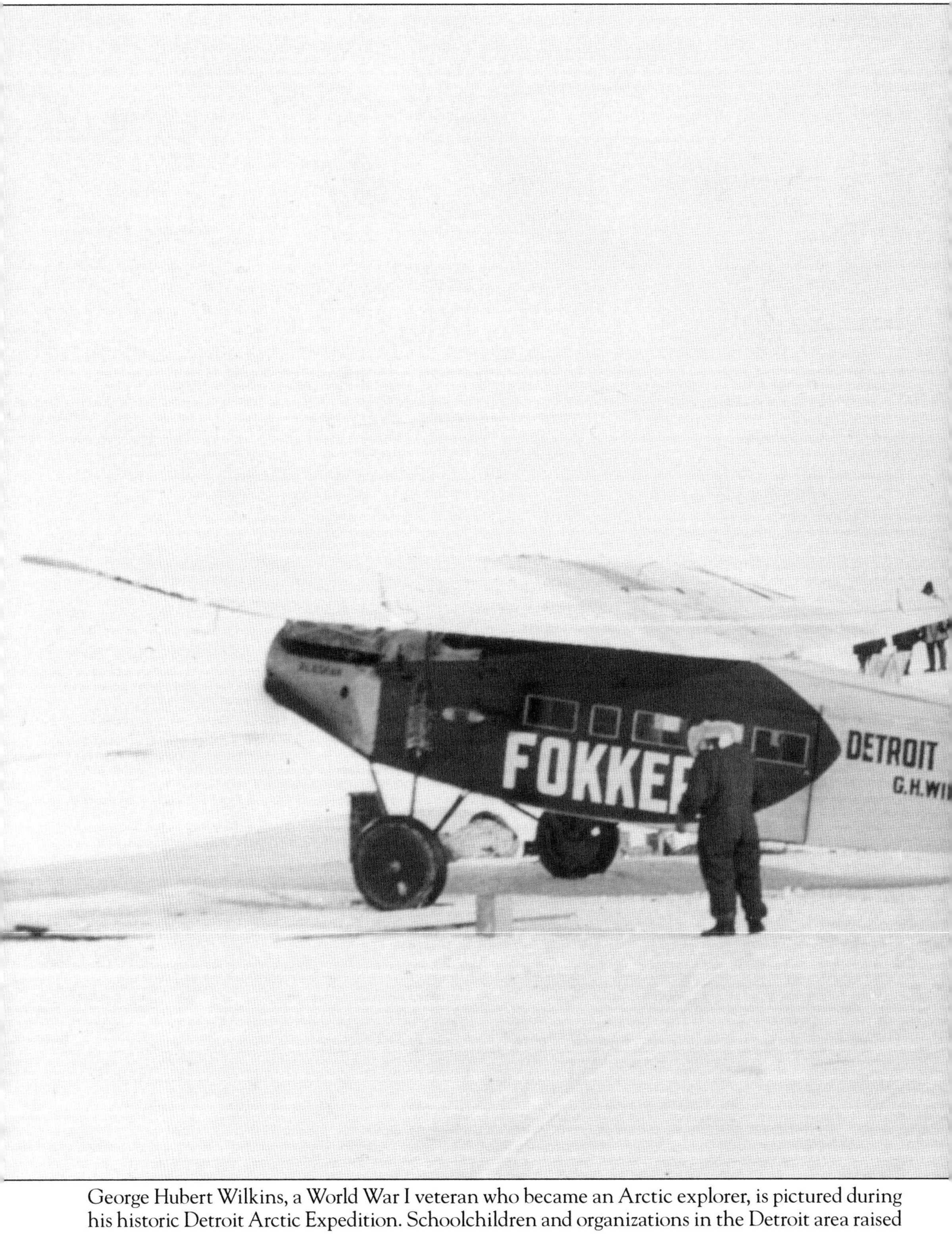

George Hubert Wilkins, a World War I veteran who became an Arctic explorer, is pictured during his historic Detroit Arctic Expedition. Schoolchildren and organizations in the Detroit area raised

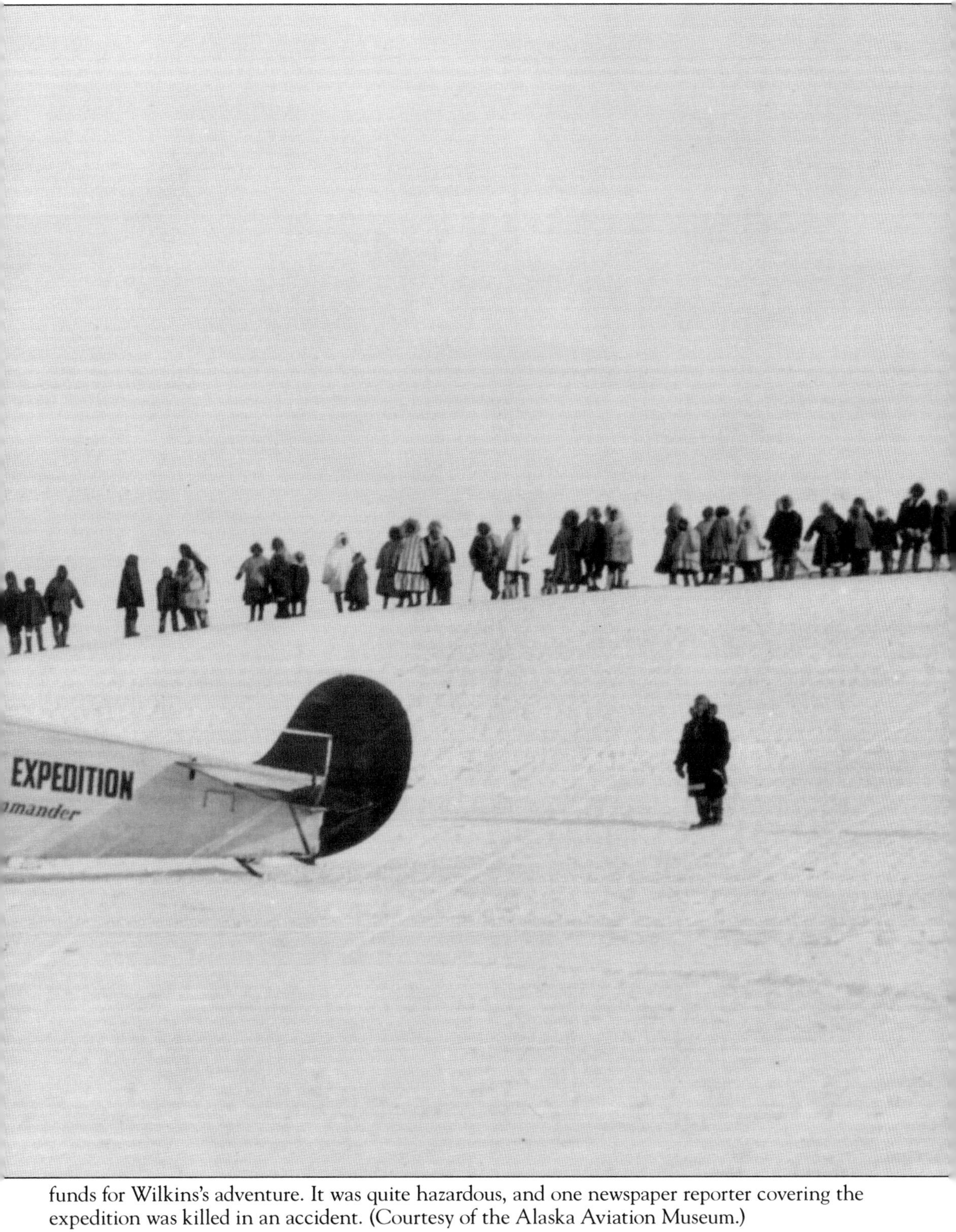

funds for Wilkins's adventure. It was quite hazardous, and one newspaper reporter covering the expedition was killed in an accident. (Courtesy of the Alaska Aviation Museum.)

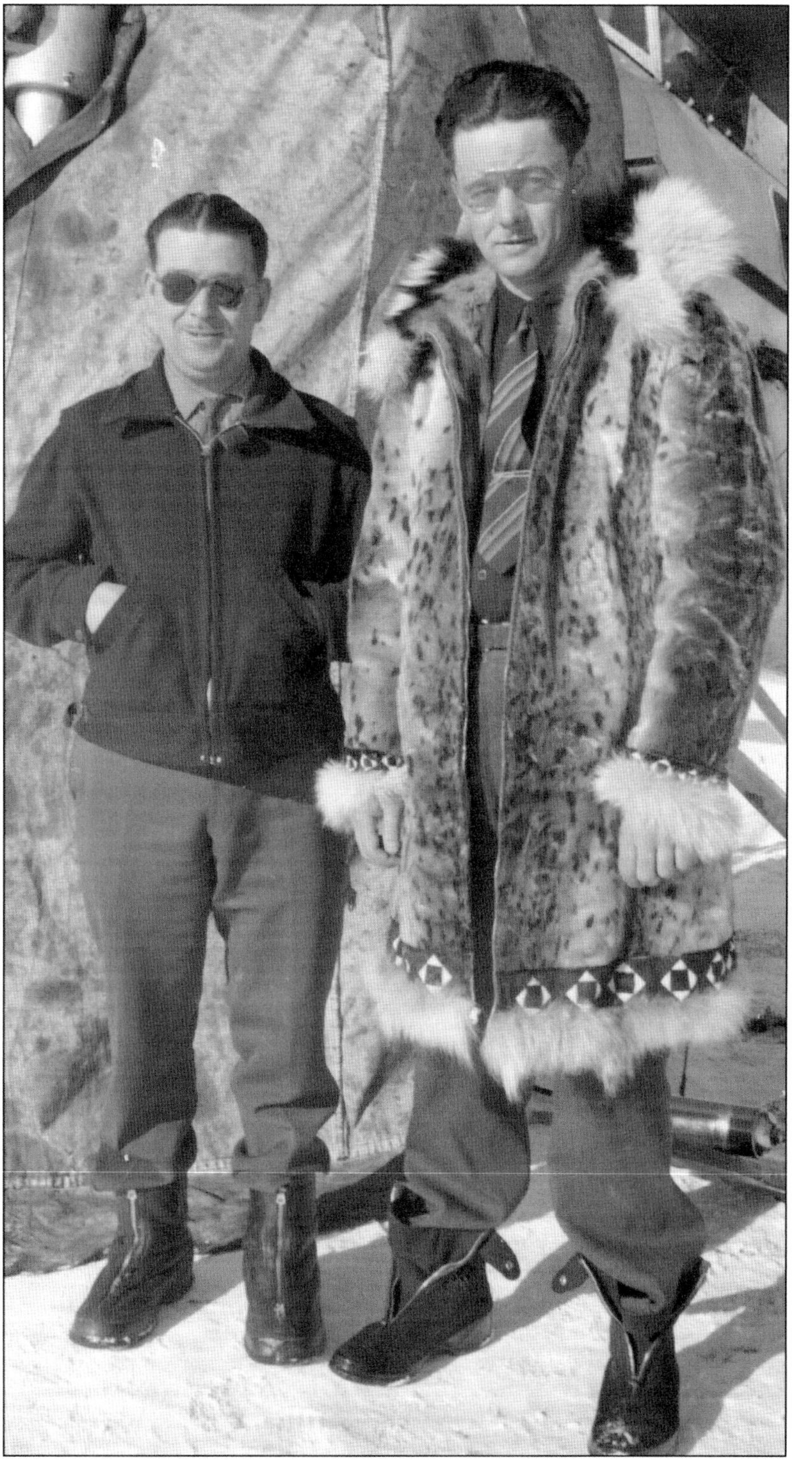

A pilot and his passenger are dressed for the day. Note the three-quarter-length spotted seal coat with Eskimo rickrack trim. The men are standing in front of a Mirrow Lockheed Vega. (Courtesy of the Alaska Aviation Museum.)

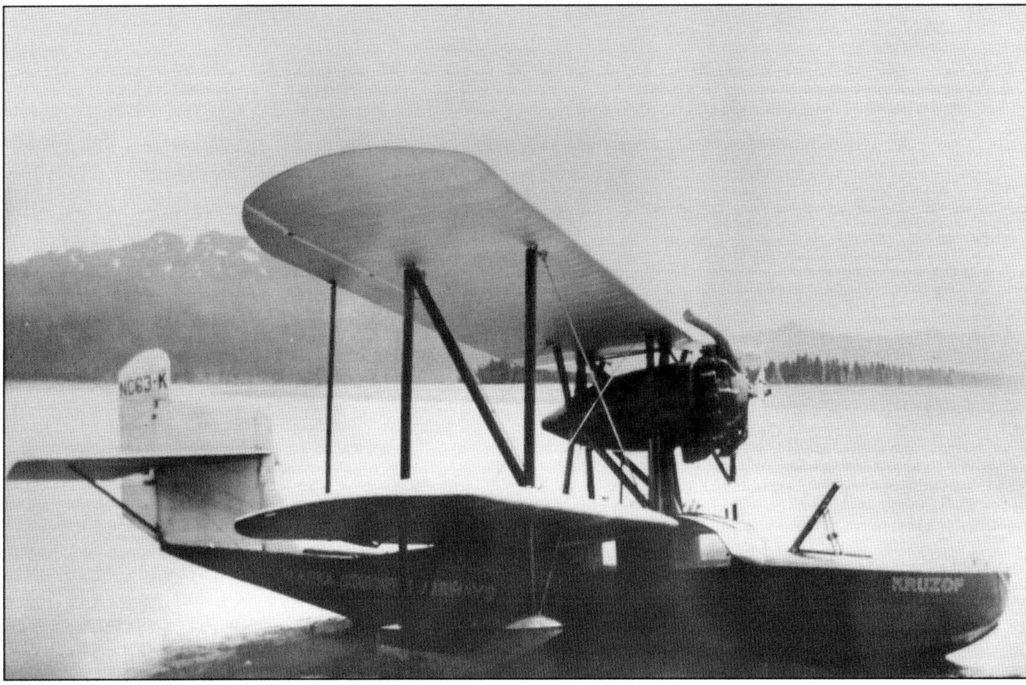

The Alaska Southern Airways Keystone-Loening Commuter K-84 *Kruzof* is seen on the beach in southeast Alaska. (Courtesy of the Alaska Aviation Museum.)

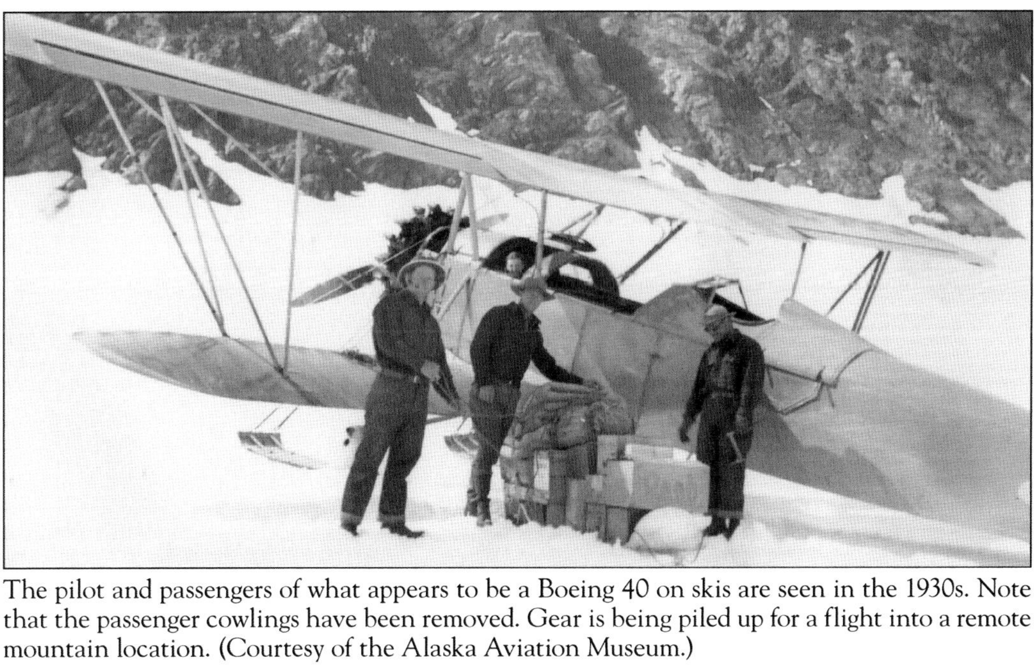

The pilot and passengers of what appears to be a Boeing 40 on skis are seen in the 1930s. Note that the passenger cowlings have been removed. Gear is being piled up for a flight into a remote mountain location. (Courtesy of the Alaska Aviation Museum.)

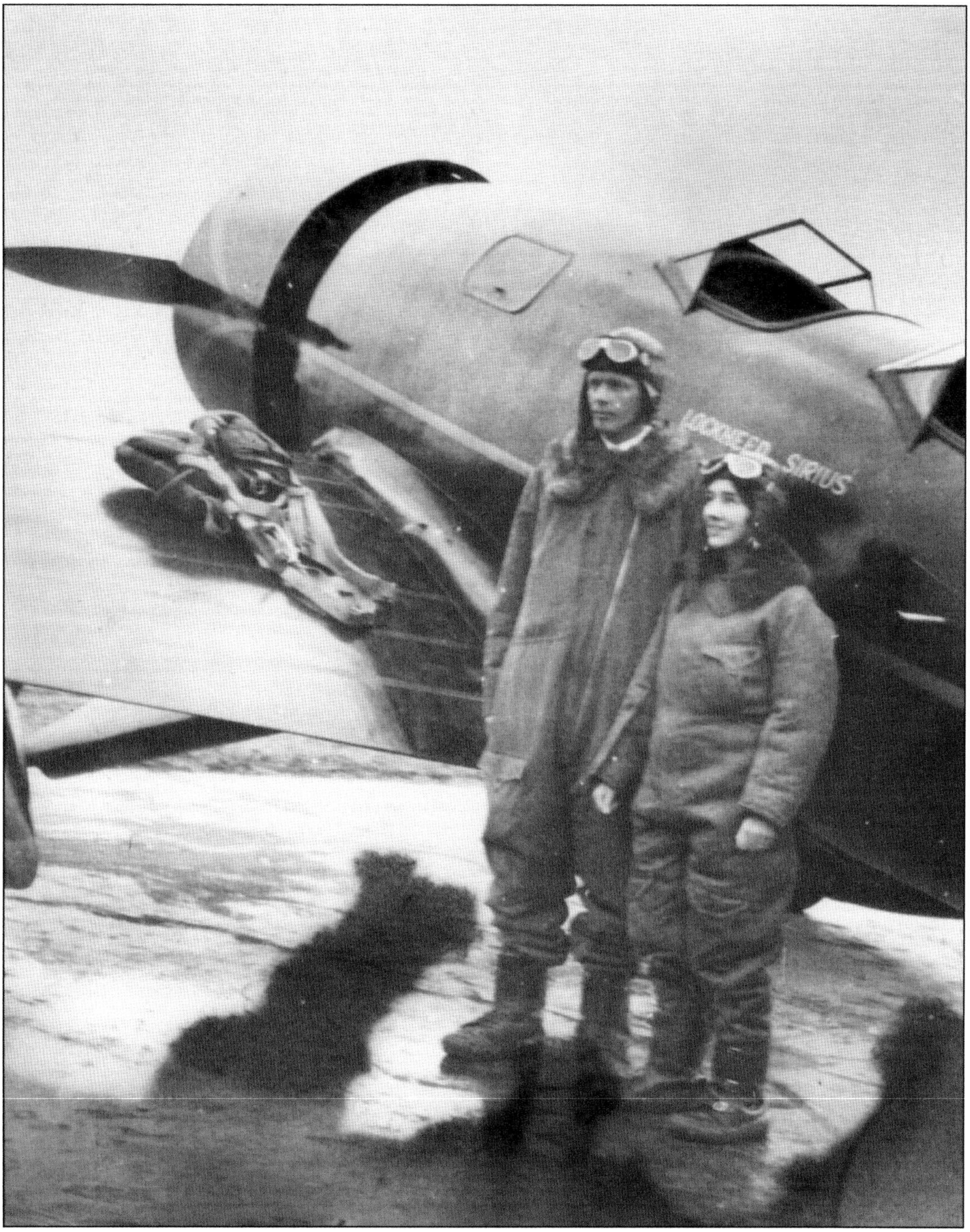

Charles and Anne Lindbergh stand next to a Lockheed Sirius at Nome, Alaska, during their flights to chart air routes to the Orient in 1931. The task lasted five and a half months and covered 30,000 miles. (Courtesy of the Alaska Aviation Museum.)

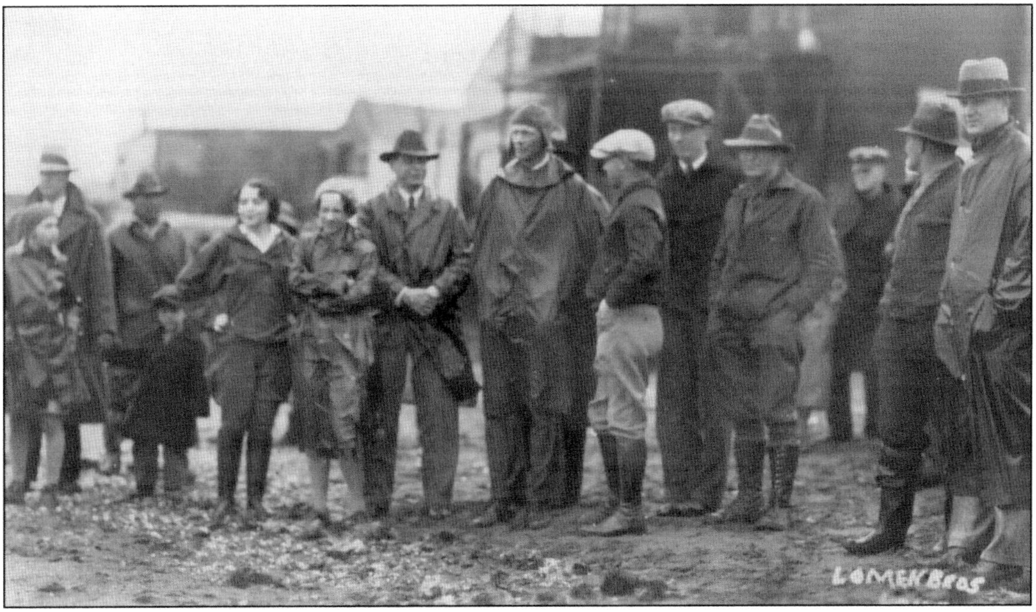

Charles (center, with pilot cap) and Anne Lindbergh (fourth from left) stand with a group of people, including their hosts, Mr. and Mrs. Grant Jackson, as they watch umiak skin-boat races off the beach at Nome, Alaska. Mr. and Mrs. Grant Jackson are between the Lindberghs. (Both, courtesy of the Alaska Aviation Museum.)

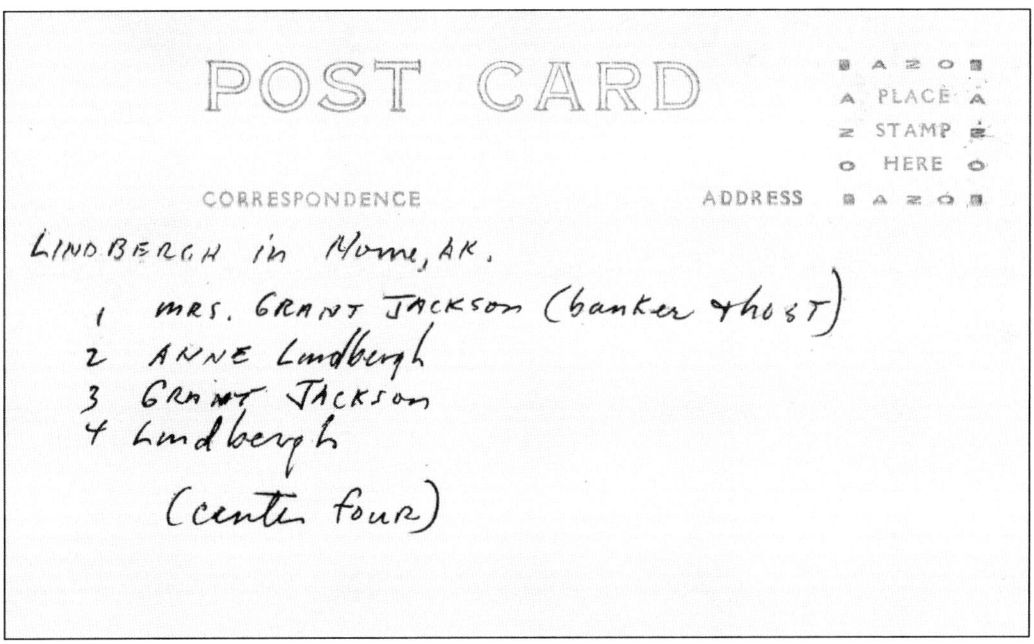
POST CARD

AZO PLACE STAMP HERE

CORRESPONDENCE

ADDRESS

LINDBERGH in Nome, AK.

1 MRS. GRANT JACKSON (banker + host)
2 ANNE Lindbergh
3 GRANT JACKSON
4 Lindbergh

(center four)

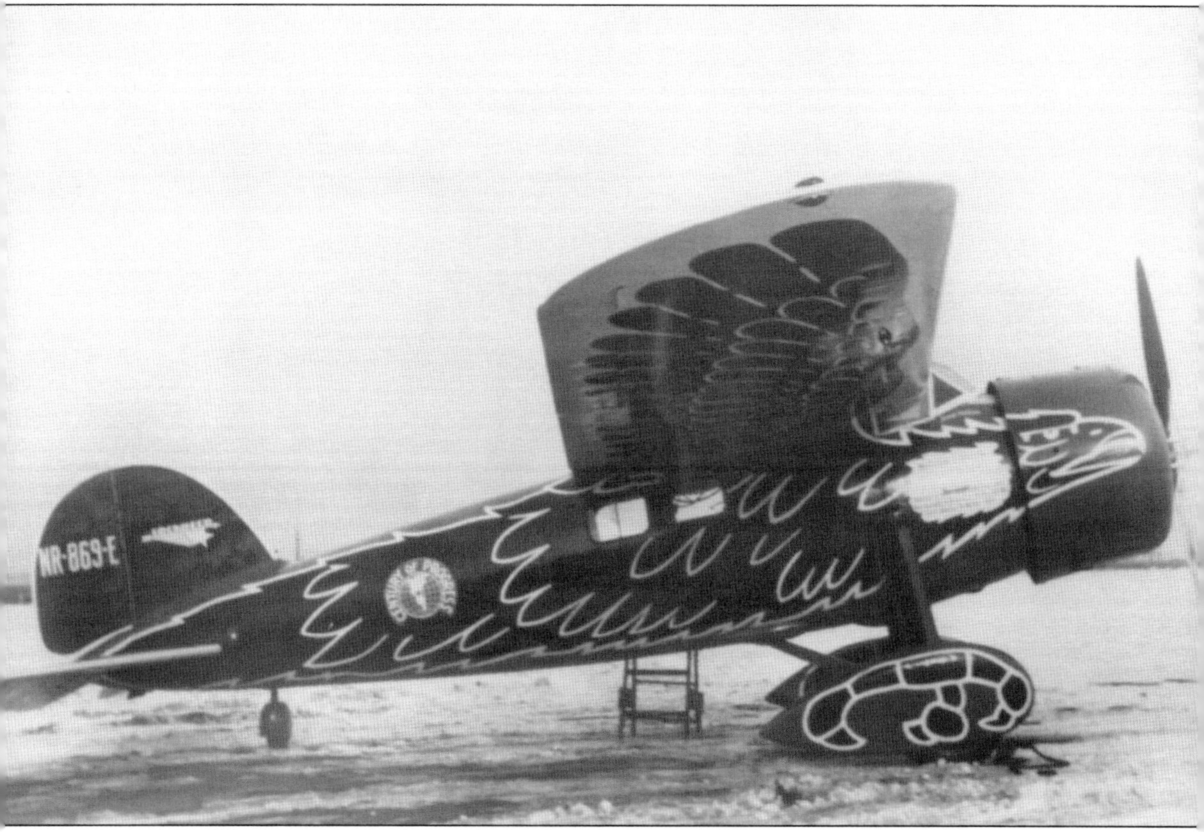

This model of the ever-popular 1930s Lockheed Vega features a fancy bird-of-prey livery. The craft, owned by Jimmy Matterns and sponsored by Standard Oil for an around-the-world flight, sits at the Seattle airport before being flown to Alaska. (Courtesy of the Alaska Aviation Museum.)

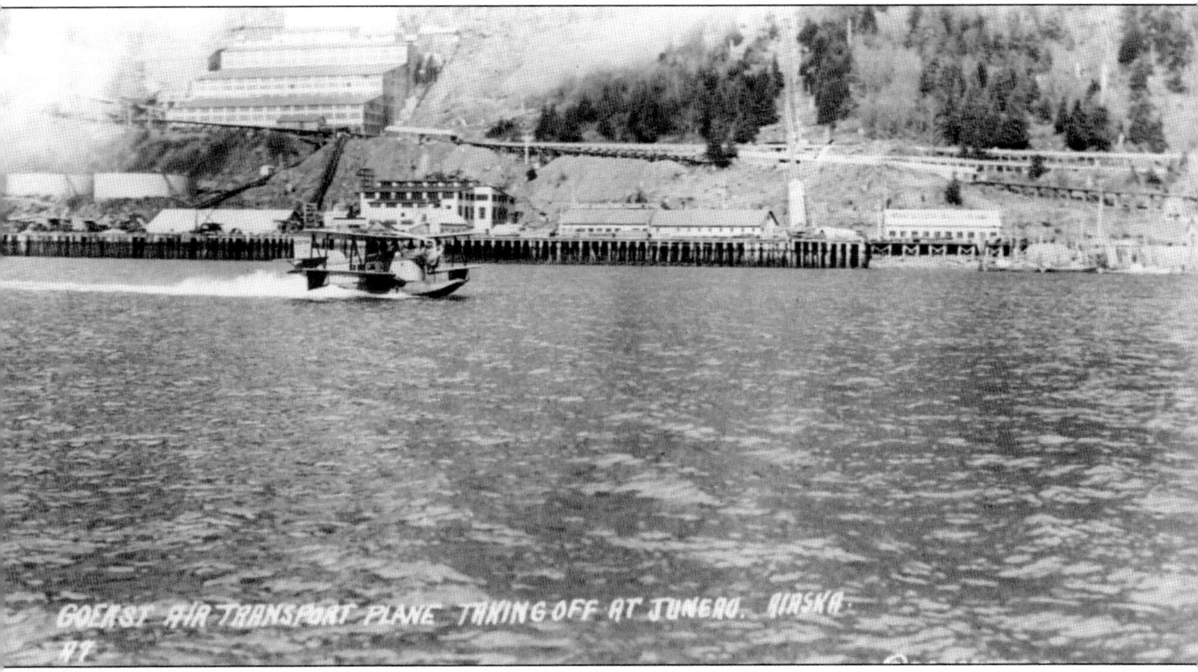

A Gorst Pacific Air Transport aircraft takes off from the Gastineau Channel between Juneau and Douglas Island in 1928. (Courtesy of the Alaska Aviation Museum.)

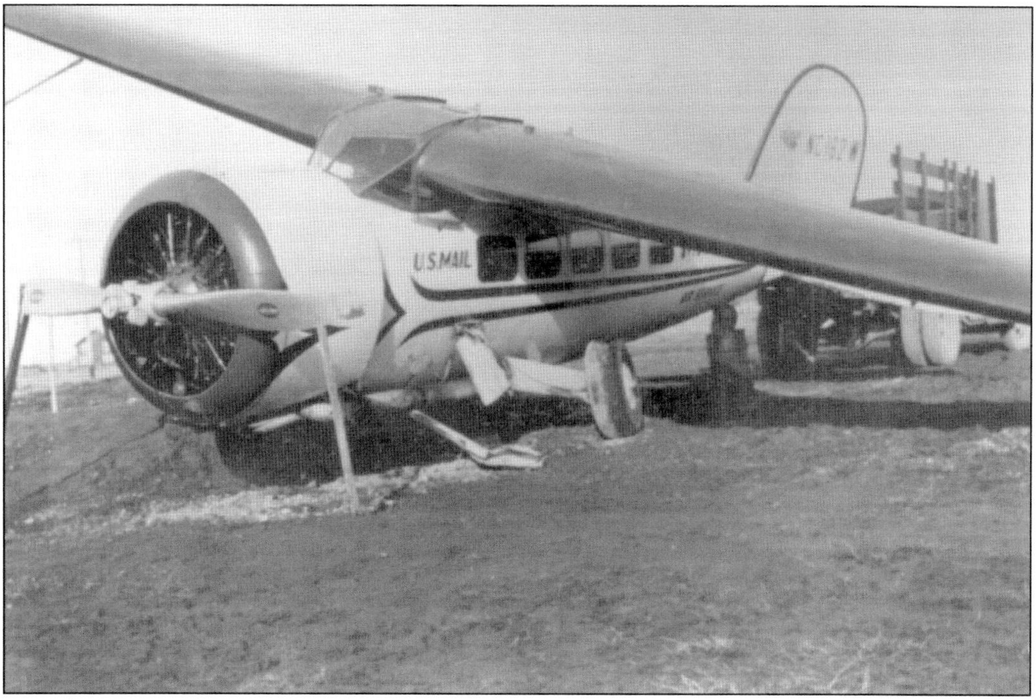

Famed pilot Wiley Post's Lockheed Vega, *Winnie Mae*, is seen here after a landing incident in Flat, Alaska, that caused him to replace the propeller during his around-the-world flight in 1933. Post was the first pilot to fly solo around the world. (Courtesy of the Alaska Aviation Museum.)

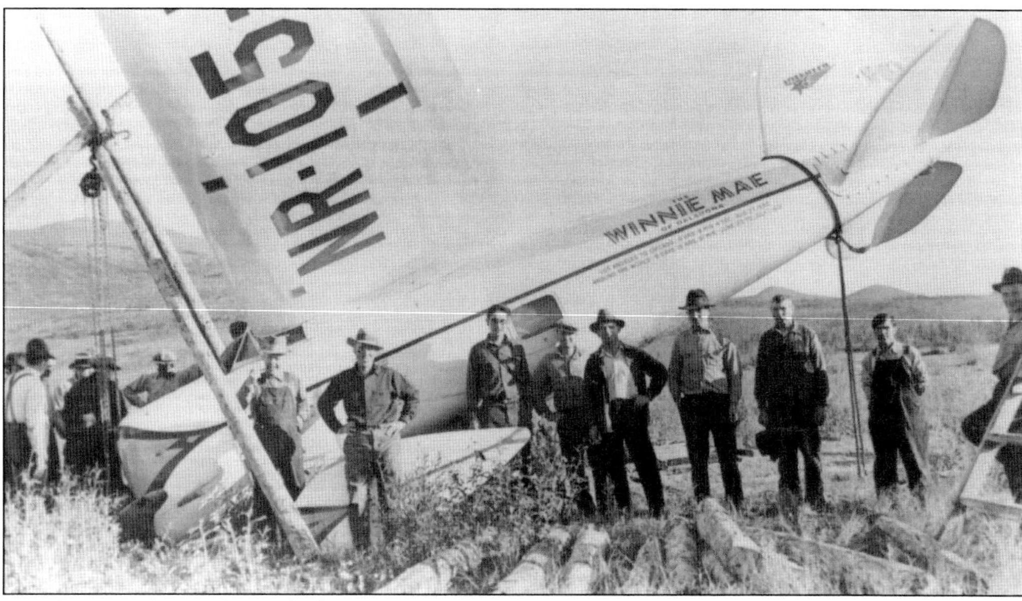

Local crews from Flat, Alaska, work on Wiley Post's Lockheed Vega, *Winnie Mae*, after a faulty landing attempt during his 1933 solo flight around the world. (Courtesy of the Alaska Aviation Museum.)

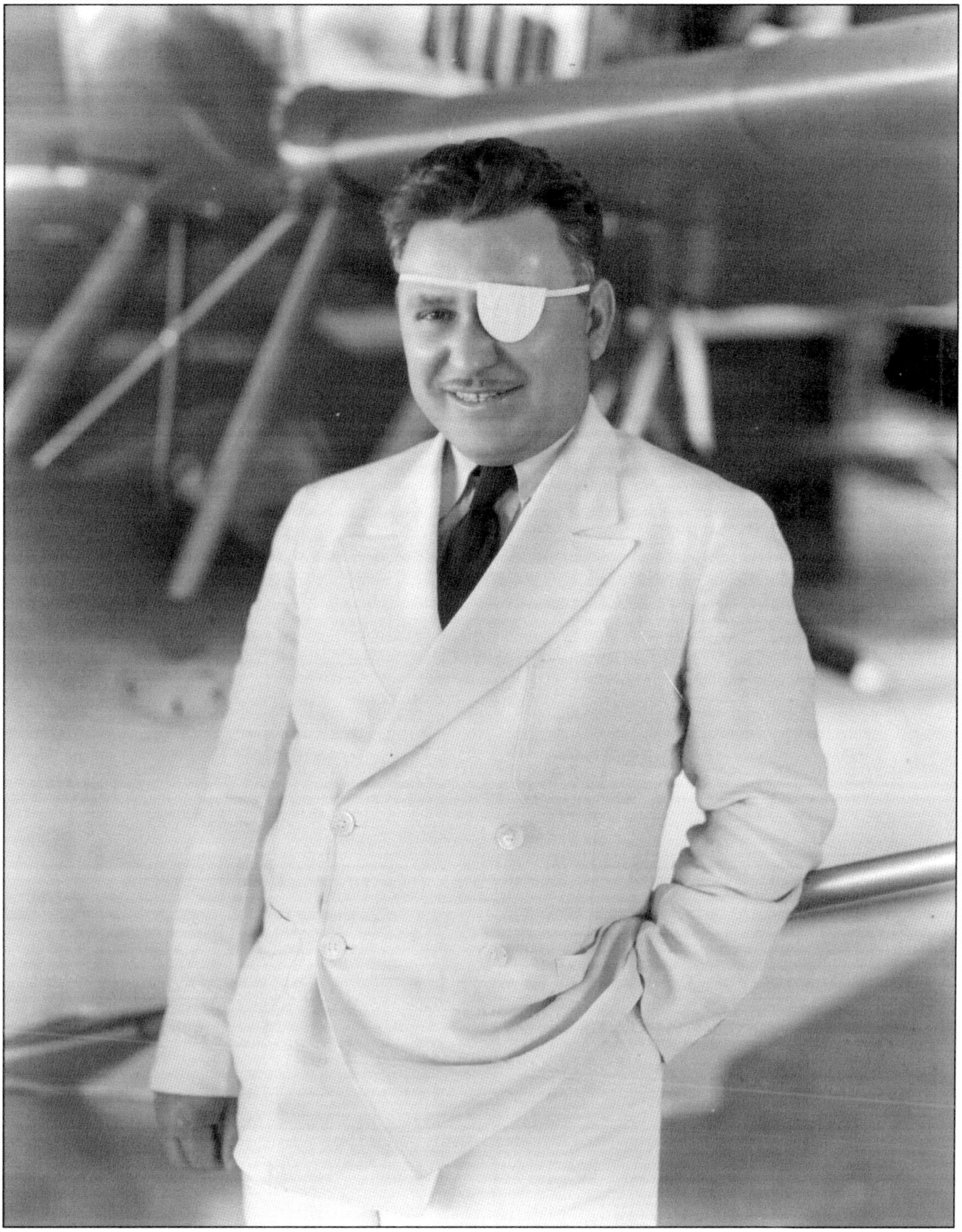

This is a rare photograph of Wiley Post dressed in a summer suit. Post and humorist Will Rogers were killed in 1935 during a takeoff attempt in a Lockheed Orion on floats near Barrow, Alaska. (Courtesy of the Alaska Aviation Museum.)

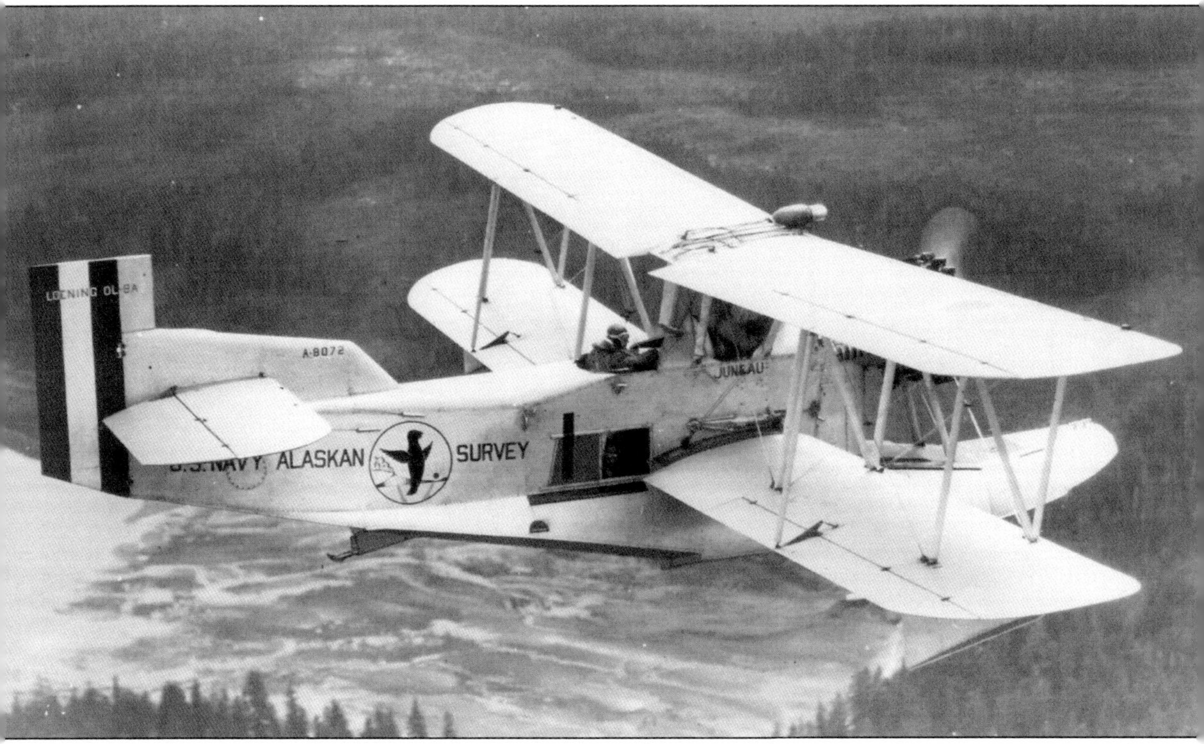

This air-to-air photograph shows a Loening plane flying over the Tongass Forest, covering 10,000 square miles in southeast Alaska, during a US Navy survey in 1926. The Navy returned in 1929 with the Loenings to complete the aerial survey of southeast Alaska. (Courtesy of the Alaska Aviation Museum.)

Two

The Golden Age

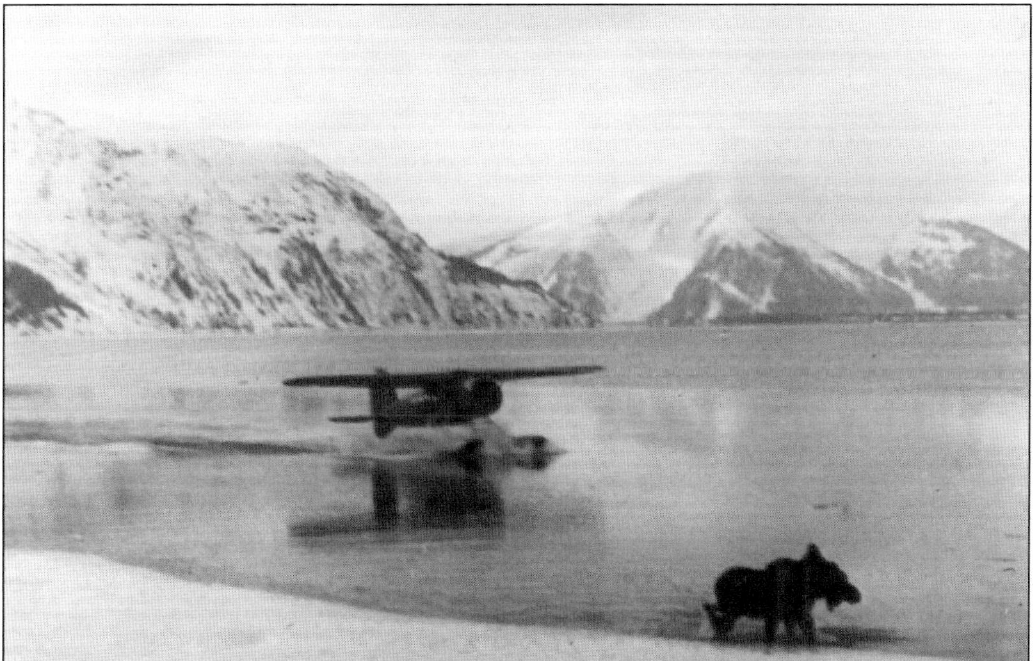

A Lockheed Vega, 47 Mike, operated by Alaska Southern Airways taxis to get a better look at a moose along the Taku Arm in southeast Alaska in 1935. (Courtesy of the Alaska Aviation Museum.)

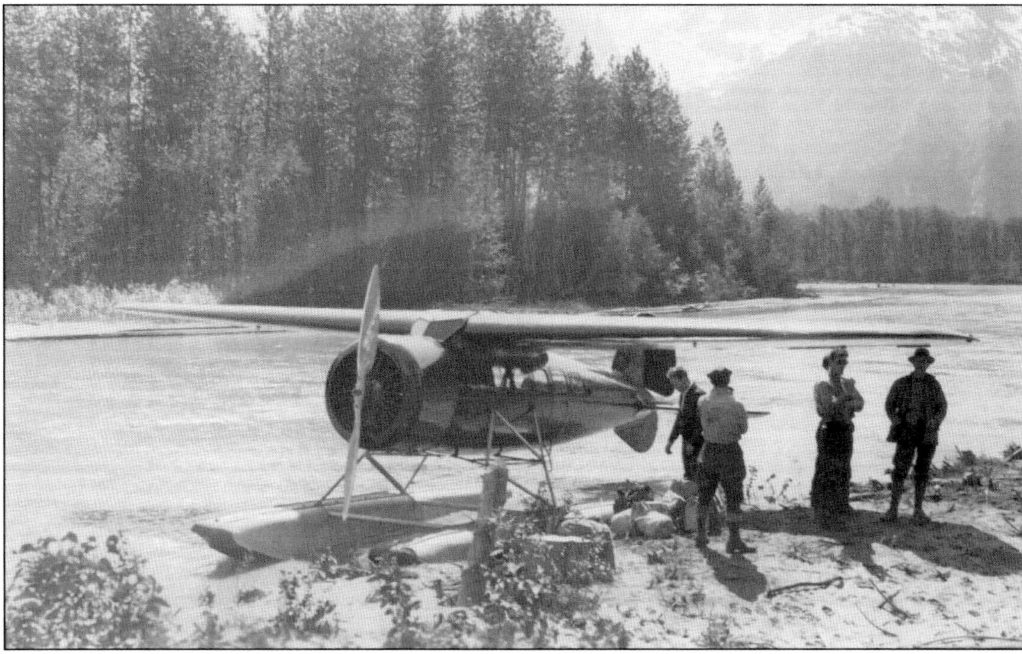

The Lockheed Vega was a fast and efficient aircraft in Alaska, using skis, floats, and wheels. Here, a group of wealthy sightseers takes a break on the Tulsequah Landing in British Columbia on a flight from the Taku River. They are traveling in an Alaska Coastal Airline aircraft. (Courtesy of the Alaska Aviation Museum.)

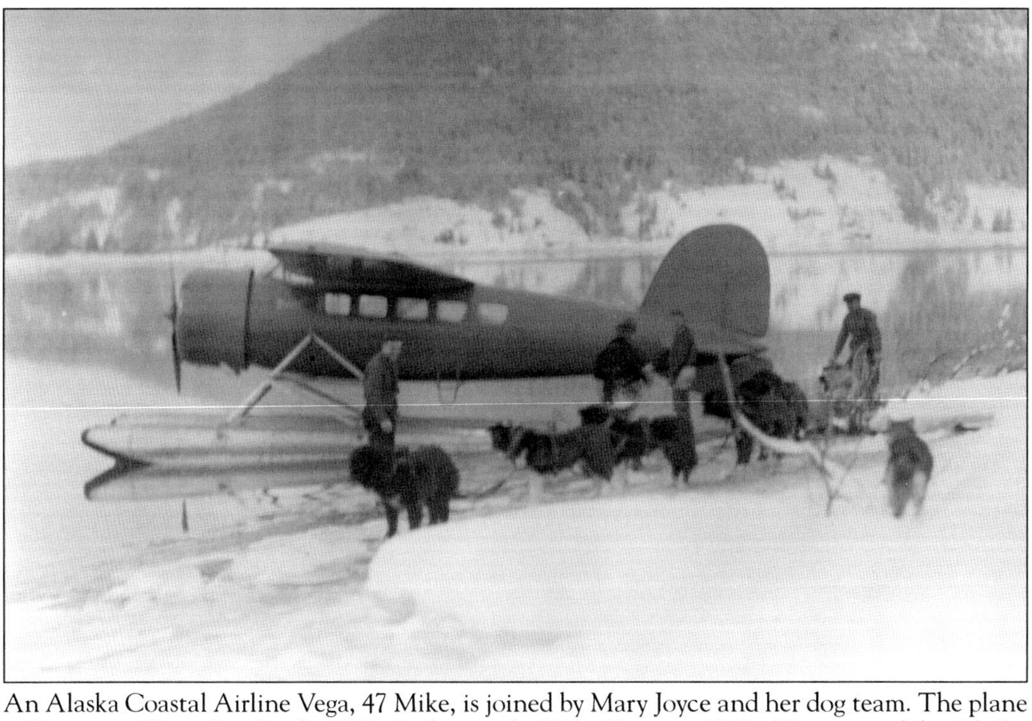

An Alaska Coastal Airline Vega, 47 Mike, is joined by Mary Joyce and her dog team. The plane is dropping off supplies for the Taku Lodge on the Taku River in 1940. (Courtesy of the Alaska Aviation Museum.)

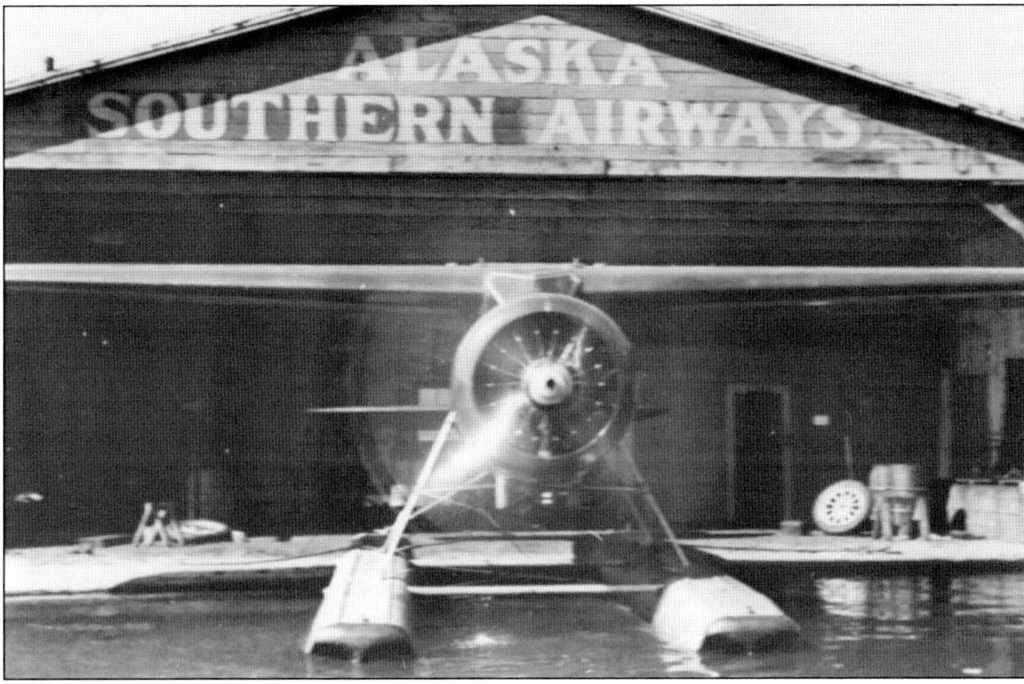

A Lockheed Vega runs up its engine at the dock of its boathouse hangar in Juneau. Alaska Southern Airways became Alaska Air Transport. The company later became Alaska Coastal Airlines, which eventually grew into Alaska Airlines. (Courtesy of the Alaska Aviation Museum.)

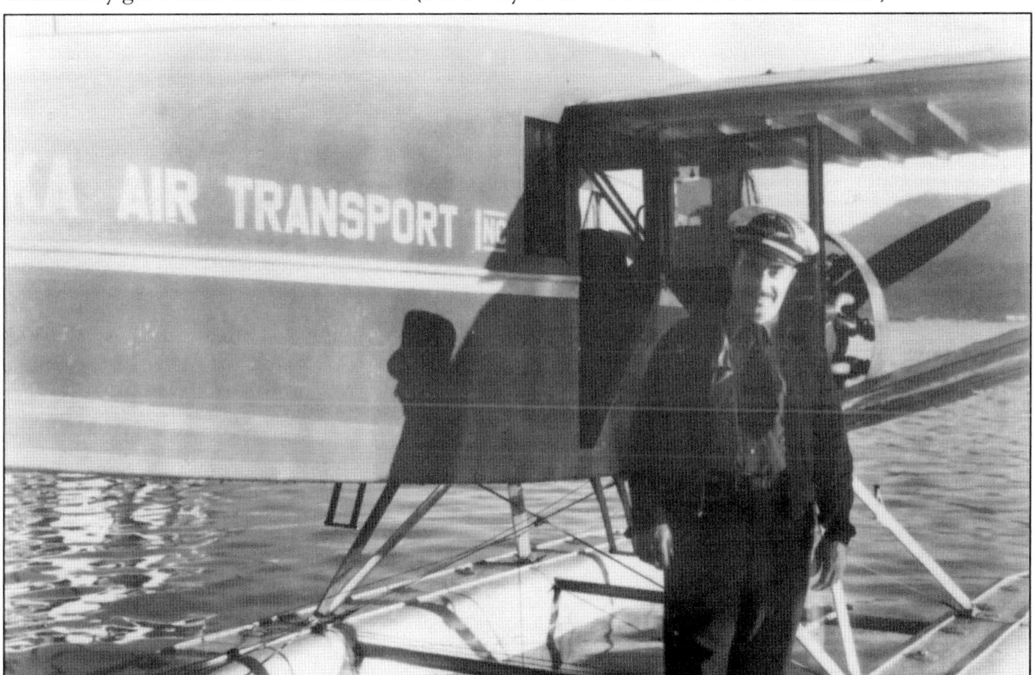

Frank Barr stands next to a Bellanca 11E operated by Alaska Air Transport. Barr was a well-known pilot in southeast Alaska in the 1930s and early 1940s. (Courtesy of the Alaska Aviation Museum.)

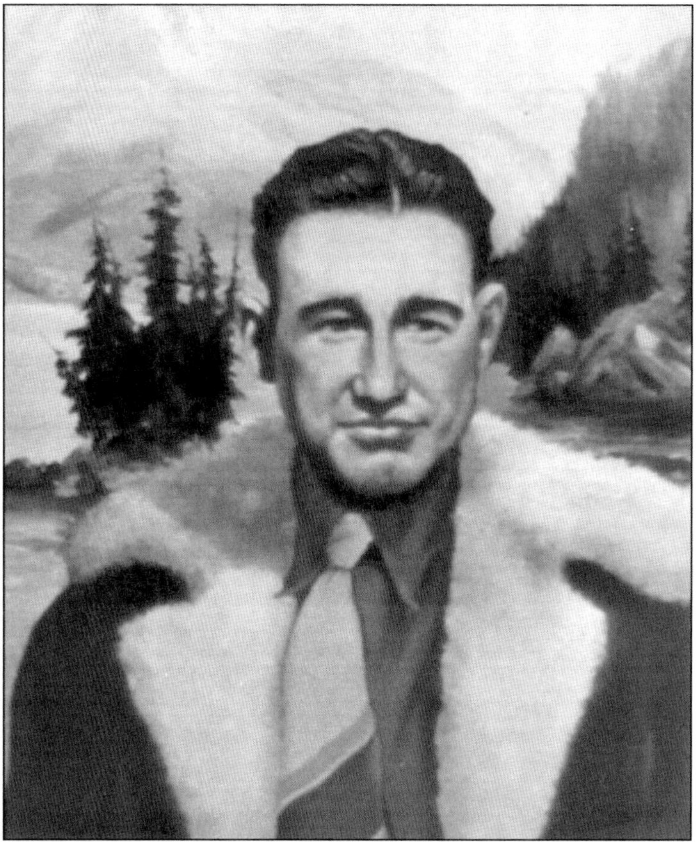

In 1934, Sheldon Bruce "Shell" Simmons started Alaska Coastal Airlines. The original name of the airline was Alaska Air Transport. Simmons, shown here in an artist's rendering of a photograph, put his company together with a wrecked aircraft, $1, and some outside investment. (Courtesy of the Alaska Aviation Museum.)

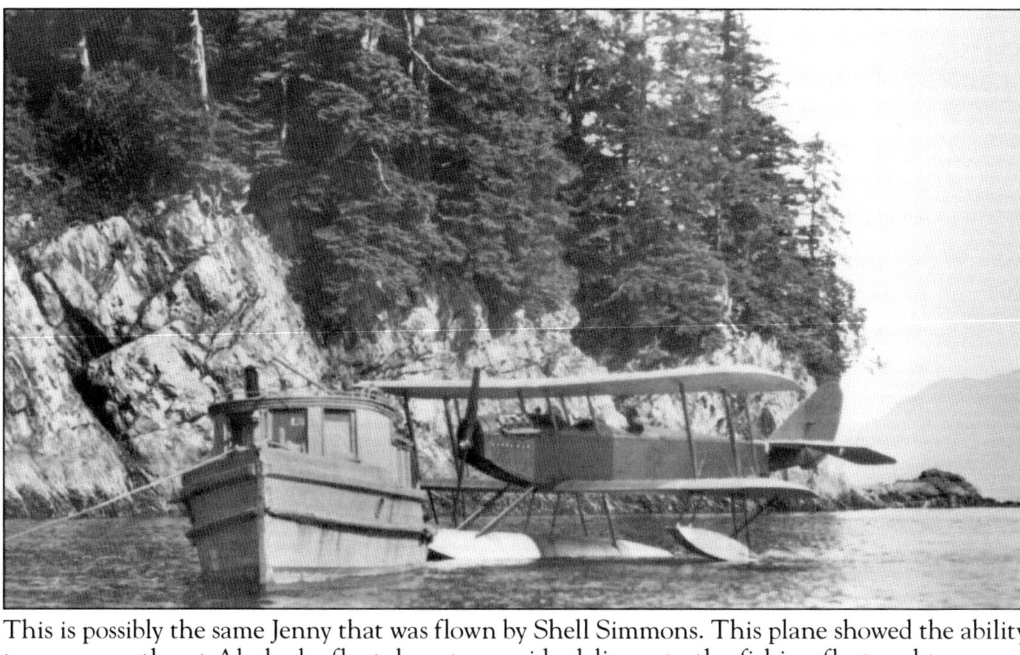

This is possibly the same Jenny that was flown by Shell Simmons. This plane showed the ability to access southeast Alaska by floatplane to provide delivery to the fishing fleet and transport between ports. (Courtesy of the Alaska Aviation Museum.)

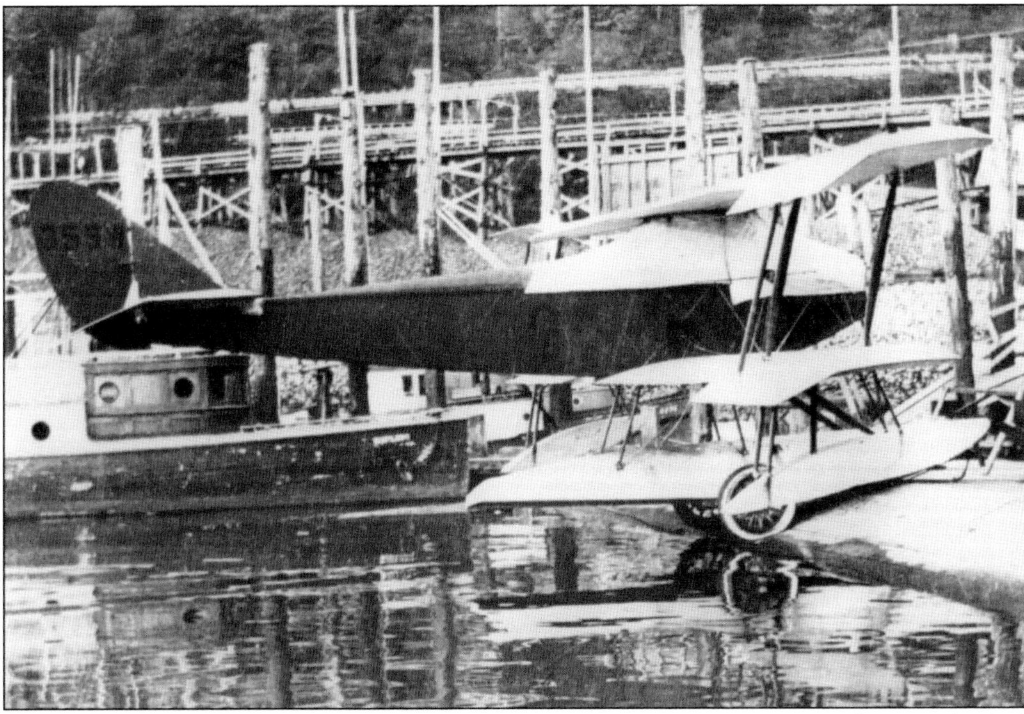

In this rare photograph of a JN-4 Jenny, the aircraft, used by Shell Simmons, is on floats on the dock along the Gastineau Channel in Juneau, Alaska. (Courtesy of the Alaska Aviation Museum.)

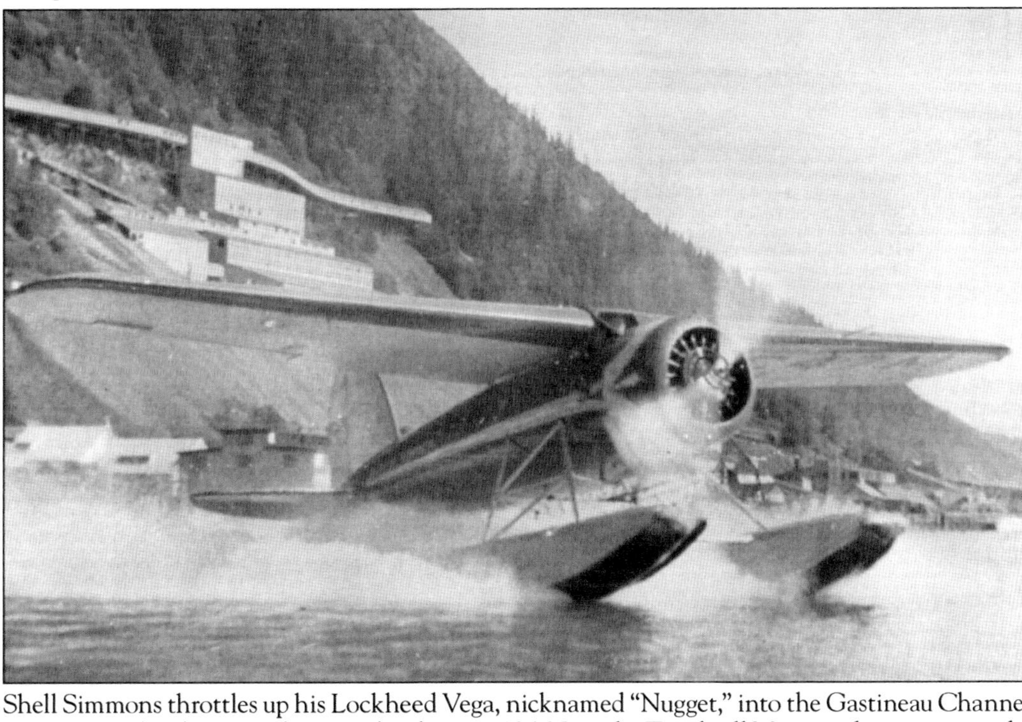

Shell Simmons throttles up his Lockheed Vega, nicknamed "Nugget," into the Gastineau Channel at Juneau in this dynamic photograph taken in 1936. Note the Treadwell Mine on the mountainside, above and behind the aircraft. (Courtesy of the Alaska Aviation Museum.)

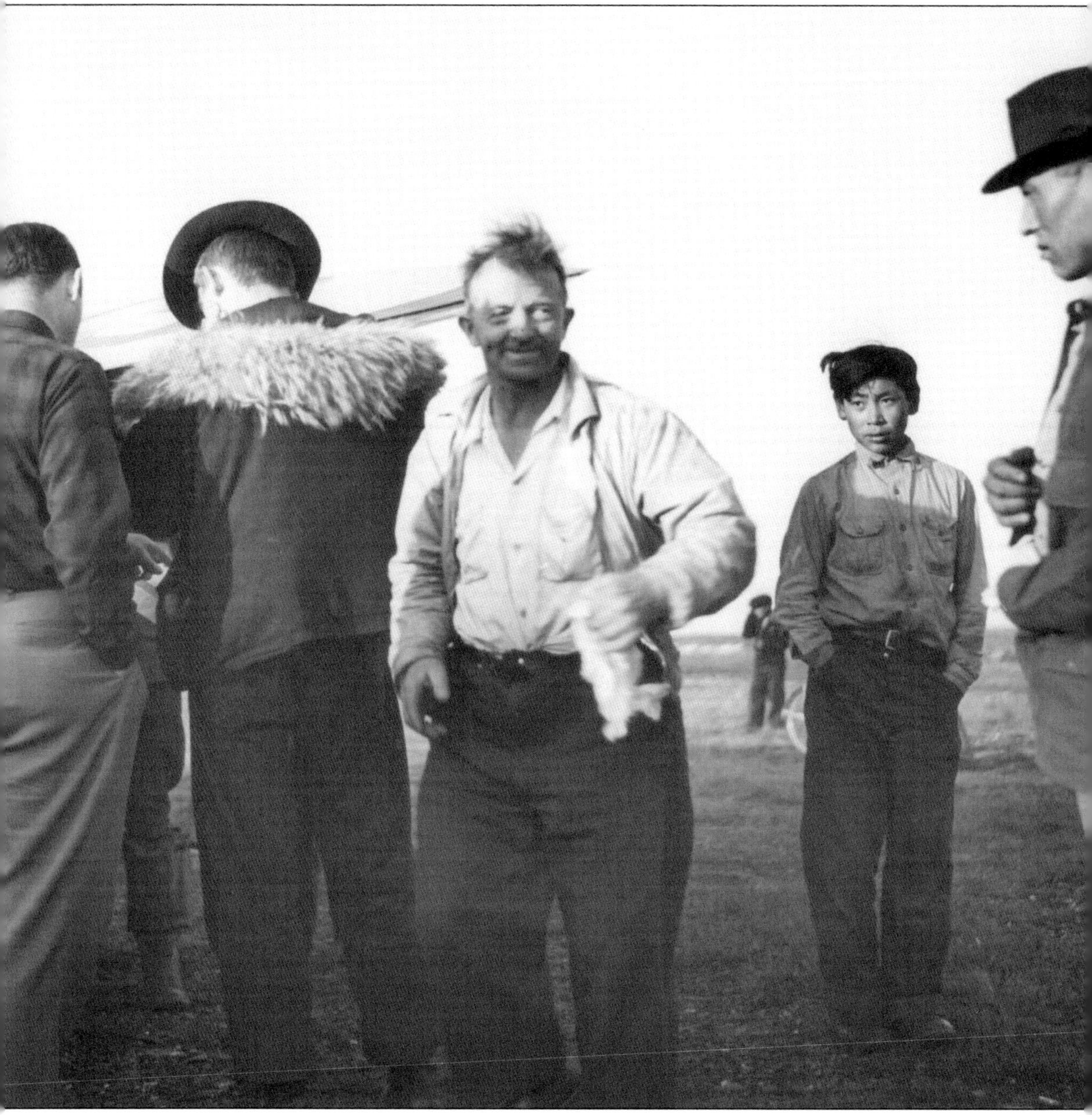

Pilot Archie Ferguson, a bombastic personality among the peoples of northwest Alaska, makes his way through a crowd after landing his aircraft in Kotzebue. Stories abound about Ferguson, who once landed his aircraft in a whiteout blizzard and was stuck in a snowdrift. He continued to fly the aircraft, not knowing that he was earthbound until a person walked up to the aircraft and waved at him. (Courtesy of the Alaska Aviation Museum.)

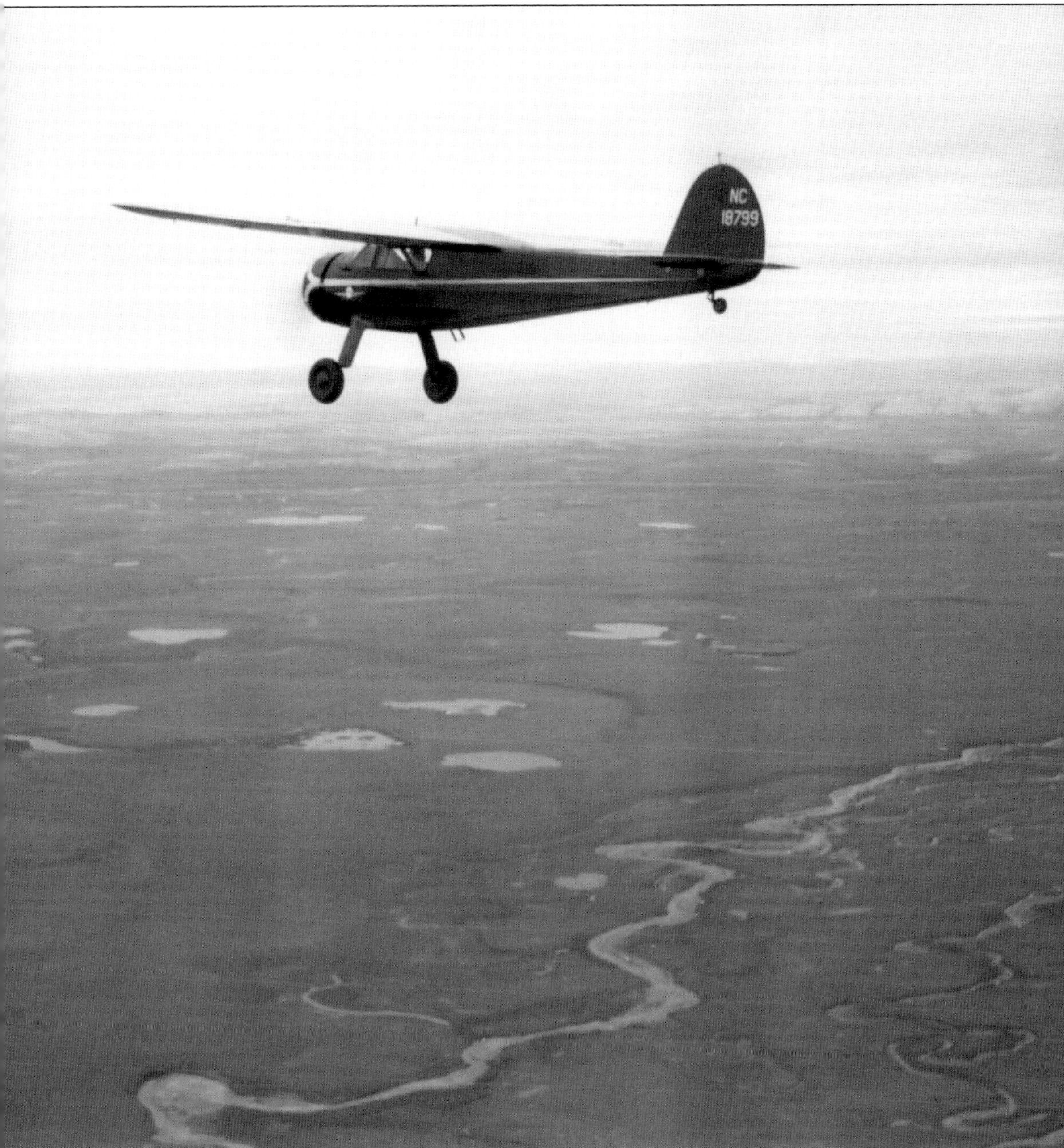

This air-to-air photograph shows Archie Ferguson flying over the tundra of northwest Alaska. Ferguson, dubbed "Alaska's Clown Prince" by the *Saturday Evening Post*, used the Cessna 165 Airmaster to service villages of the Kobuk-Seward Peninsula from the 1940s to the 1960s. Ferguson calmed his passengers' uneasiness by telling them not to worry, they were all insured for $10,000. (Courtesy of the Alaska Aviation Museum.)

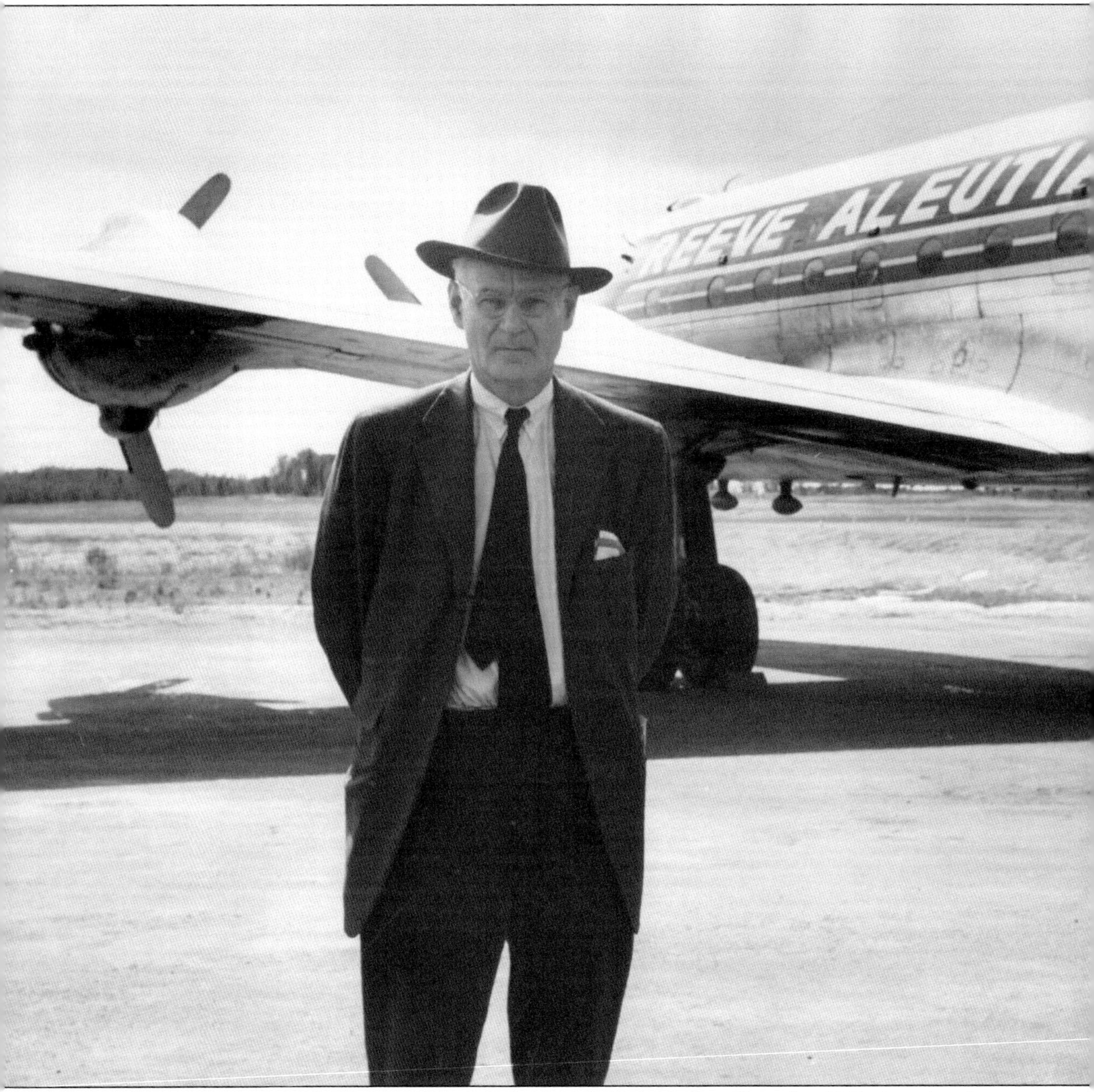

Bob Reeve poses with Reeve Aleutian Airlines' (RAA) first Douglas DC-4 at Anchorage International Airport. RAA's fleet of DC-3s and C-47s gave way to the newer, faster Douglas aircraft in the late 1950s. (Courtesy of the Alaska Aviation Museum.)

Bob Reeve stands under a C-47 purchased as surplus from the US Army Air Force after World War II. (Courtesy of the Alaska Aviation Museum.)

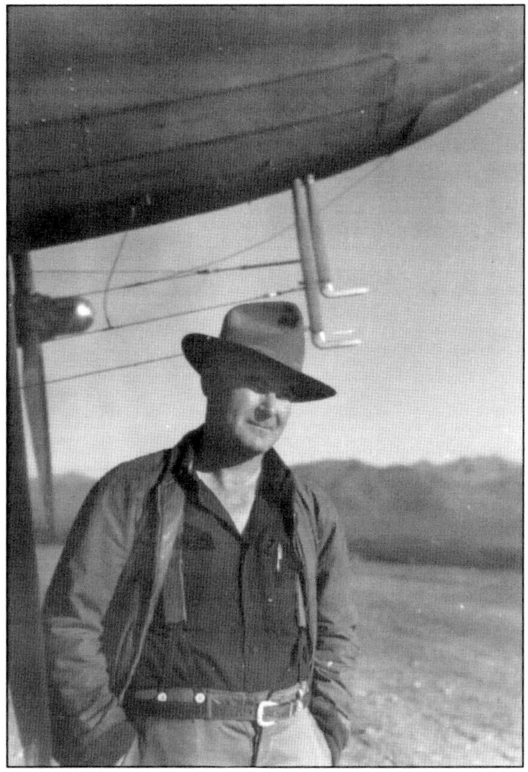

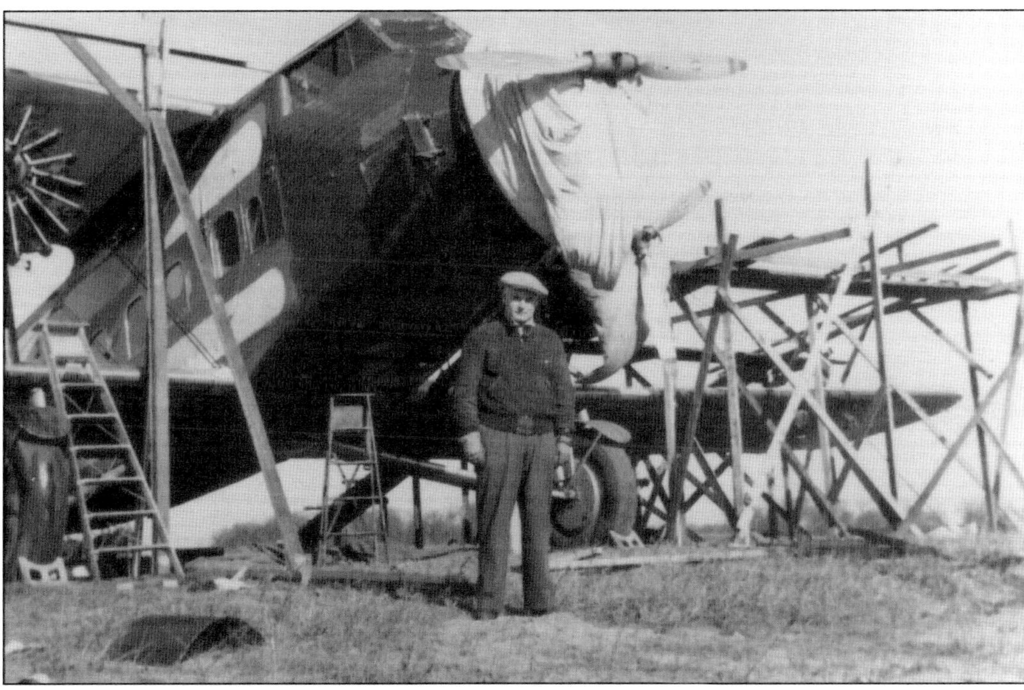

Known as the world's best glacier ski pilot, with over 2,000 glacier landings, Bob Reeve stands under the nose of a Boeing 80A. Scaffolding has been erected for a wing repair. (Courtesy of the Alaska Aviation Museum.)

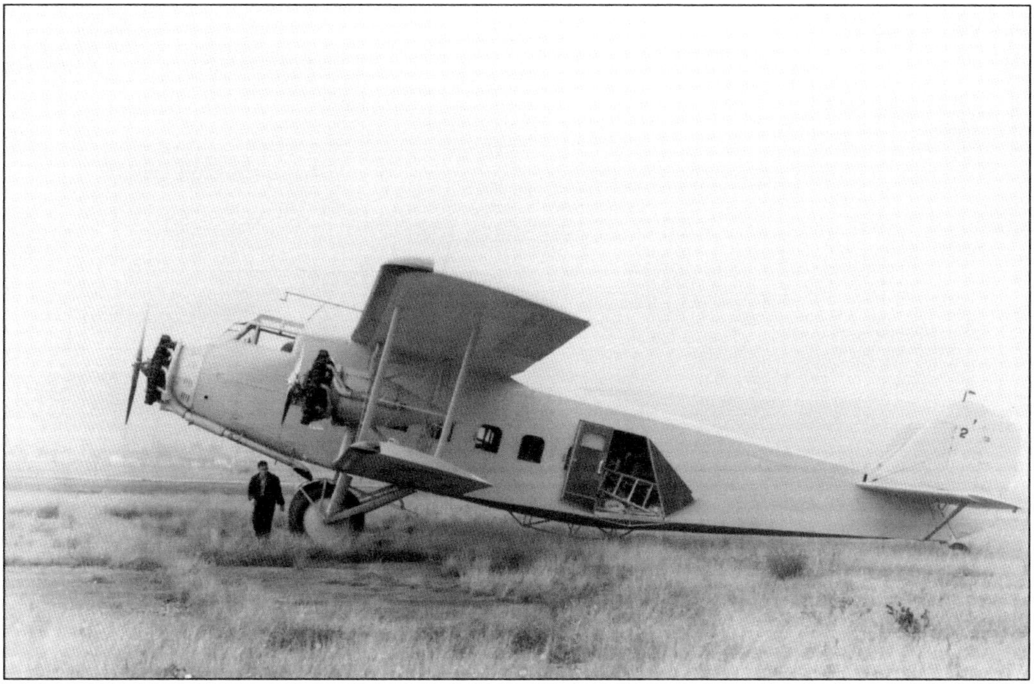

This is a rare photograph of a Reeve Airways Boeing 80A, called the *Yellow Pearl*, in Valdez, Alaska. (Courtesy of the Alaska Aviation Museum.)

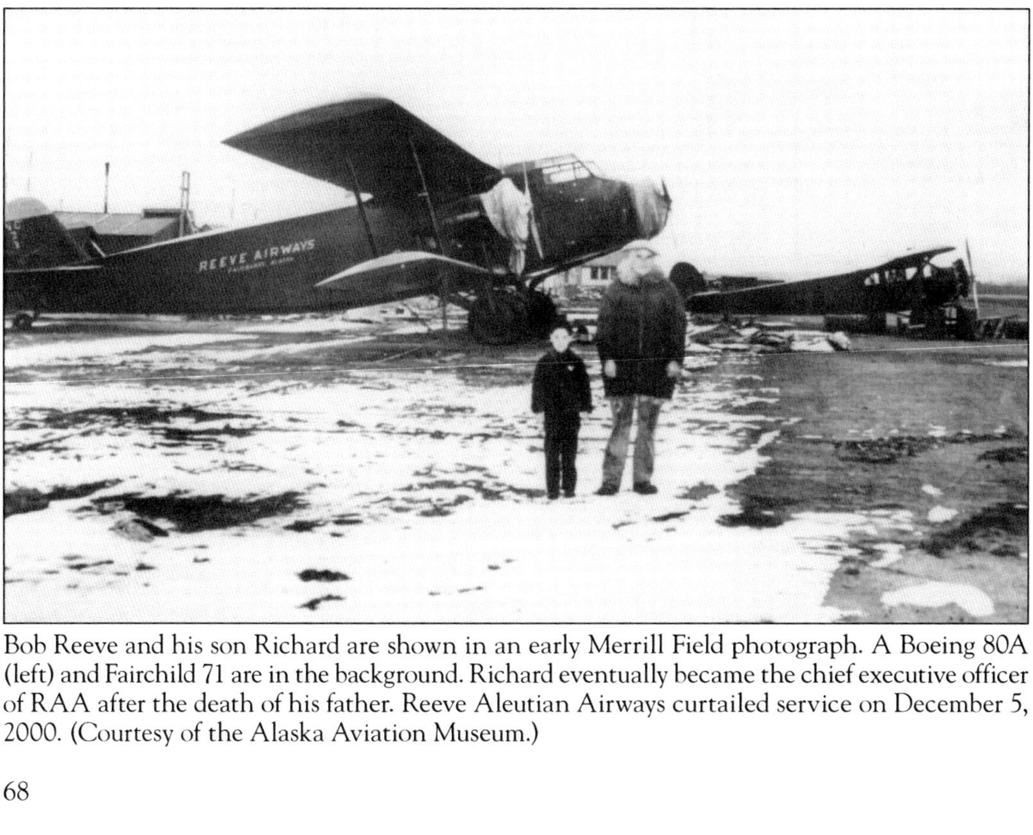

Bob Reeve and his son Richard are shown in an early Merrill Field photograph. A Boeing 80A (left) and Fairchild 71 are in the background. Richard eventually became the chief executive officer of RAA after the death of his father. Reeve Aleutian Airways curtailed service on December 5, 2000. (Courtesy of the Alaska Aviation Museum.)

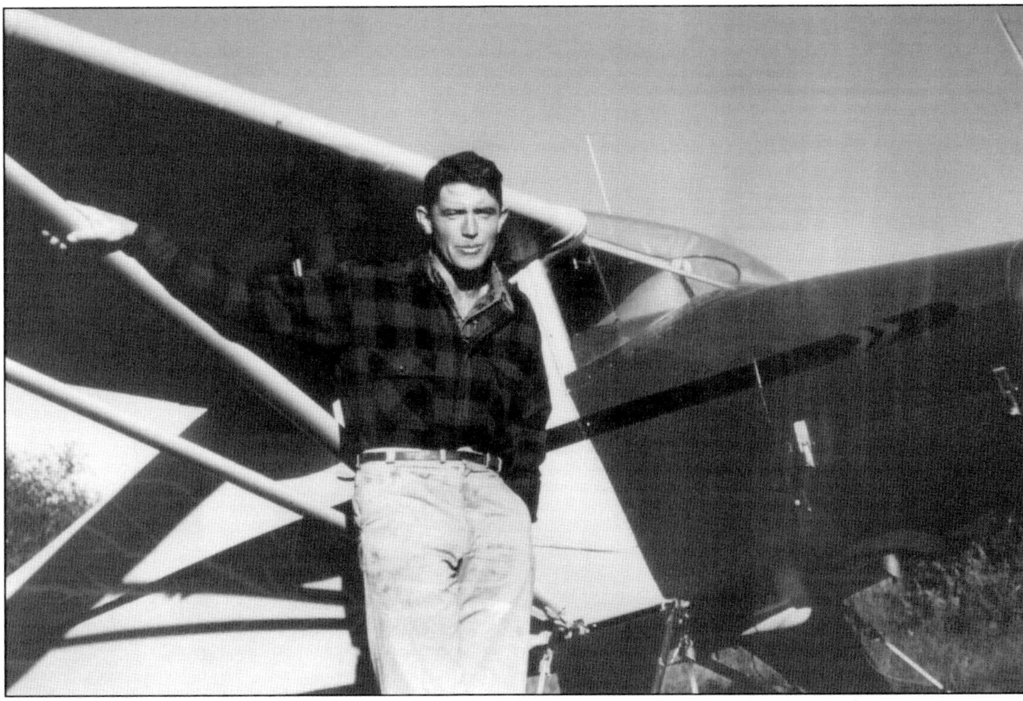

Famed Alaska mountain and glacier pilot Don Sheldon is shown with one of his early Piper aircraft at the Talkeetna airport. (Courtesy of the Alaska Aviation Museum.)

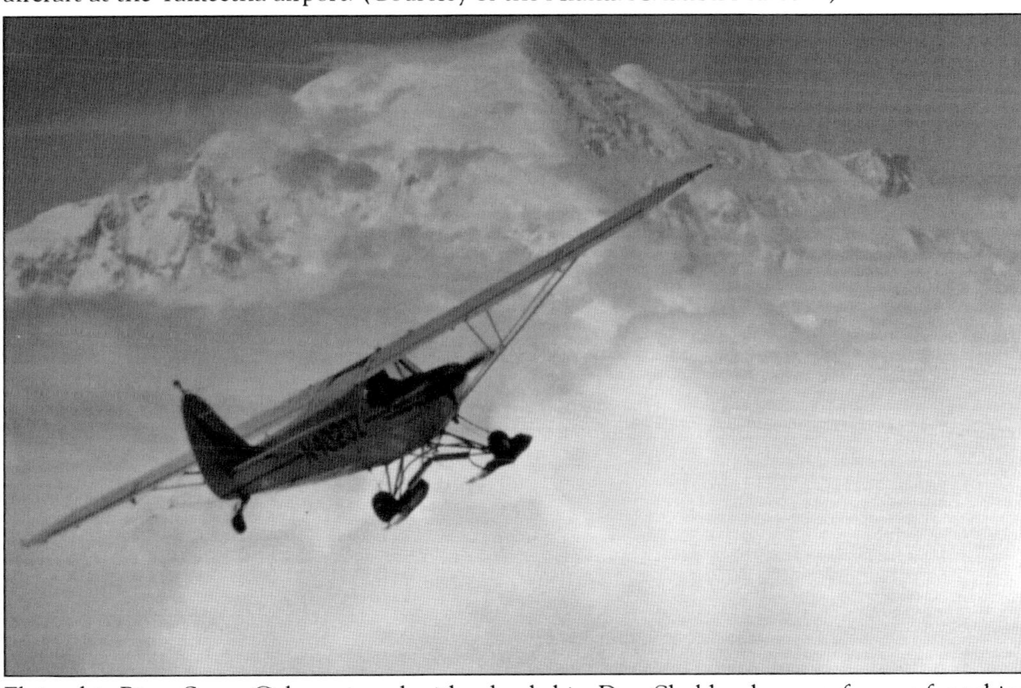

Flying his Piper Super Cub equipped with wheel skis, Don Sheldon became famous for taking mountaineers into the Alaska Range. This photograph, used for the cover of the book *Wager with the Wind*, shows the aircraft in flight near 17,402-foot Mount Foraker over the Kahiltna Glacier. (Courtesy of the Alaska Aviation Museum.)

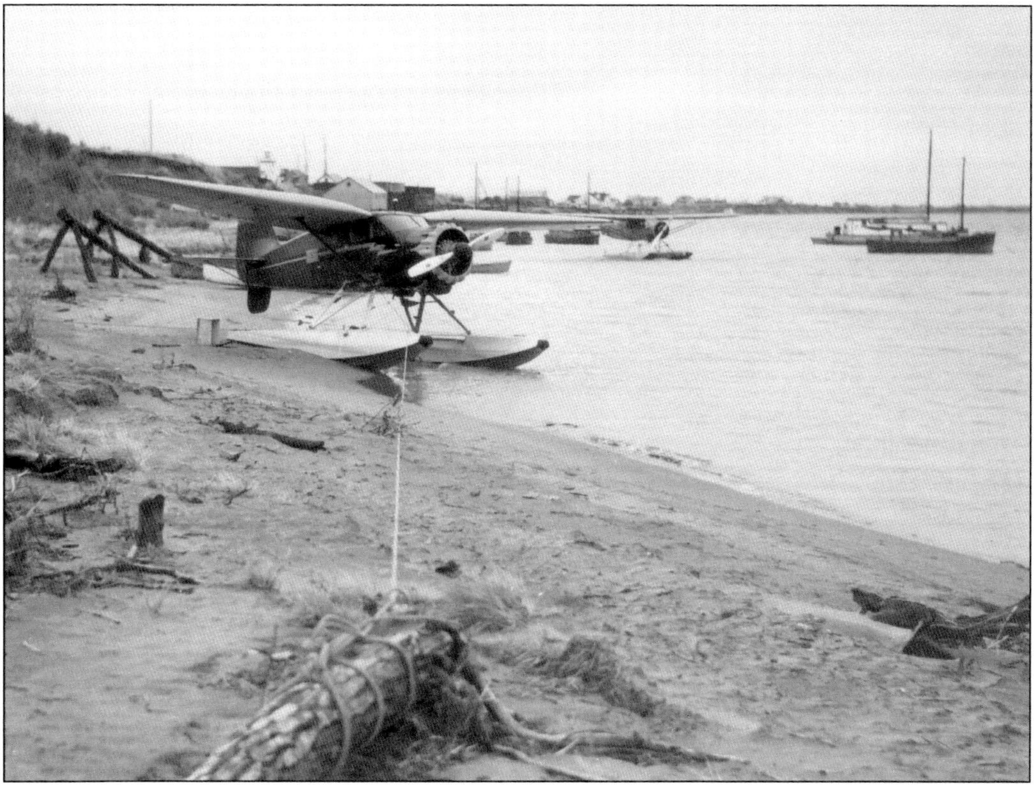

A Stinson SR9B sits on the shore of Bristol Bay, tied down to driftwood. Note the Travel Air on floats and the fishing boats of the day that used sails. (Courtesy of the Alaska Aviation Museum.)

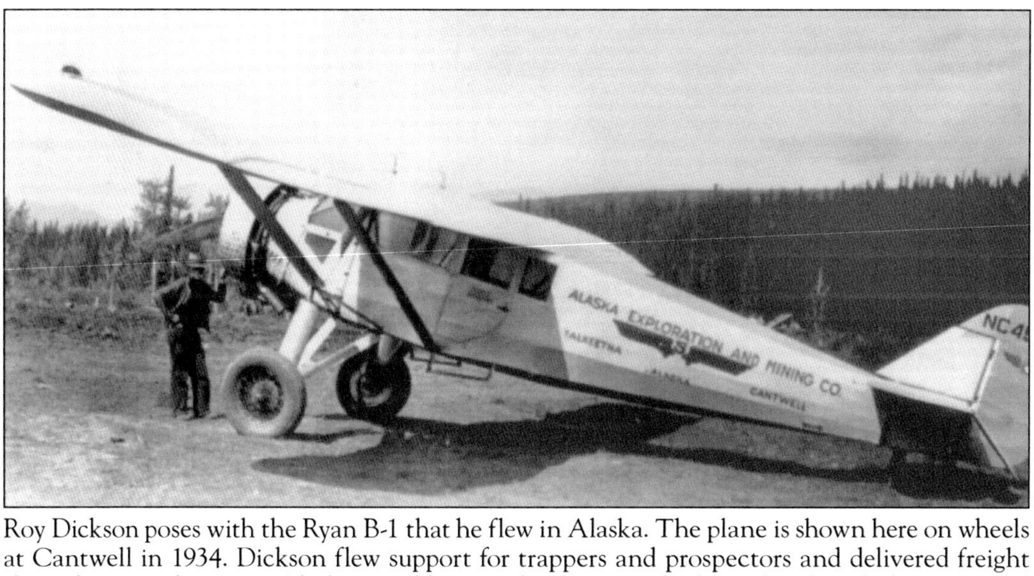

Roy Dickson poses with the Ryan B-1 that he flew in Alaska. The plane is shown here on wheels at Cantwell in 1934. Dickson flew support for trappers and prospectors and delivered freight throughout southwestern Alaska, in addition to hauling people through Lake Clark Pass to and from Anchorage from 1934 to 1941. (Courtesy of the Alaska Aviation Museum.)

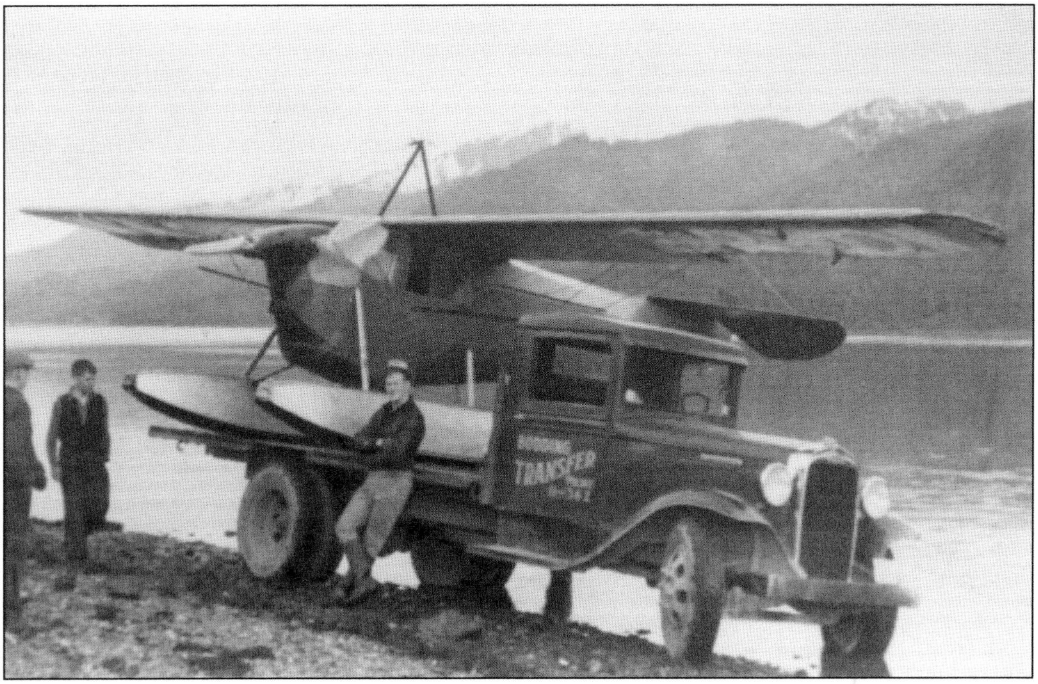

An Aeronica C3 Bathtub on floats is being carried by a truck of the Bodding Transport Company. The photograph was taken at the water's edge in southeast Alaska. (Courtesy of the Alaska Aviation Museum.)

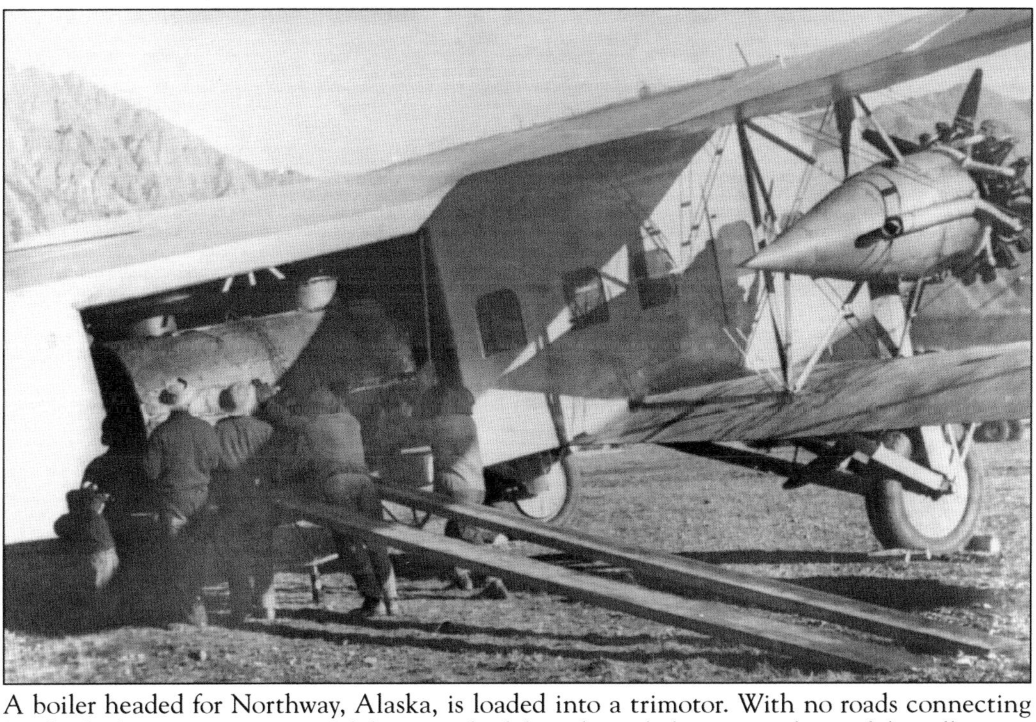

A boiler headed for Northway, Alaska, is loaded into a trimotor. With no roads connecting landlocked communities, aircraft became the life and supply lines in and out of the villages in Alaska. (Courtesy of the Alaska Aviation Museum.)

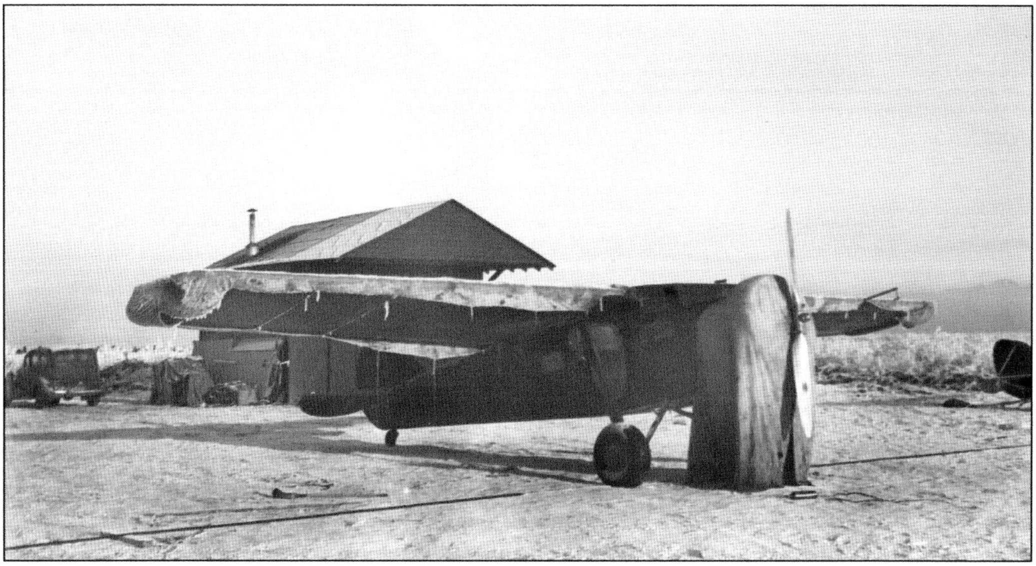

One of Jack Peck's planes sits with an engine covering, used to heat up the engine before a flight. (Courtesy of the Alaska Aviation Museum.)

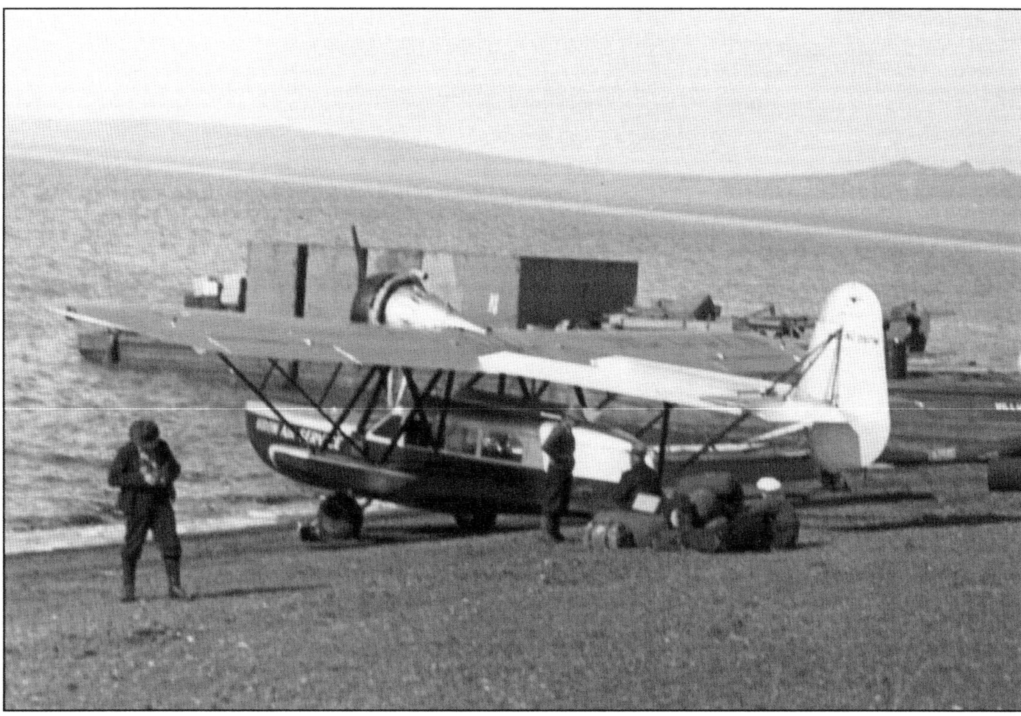

A Mirow Air Service Loening sits on the beach as its passengers and their cargo wait for their flight. (Courtesy of the Alaska Aviation Museum.)

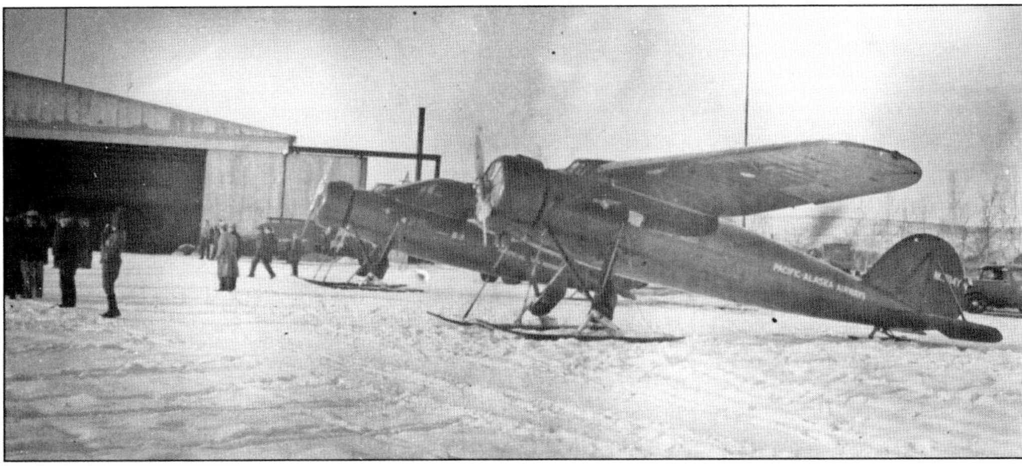

A pair of Consolidated Fleetstar Model 20 aircraft used by Pacific Alaska Airways, a subsidiary of Pan American World Airways, sits ready to fly as part of the airline's network of flights in Alaska and the Northwest. The airline was absorbed by Pan Am in 1941. (Courtesy of the Alaska Aviation Museum.)

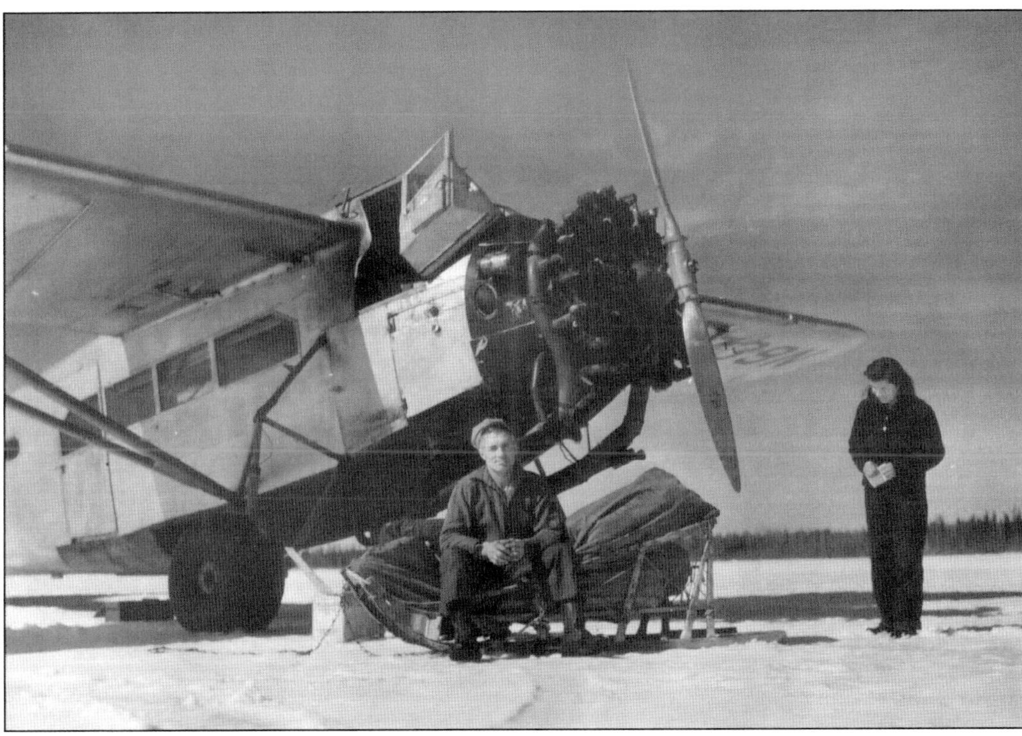

Pilot Frank Barr sits on a load of US Postal Service mail in front of a Fairchild Pilgrim belonging to Harold Gillam at Stoney River, Alaska. Passenger Margaret White examines the sled. (Courtesy of the Alaska Aviation Museum.)

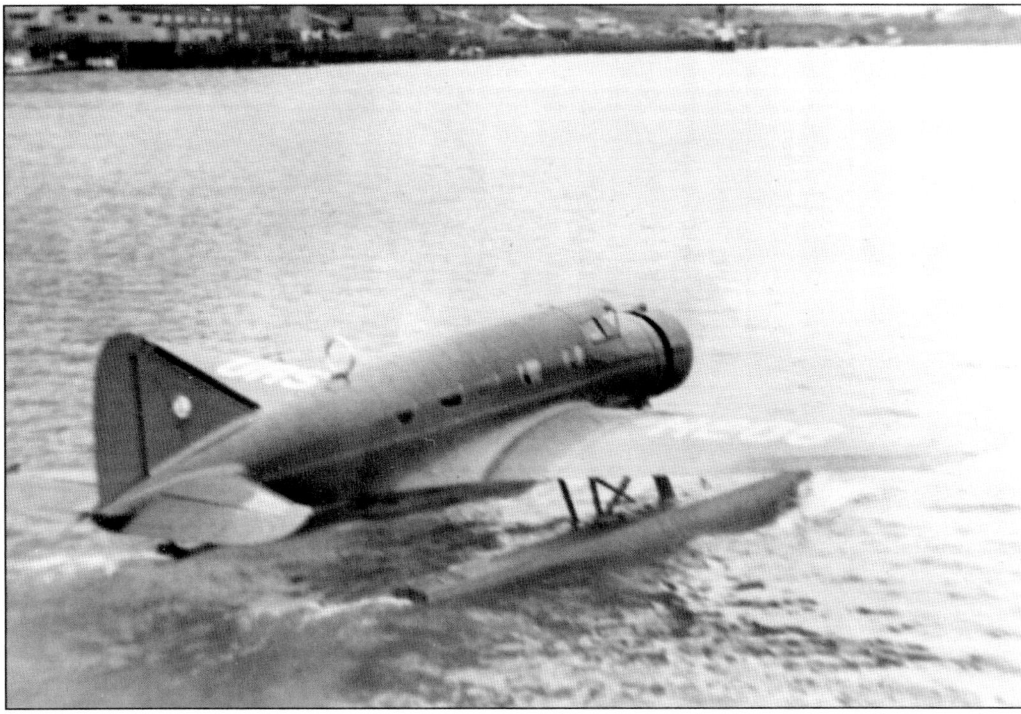

Seen here is the Vultee V1AS on pontoons flown by Sigizmund Levanevsky on his 1936 long-distance trip from Santa Monica to Moscow. (Courtesy of the Alaska Aviation Museum.)

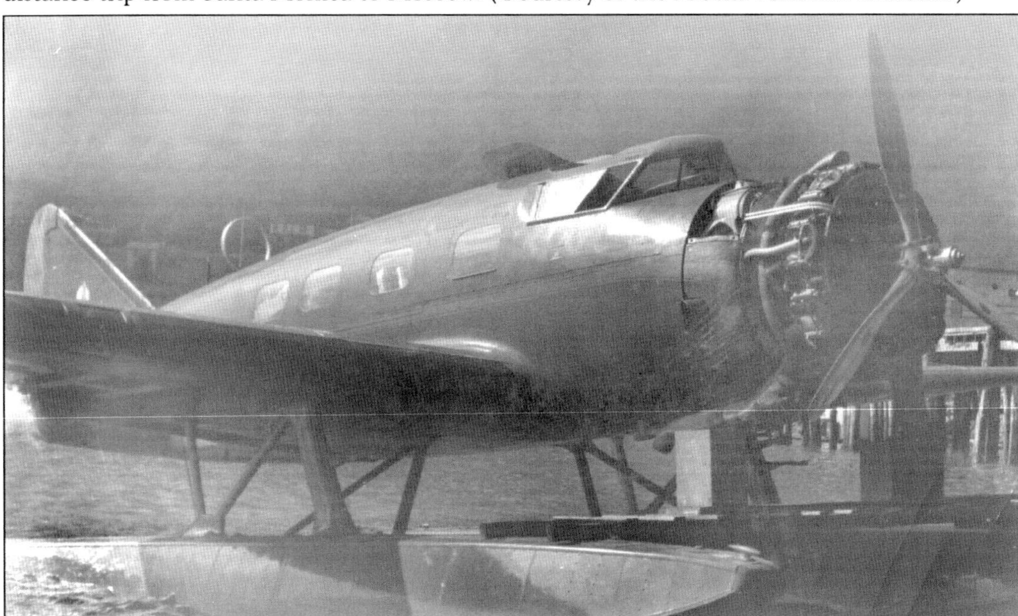

Levanevsky rescued Jimmy Mattern, who was forced down near Anadyr during an attempted flight around the world. Levanevsky flew from Anadyr to Nome in 1933. He was lost over the Arctic Ocean while flying a Bolkhovitinov DB-A long-range bomber. He and the plane's six-man crew were on a flight from Moscow to the United States via the North Pole. (Courtesy of the Alaska Aviation Museum.)

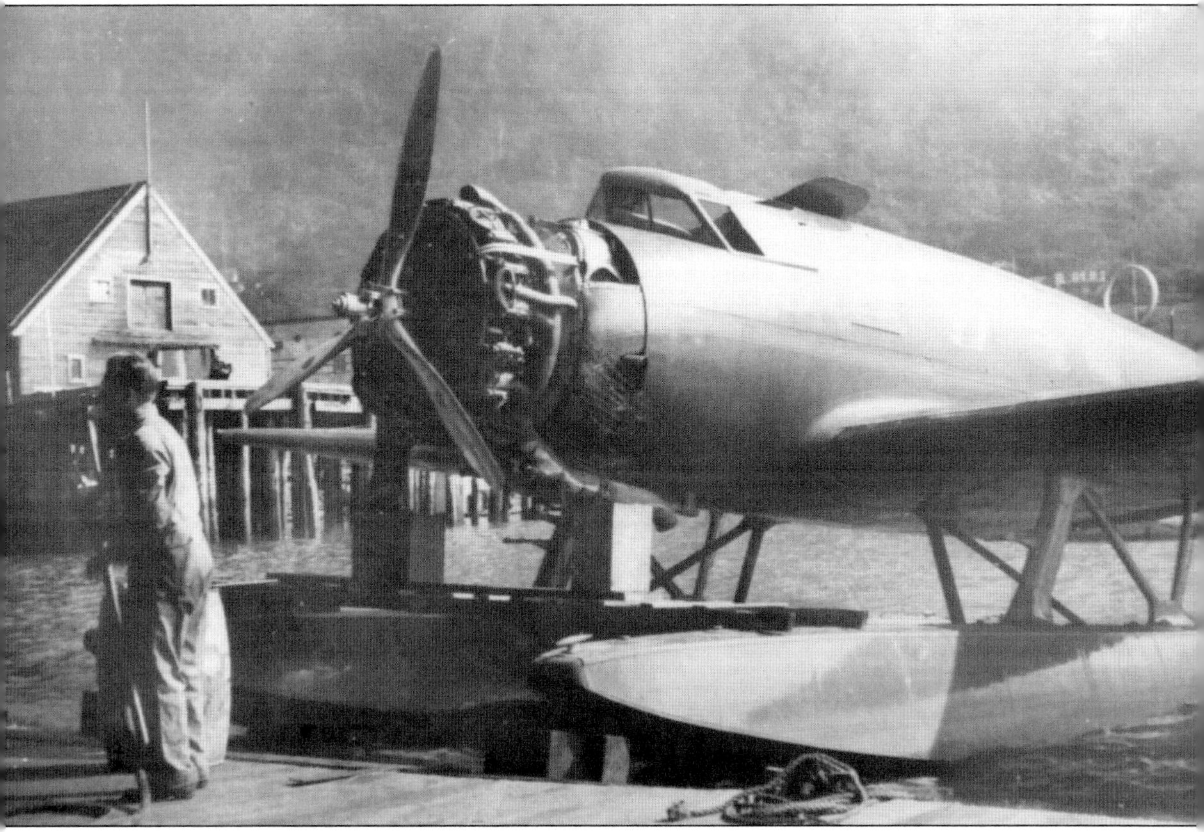

This Levanevsky Vultee V-1 was the sole V-1AS twin-EDO float version of the V-1A, built for the Soviet government. It featured additional fuel tanks in the cabin, an enlarged vertical tail, and a special cold-weather cowling. It took pilots Sigismund Levanevsky and Victor Levchenko five and a half weeks during August and September 1936 to fly the aircraft the 10,000 miles from Santa Monica to Moscow, via Alaska and Siberia. Levanevsky is on the left. (Courtesy of the Alaska Aviation Museum.)

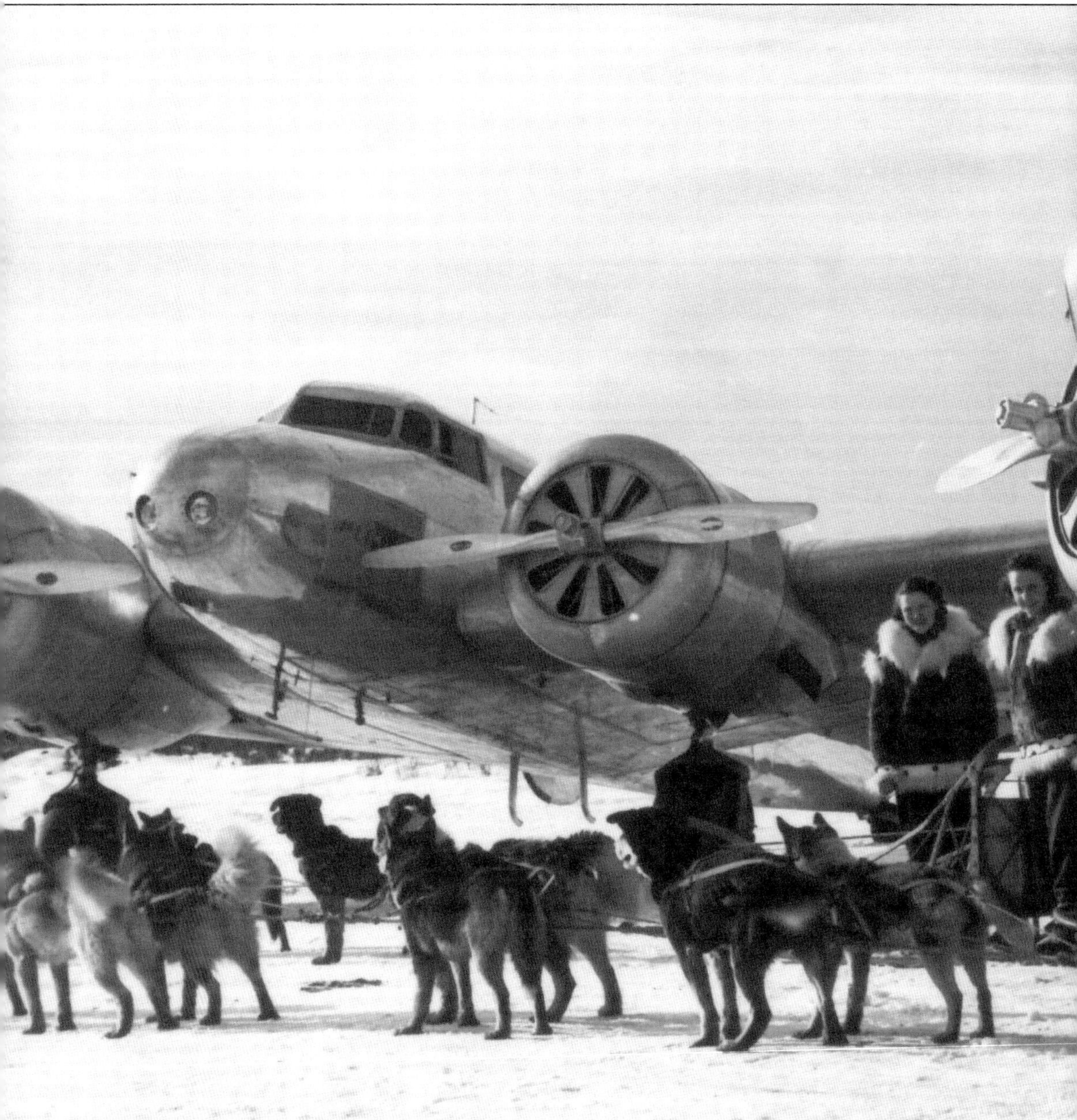

This stylized image of Alaska aviation was not far from reality, as dog teams were used in the early days of air transport to pick up passengers from airports and take them to villages. This

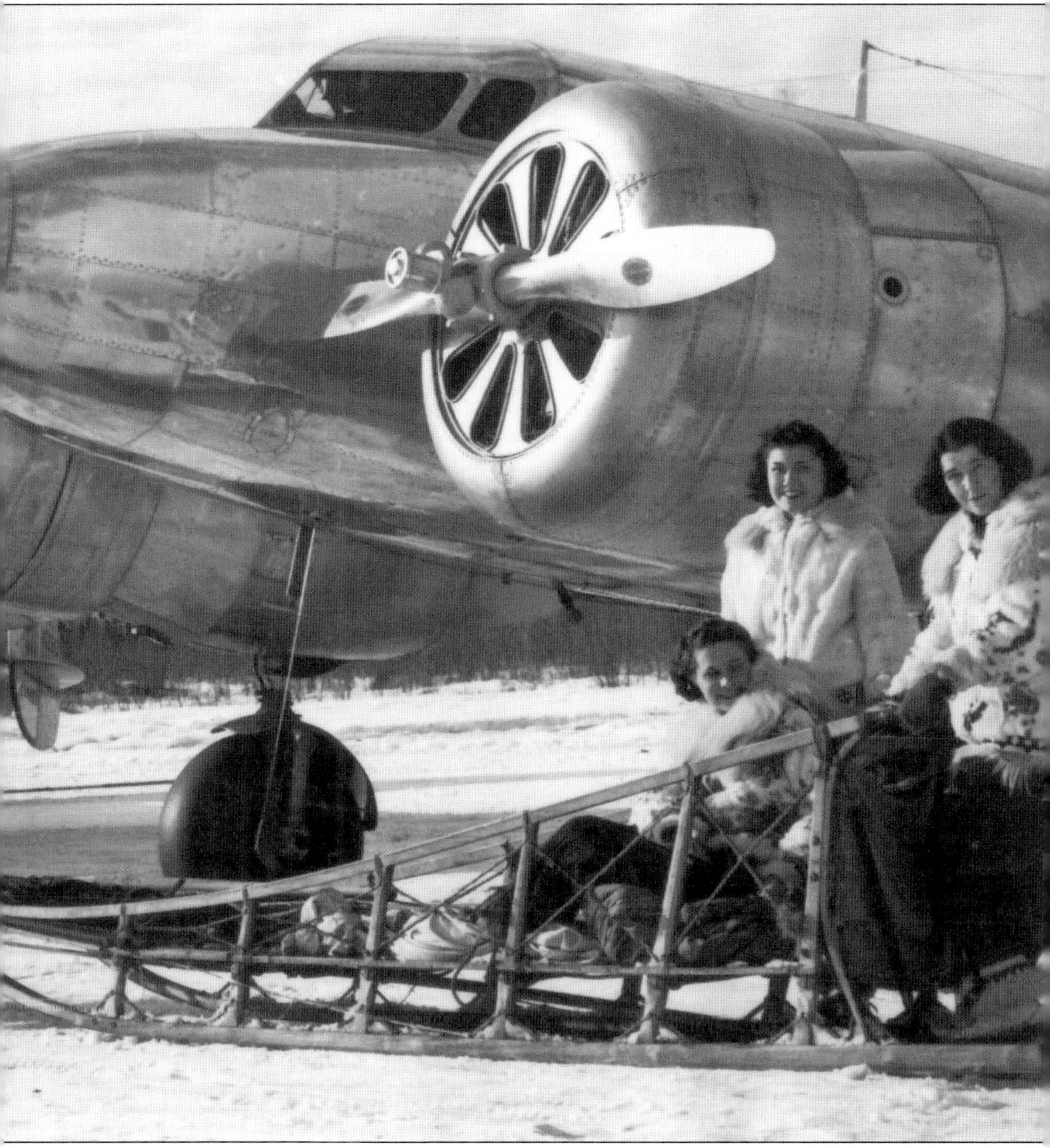

photograph comes from a Wien exhibit at the Alaska Aviation Museum. (Courtesy of the Alaska Aviation Museum.)

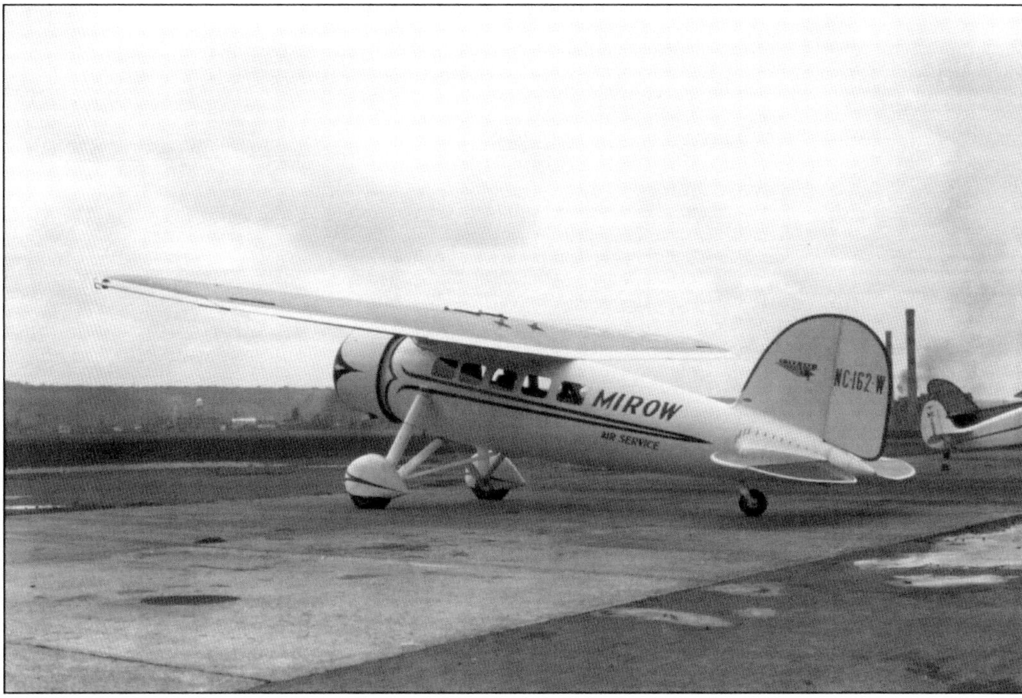

A Mirow Air Service Lockheed Vega is shown on the ramp. The Vega became the aircraft of choice, due to its streamlined fuselage, which gave the aircraft a better cruise speed and allowed for improved fuel consumption for a larger passenger plane. (Courtesy of the Alaska Aviation Museum.)

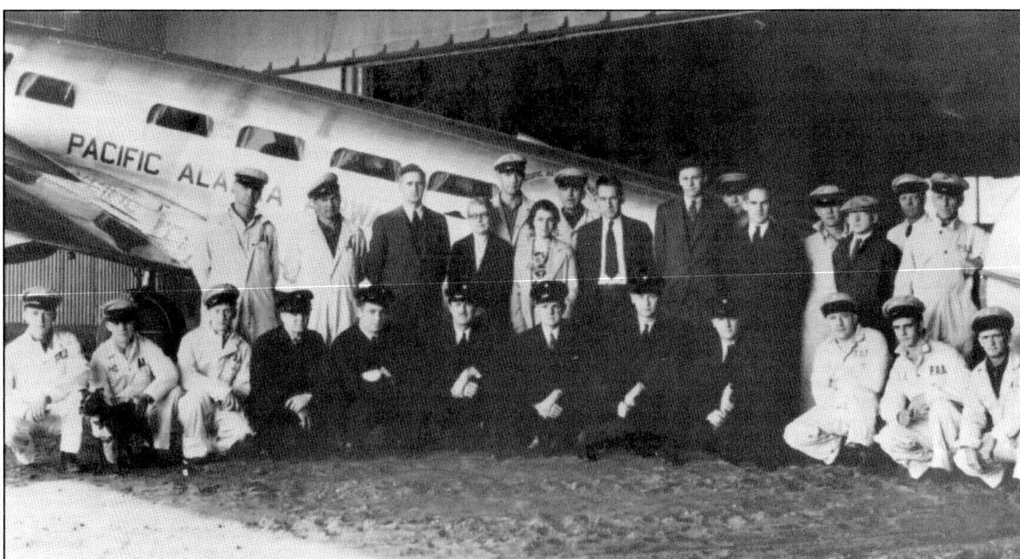

Some of the employees of Pacific Airways gather for a group photograph in Juneau in 1939. (Courtesy of the Alaska Aviation Museum.)

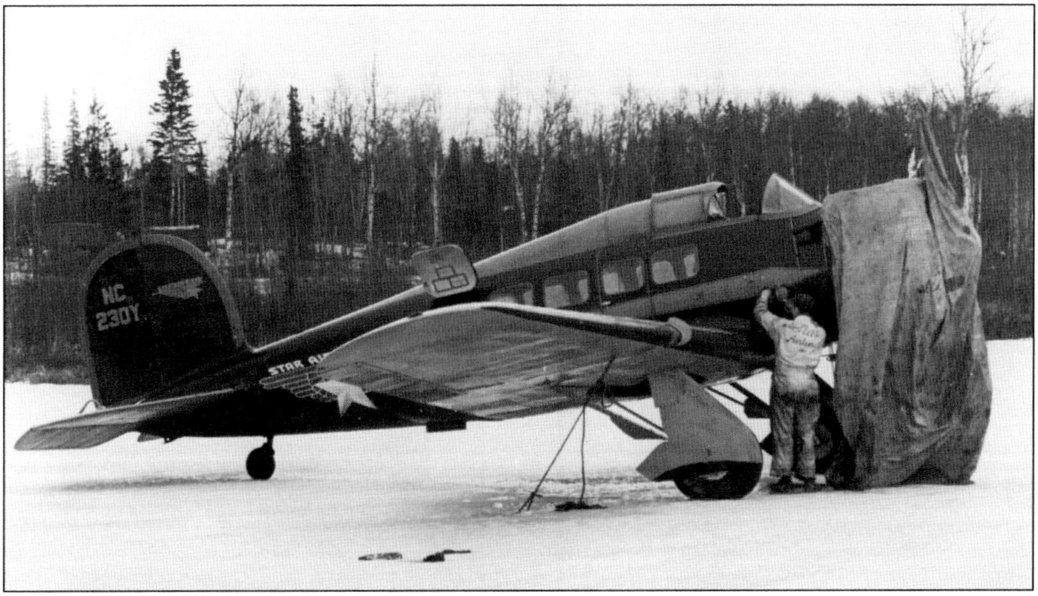

A Star Airlines mechanic checks out a Lockheed Orion before one of its extended bush flights. (Courtesy of the Alaska Aviation Museum.)

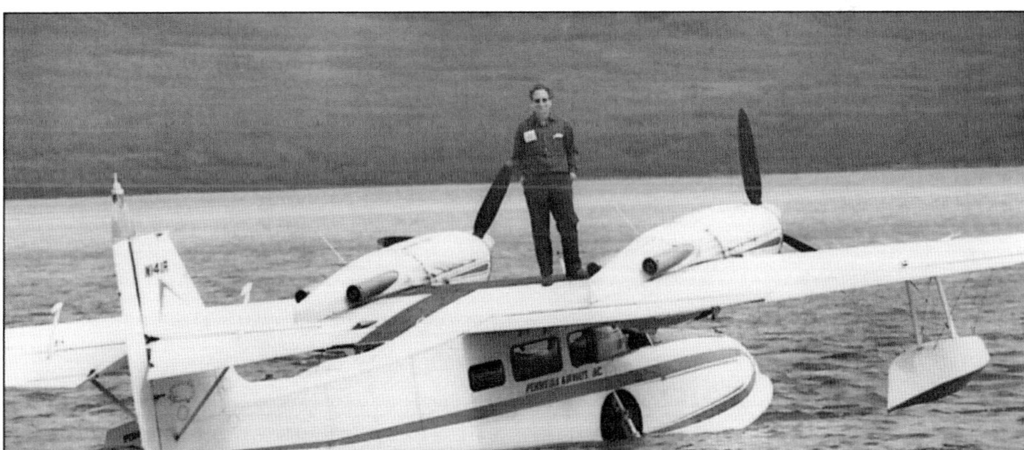

Orin Seybert, founder of Peninsula Airways, stands on top of a Grumman Widgeon, used for transporting fishermen to and from fishing boats. The aircraft also serviced the Alaska Peninsula. (Courtesy of Orin Seybert Collection.)

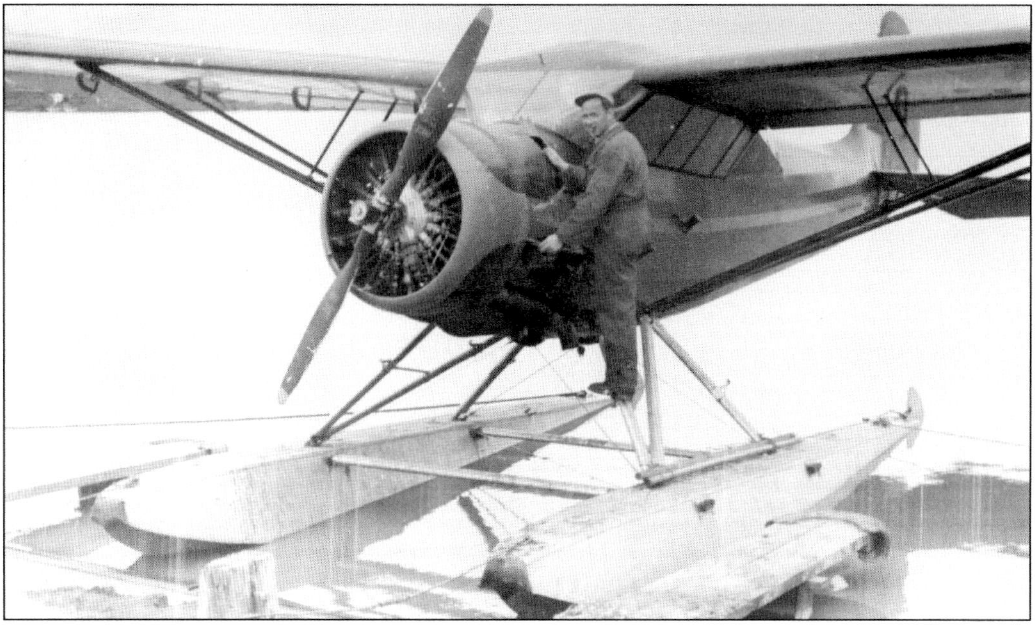

Bush pilot Don Wolforth is pictured during a preflight check of his Stinson aircraft, used by the Alaska Department of Fish and Game. (Courtesy of the Alaska Aviation Museum.)

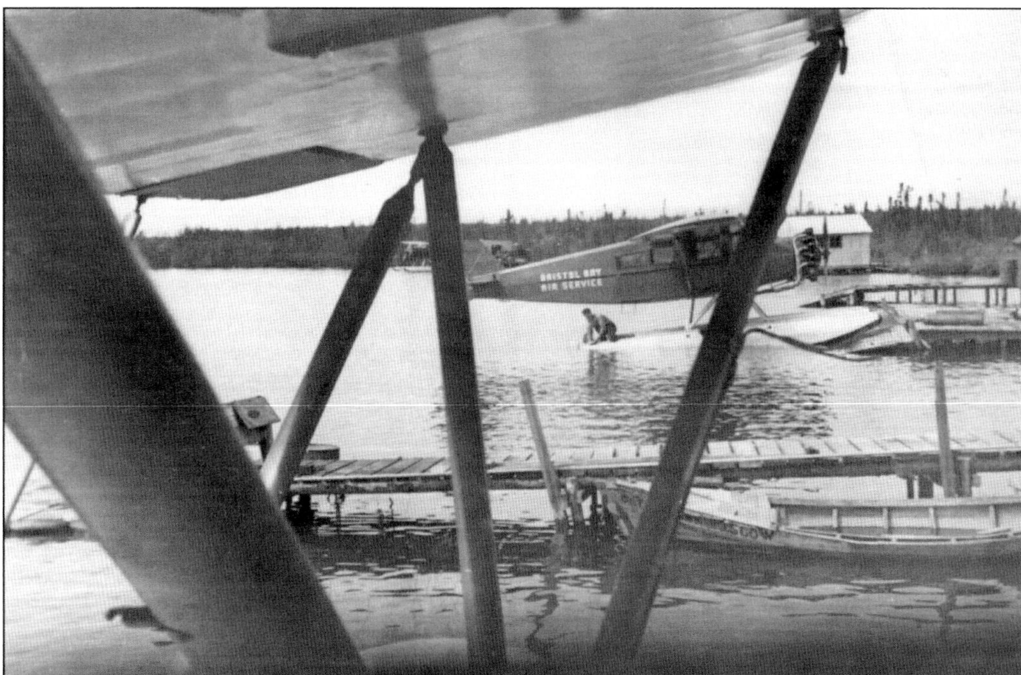

A Bristol Bay Air Service pilot cleans his aircraft after making a successful flight back to the tie-down somewhere in Bristol Bay. (Courtesy of the Alaska Aviation Museum.)

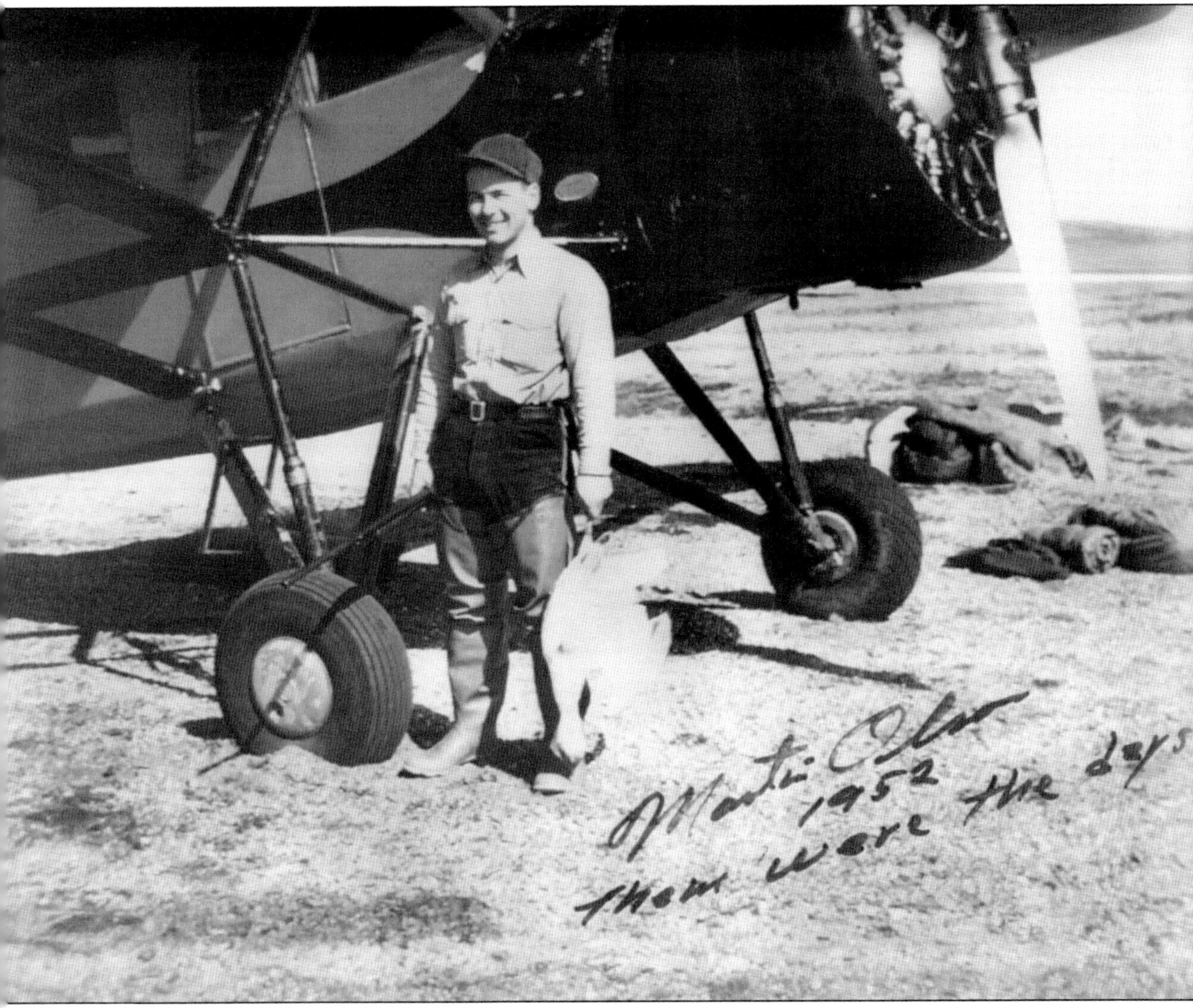

Martin Olson of Olson Air, which operated to the villages of the Seward Peninsula, stands with his catch in front of a Stinson SRJR. (Courtesy of the Alaska Aviation Museum.)

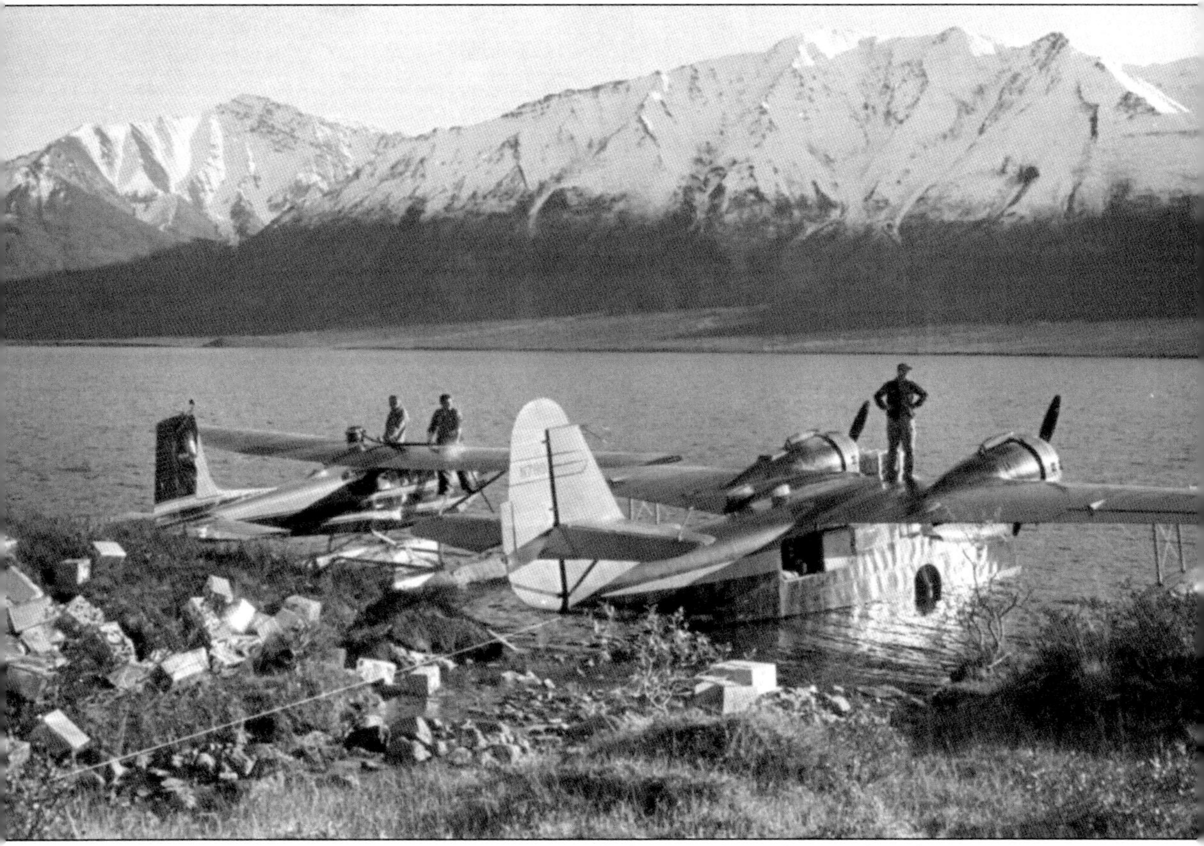

At left, pilots refuel their Cessna 180 after a flight. On the right, a pilot of a Grumman Goose takes in the view across an Alaskan lake. (Courtesy of the Alaska Aviation Museum.)

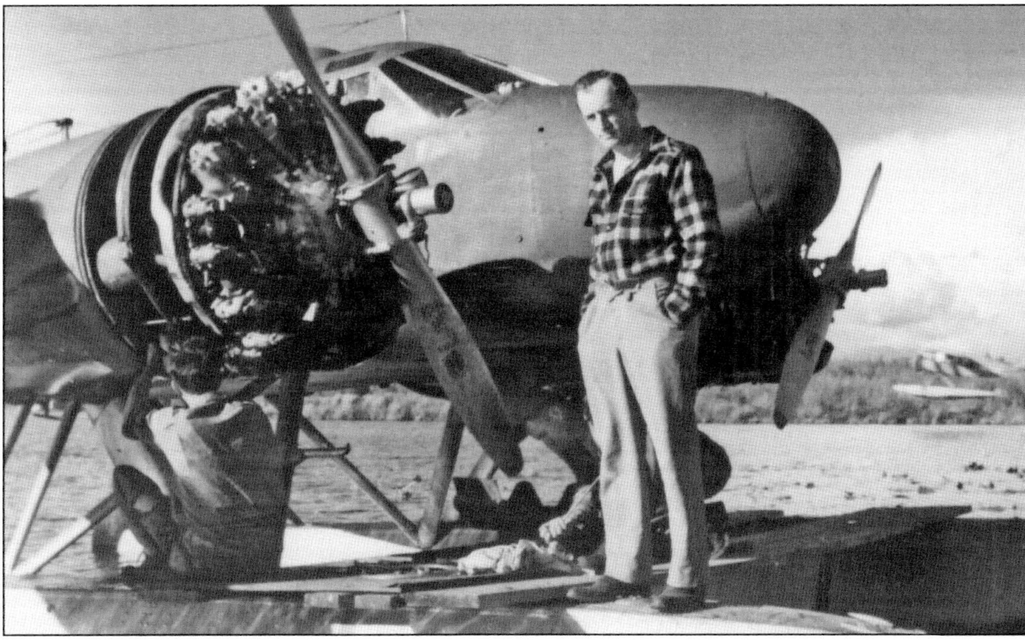

The pilot of this twin Beechcraft on floats supervises a mechanical repair to his aircraft. (Courtesy of the Alaska Aviation Museum.)

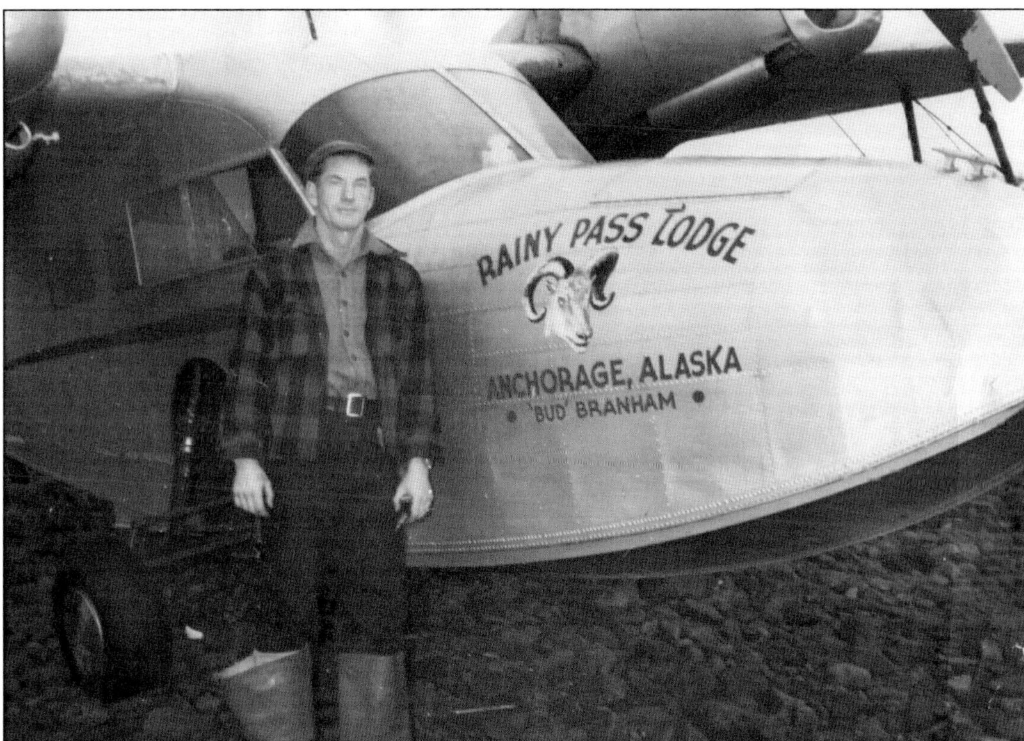

Alaska had many well-known bush pilots. Here, Bud Branham, a popular pilot from Bristol Bay to Lake Minchumina, stands next to his Grumman Widgeon. The plane was used to access Rainy Pass Lodge in the Alaska Range. (Courtesy of the Alaska Aviation Museum.)

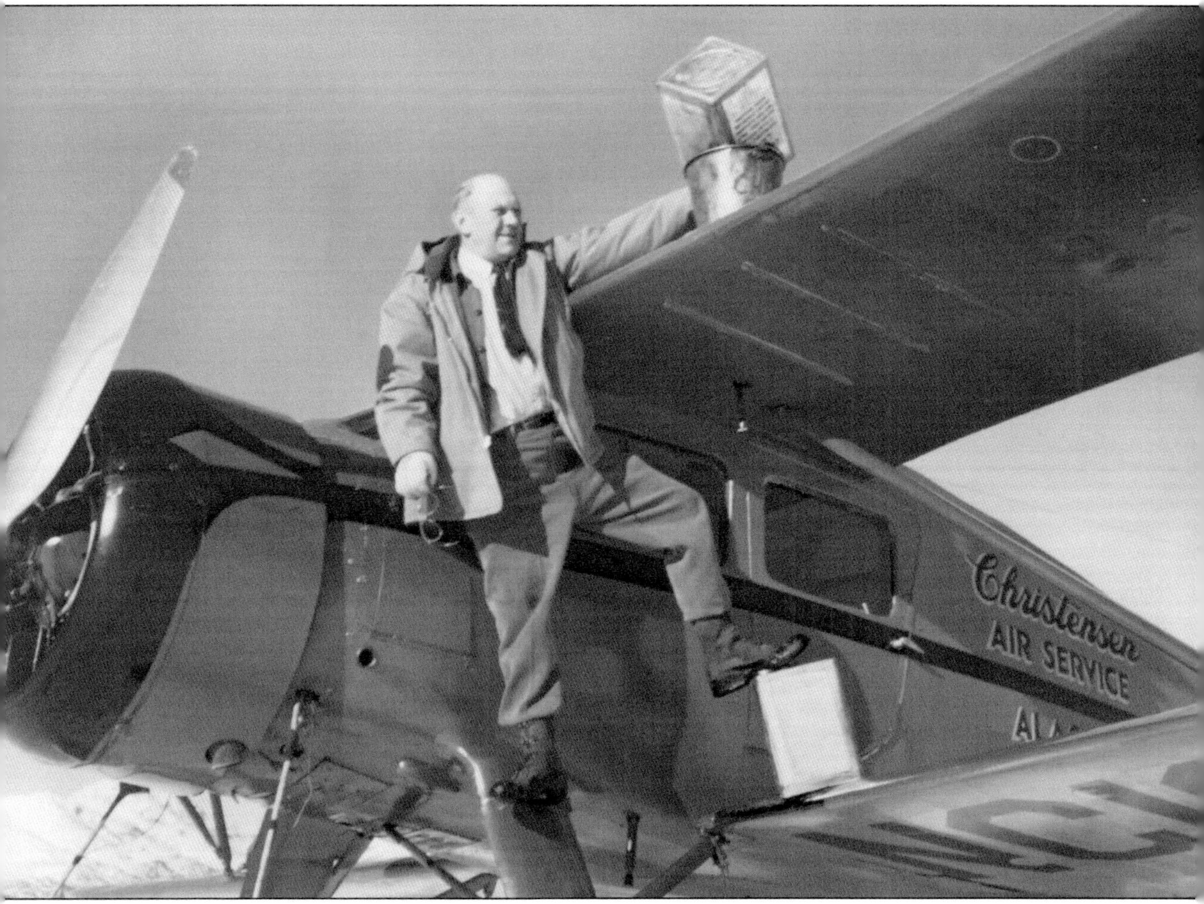

Bush pilot Chris Christianson adds fuel, bush-pilot style. He is using cans, a funnel, and a chamois to strain it. (Courtesy of the Alaska Aviation Museum.)

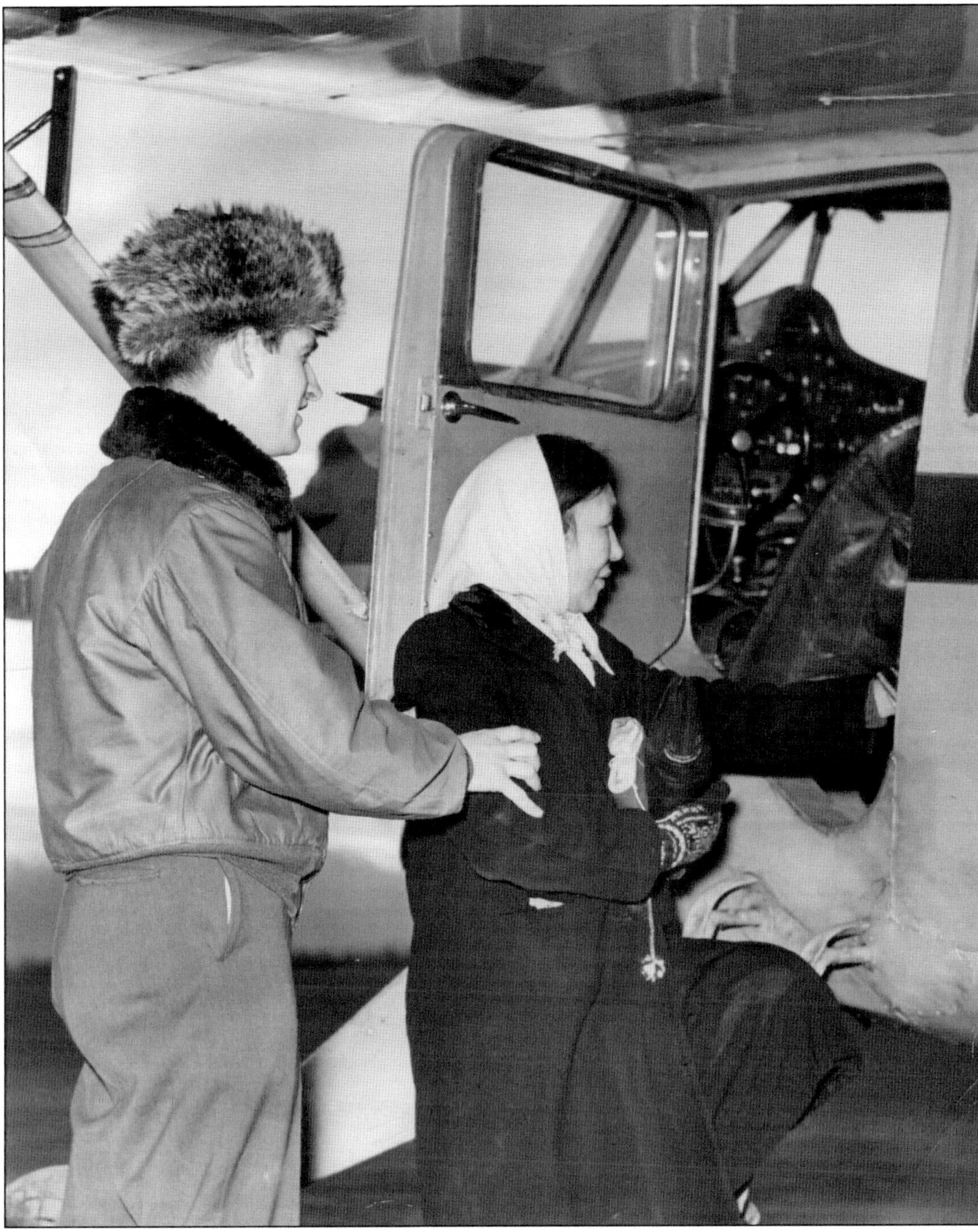

A bush pilot helps a passenger into his plane. Many of the villagers in Alaska were on a first-name basis with the pilots in the early years of Alaska aviation. (Courtesy of the Alaska Aviation Museum.)

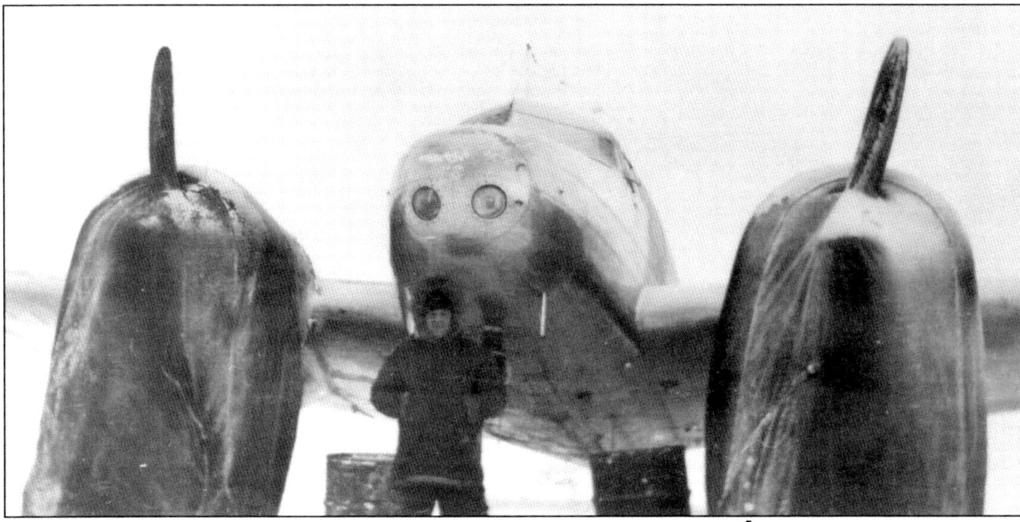

An unidentified pilot stands under the belly of his aircraft while the engines are being heated up before a winter flight. (Courtesy of the Alaska Aviation Museum.)

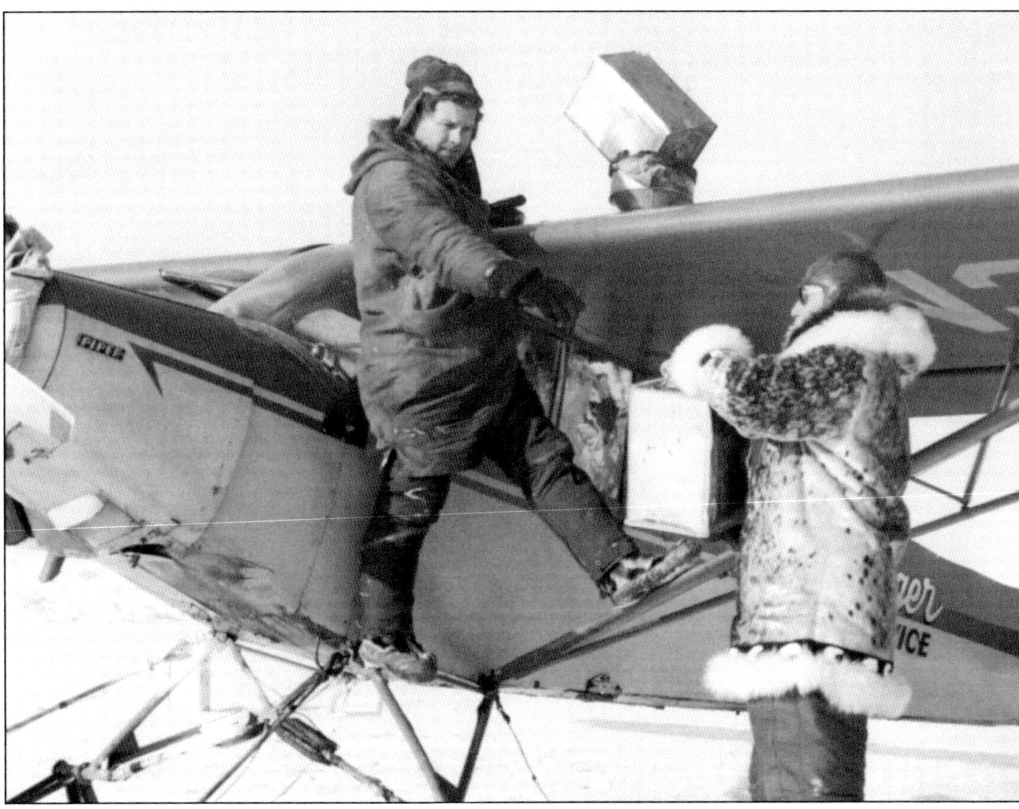

Leon Shellabarger (left), born and raised in Skwentna, Alaska, gets fueling help from a passenger dressed for winter flying. Shellabarger's plane is a Piper Super Cub on skis. (Courtesy of the Alaska Aviation Museum.)

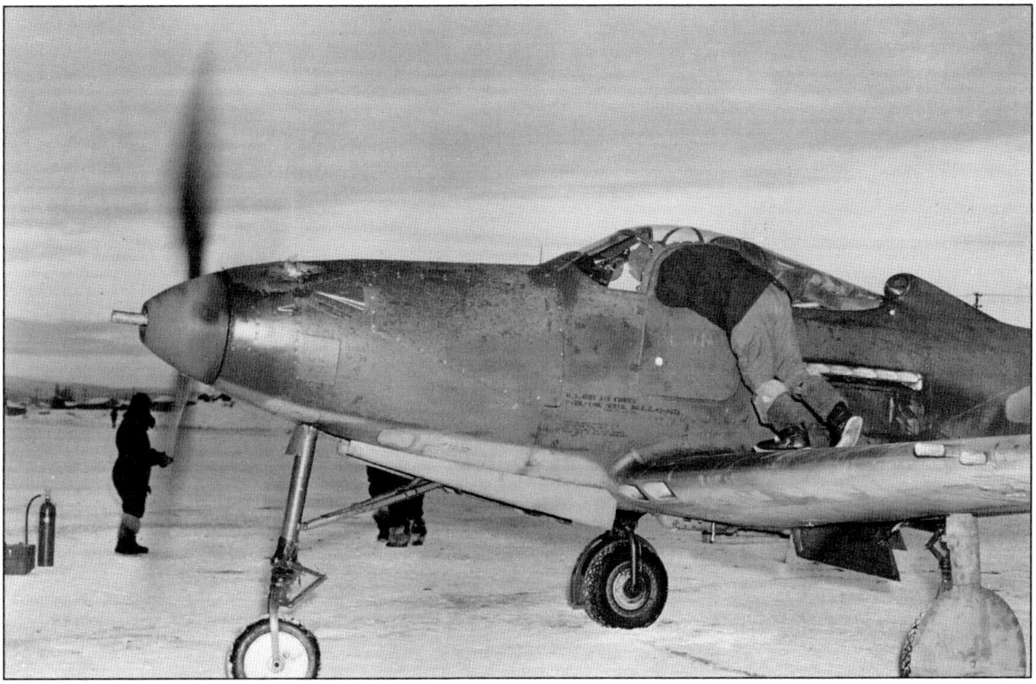

This pilot is checking the radio of a P-39 plane before taking off for Siberia in 1943 or 1944. The US military ran major operations out of Alaska during World War II. (Courtesy of the Library of Congress.)

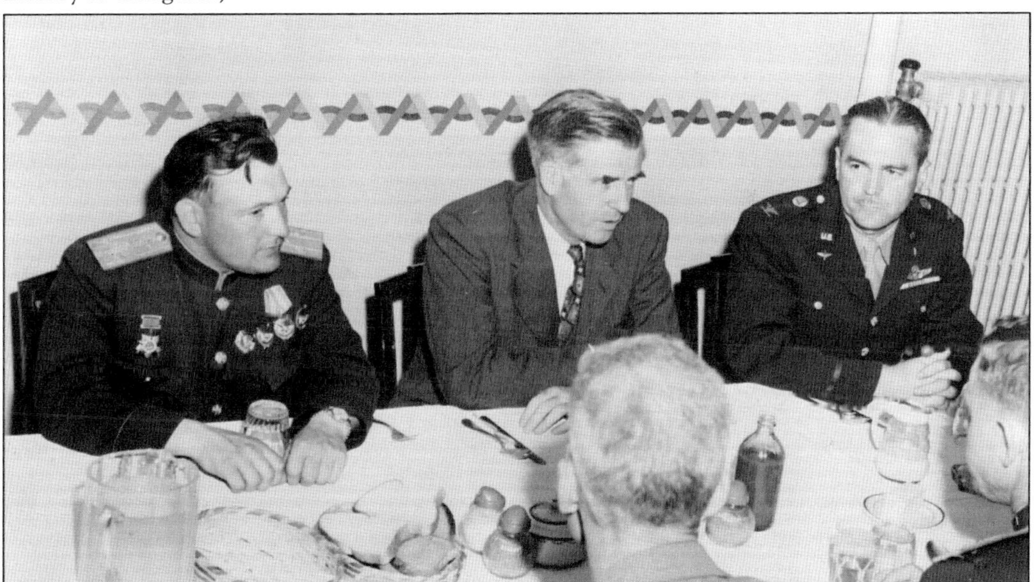

In 1944, Vice Pres. Henry A. Wallace returned from China and Siberia to dine at Ladd Field in Fairbanks with Russian and American airmen who flew Lend-Lease planes to Russia. The flights were conducted through the Alaskan wing of the Air Transport Command. Pictured here are, from left to right, Col. N.S. Vasin, commanding officer of the Russian Air Force's 1st Aviation Ferrying Regiment, who was stationed at Nome, Alaska; Wallace; and Col. Russell Keiller, commanding officer of Ladd Field. (Courtesy of the Library of Congress.)

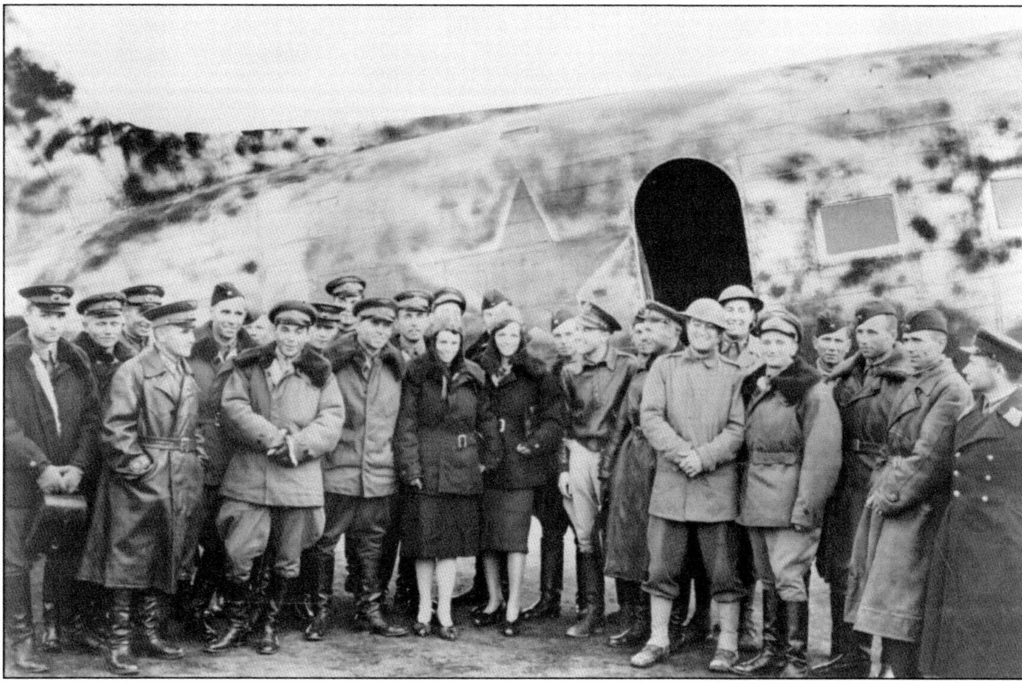

The first Russian military mission to Alaska arrives at Nome in the summer of 1942. The men in the tin hats and riding breeches are Americans. Note the camouflage on the Russian transport plane. (Courtesy of the Library of Congress.)

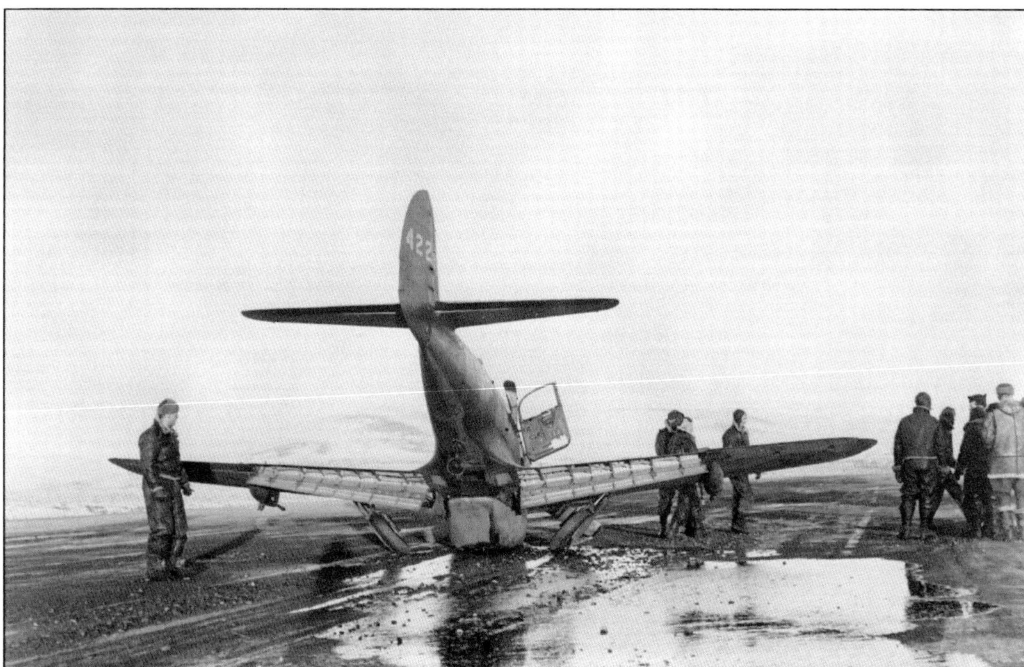

This wrecked plane in Nome, Alaska, is probably at the Alaska wing base of the Air Transport Command in 1943 or 1944. Indeed, flying conditions around Nome were perilous, and such incidents were bound to happen. (Courtesy of the Library of Congress.)

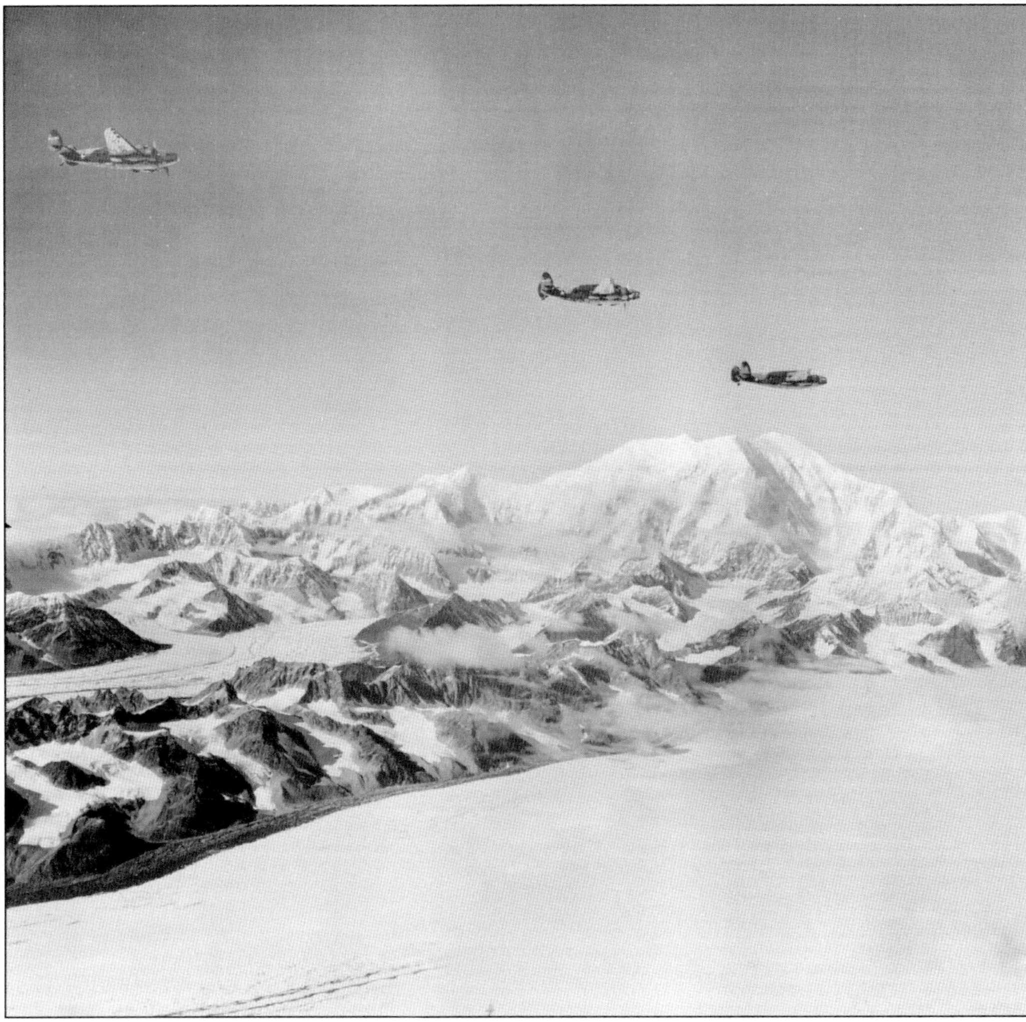

In February 1942, US warplanes—A-29 light bombers—fly over the mountains of Alaska. Mount McKinley is in the background. (Courtesy of the Library of Congress.)

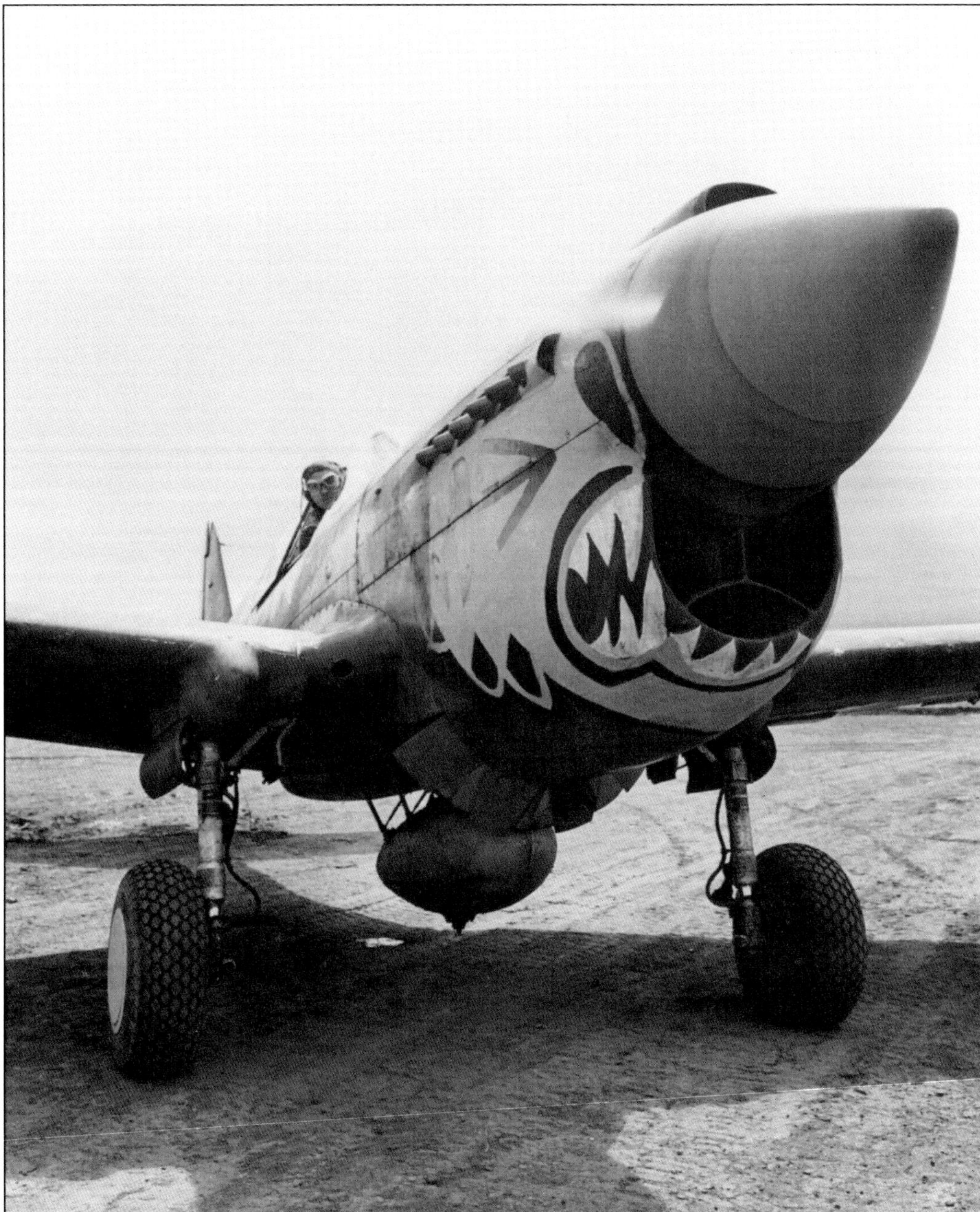

Pictured here during World War II is one of the redoubted "Flying Tigers," ready to take off from an Alaskan site. The plane is a Curtis P-40 Warhawk fighter. (Courtesy of the Library of Congress.)

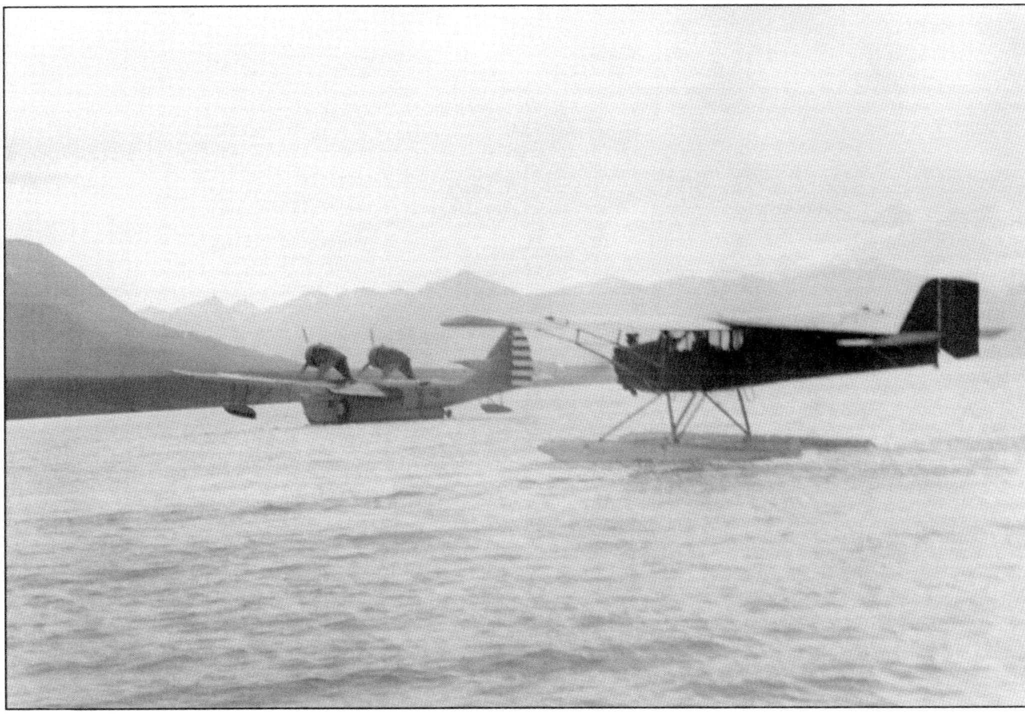

A Navy Grumman Albatross (left) and a Curtiss Robin meet up on Klutina Lake during World War II. (Courtesy of the Alaska Aviation Museum.)

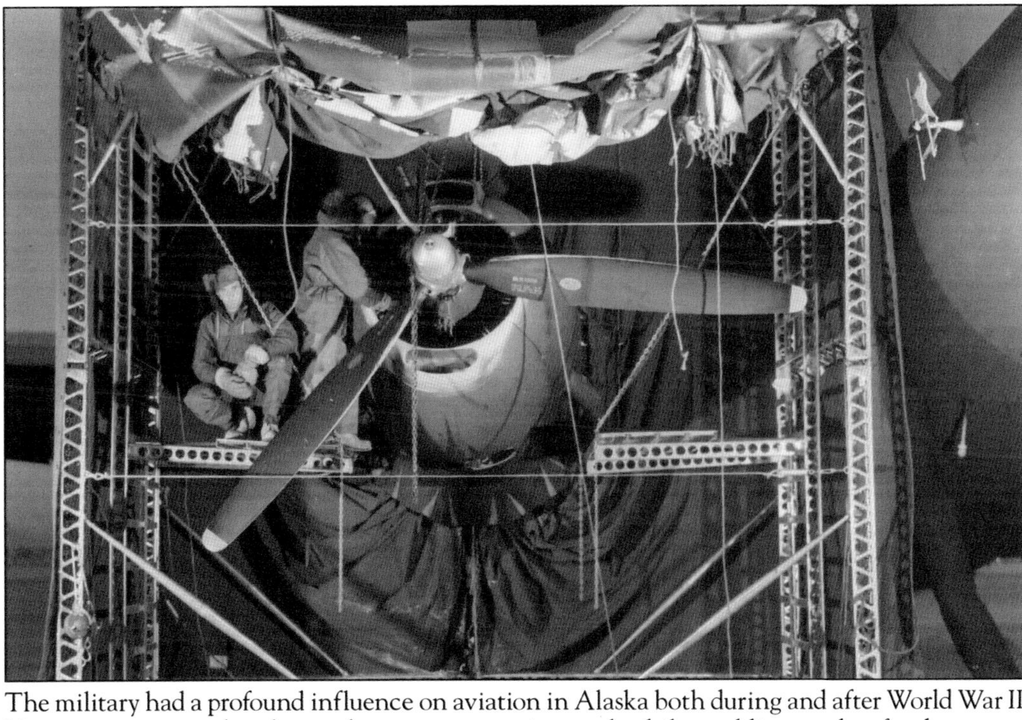

The military had a profound influence on aviation in Alaska both during and after World War II. Here, a transport or bomber undergoes some engine work while a soldier watches for the enemy. (Courtesy of the Alaska Aviation Museum.)

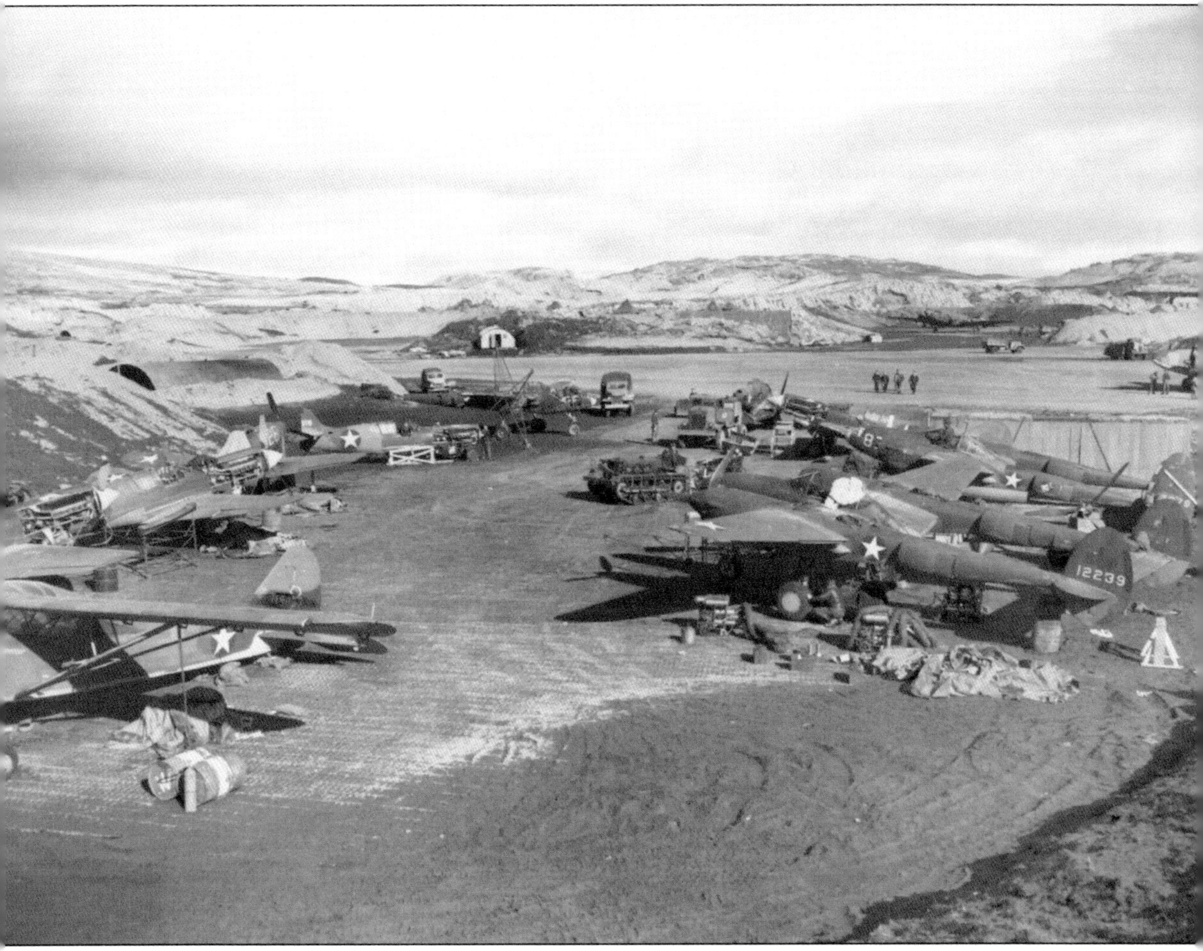

Dutch Harbor became the central point of defense readiness during World War II. This photograph shows P-38, P-39, and P-40 aircraft being assembled for use to defend the Aleutian Islands. Metal matting can still be found near the airport in Dutch Harbor. (Courtesy of the Alaska Aviation Museum.)

Three

MODERN DAYS

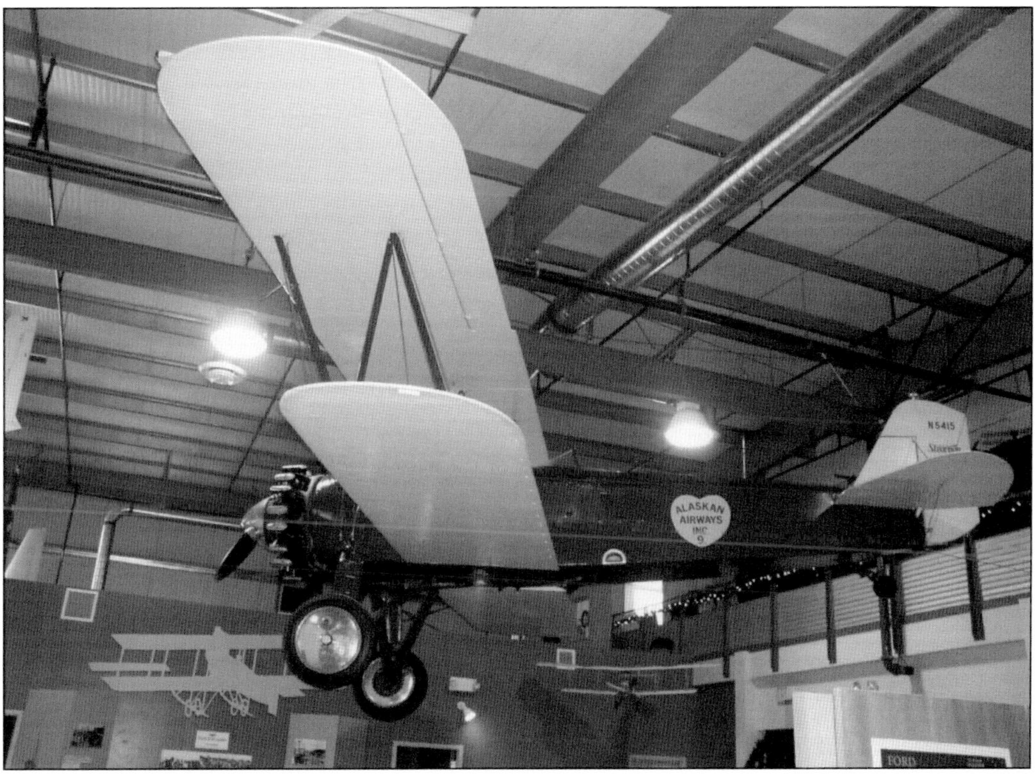

The Alaska Aviation Museum has been open to the public for 25 years. The museum was created in 1988 to display the history of aviation in Alaska as well as to restore vintage planes. Throughout its history, the museum has grown significantly, gaining more vintage planes and more detailed exhibits. The museum gives visitors the chance to get a picture of what flying in Alaska was like in the early years of aviation. (Courtesy of the Alaska Aviation Museum.)

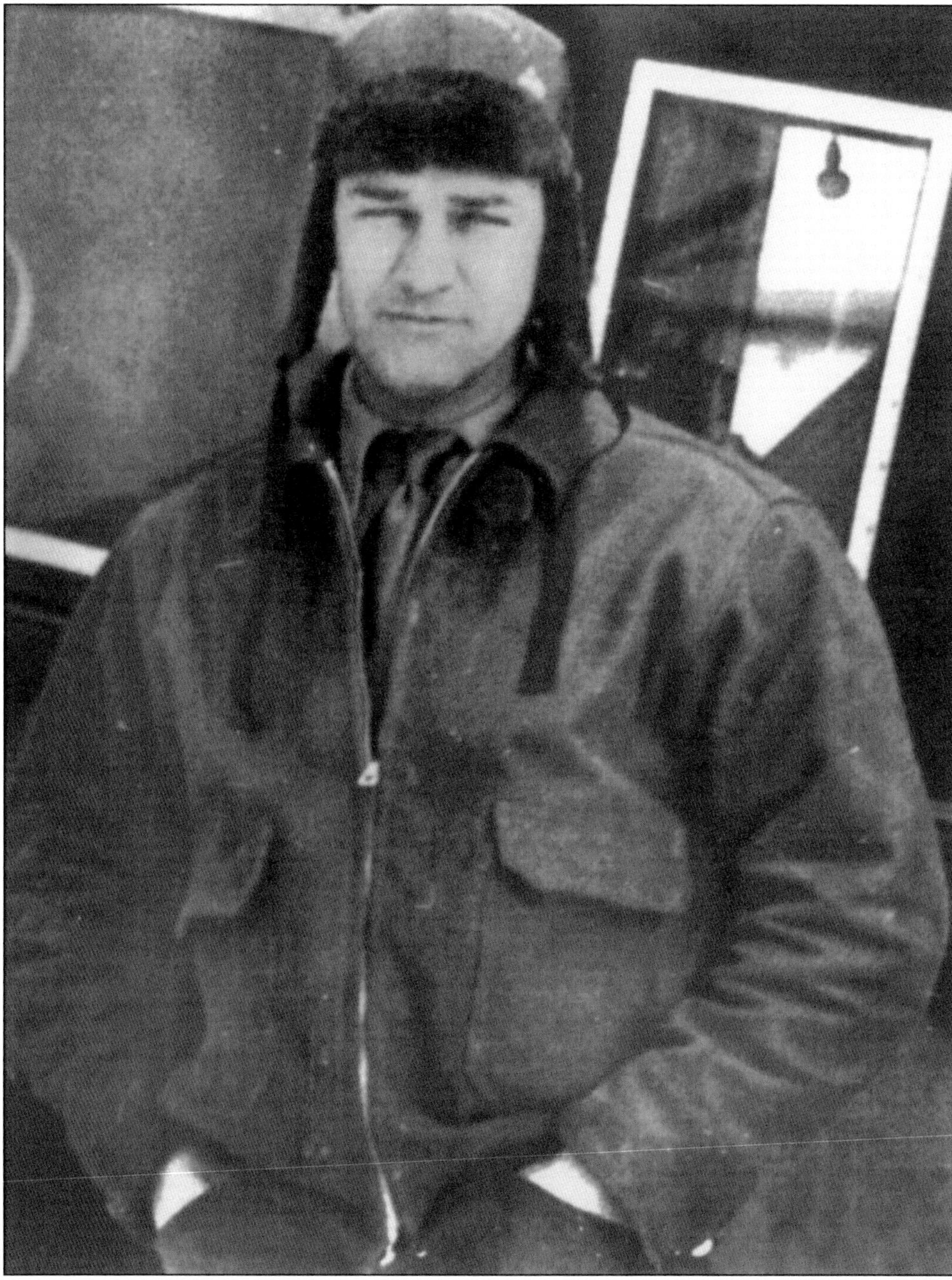

Art Woodley was inducted into the Alaska Aviation Museum Hall of Fame in 2008. Woodley learned to fly in the Army Air Corps in 1928. His brother George was a Catholic priest who owned a Bellanca that he used for his missionary work. When Father George was assigned to Nulato, he and Art flew the plane to Anchorage. Eventually, Art Woodley founded Woodley Airways in 1932 with a four-place Travel Air and a Waco, also with four seats. Woodley mostly flew in the Bristol Bay area, flying mail. He later changed the company's name to Pacific Northern Airway, then Pacific Northern Airlines. Known as PNA, it eventually merged with Western Airlines in 1967, with Woodley as vice president. He retired in 1971 and died at his home in Bellevue, Washington, on May 28, 1990. (Courtesy of the Alaska Aviation Museum.)

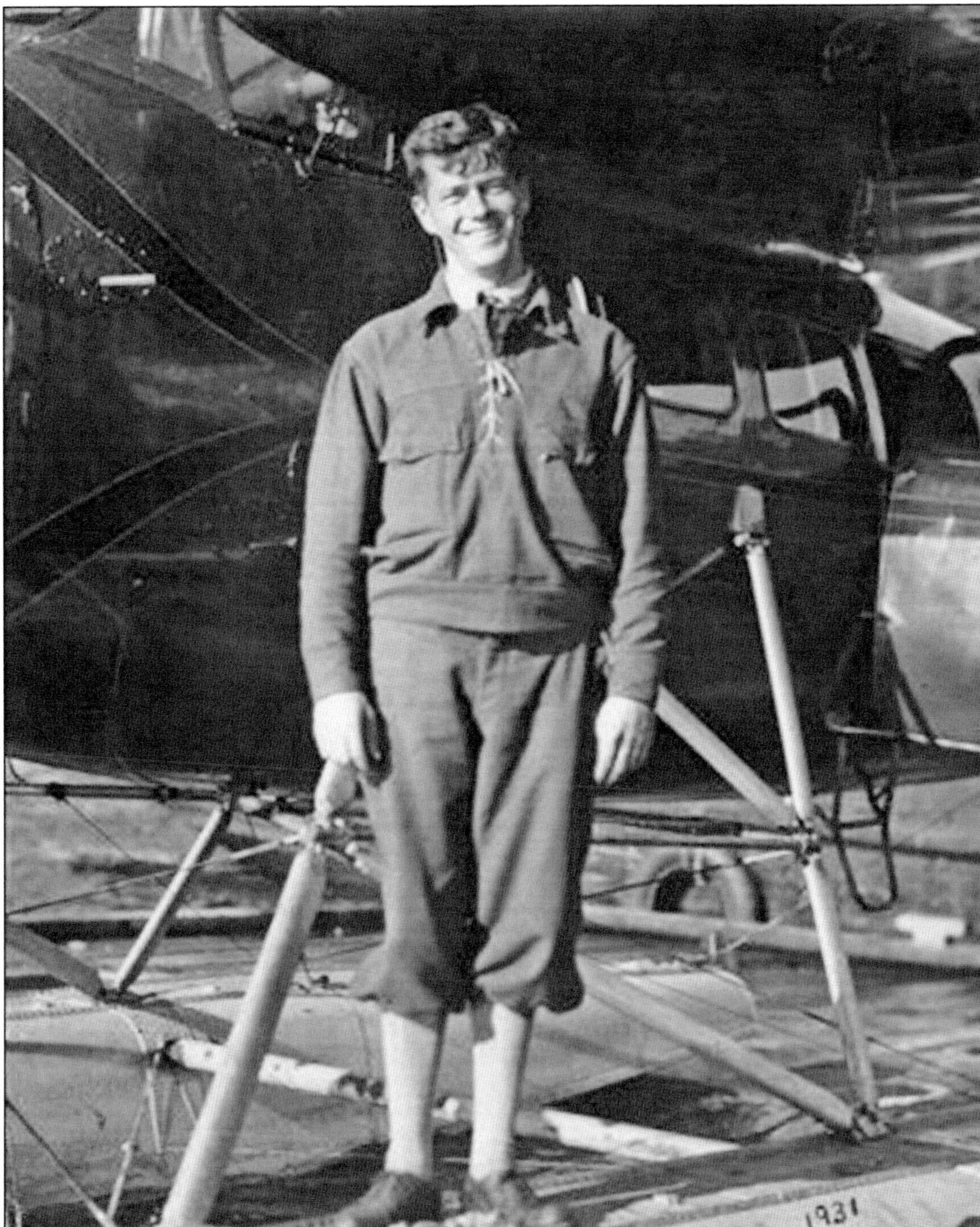

Robert E. "Bob" Ellis was born in St. Albans, Vermont, on January 20, 1903. Ellis attended the US Naval Academy, where he received navigation and flight training. He plotted a course for a flight from Seattle to Juneau on an Alaska Washington Airways Lockheed Vega. Ellis participated in the flight, which started his long aviation career in Alaska. In 1936, he purchased a Waco floatplane and established Ellis Air Transport, later called Ellis Air Lines, in Ketchikan. The company merged with Alaska Coastal Airlines in 1965 to become Alaska Coastal–Ellis Airlines, a forerunner of Alaska Airlines in 1968. Ellis was a senator in the Alaska Territorial Legislature from 1955 to 1958. He died in 1994 at his home in Ketchikan. (Courtesy of the Alaska Aviation Museum.)

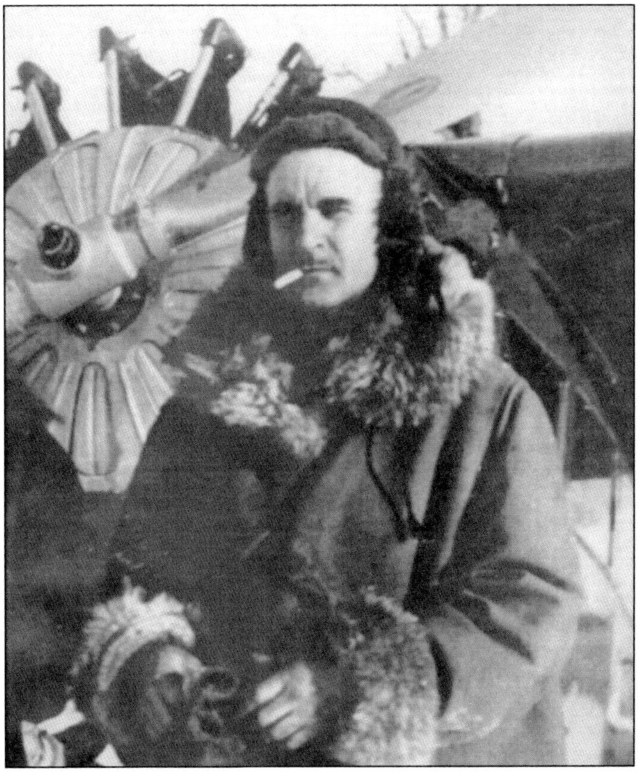

Robert "Bob" Campbell Reeve was born on March 27, 1902, in Waunakee, Wisconsin. He obtained his commercial pilot's license in 1928 and flew airmail runs in South America. Reeve, who stowed away to make passage to Valdez, repaired Owen Meals's Eaglerock biplane, which Meals had crashed. Reeve then leased the plane and started a charter business, flying the Copper River area and interior. Reeve left Valdez in the early 1940s and went to Fairbanks, then to Anchorage, where he made scheduled runs along the Aleutian chain. (Courtesy of the Alaska Aviation Museum.)

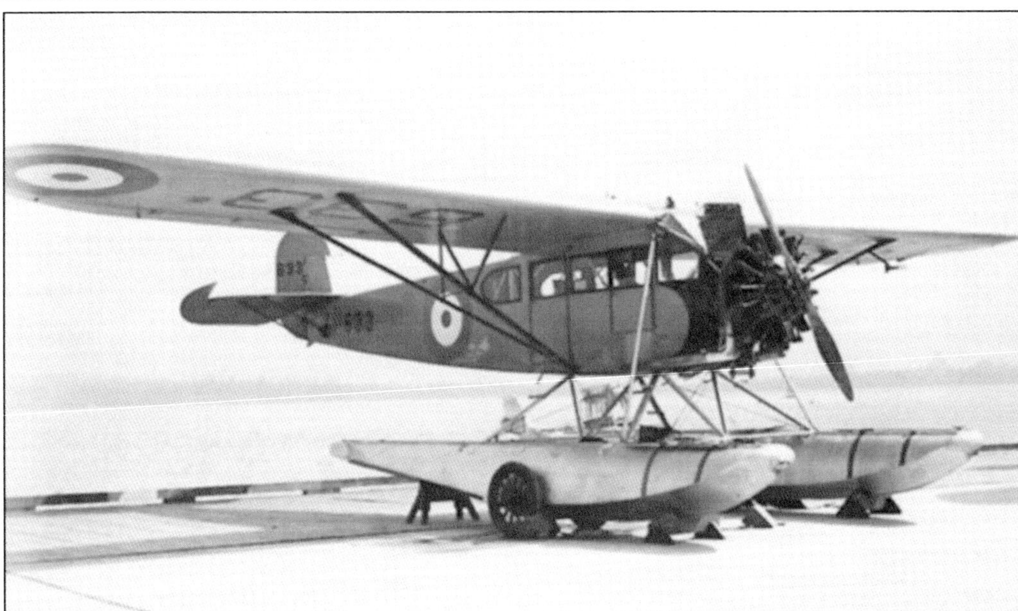

In 1947, Bob Reeve founded Reeve Aleutian Airlines, based in Anchorage. The company serviced not only the Aleutian chain but also the Russian Far East. In 1975, Reeve was inducted into the National Aviation Hall of Fame. He entered the International Aerospace Hall of Fame in 1980 and the Alaska Aviation Museum Hall of Fame in 2005. Reeve died on August 25, 1980, in Anchorage. (Courtesy of the Alaska Aviation Museum.)

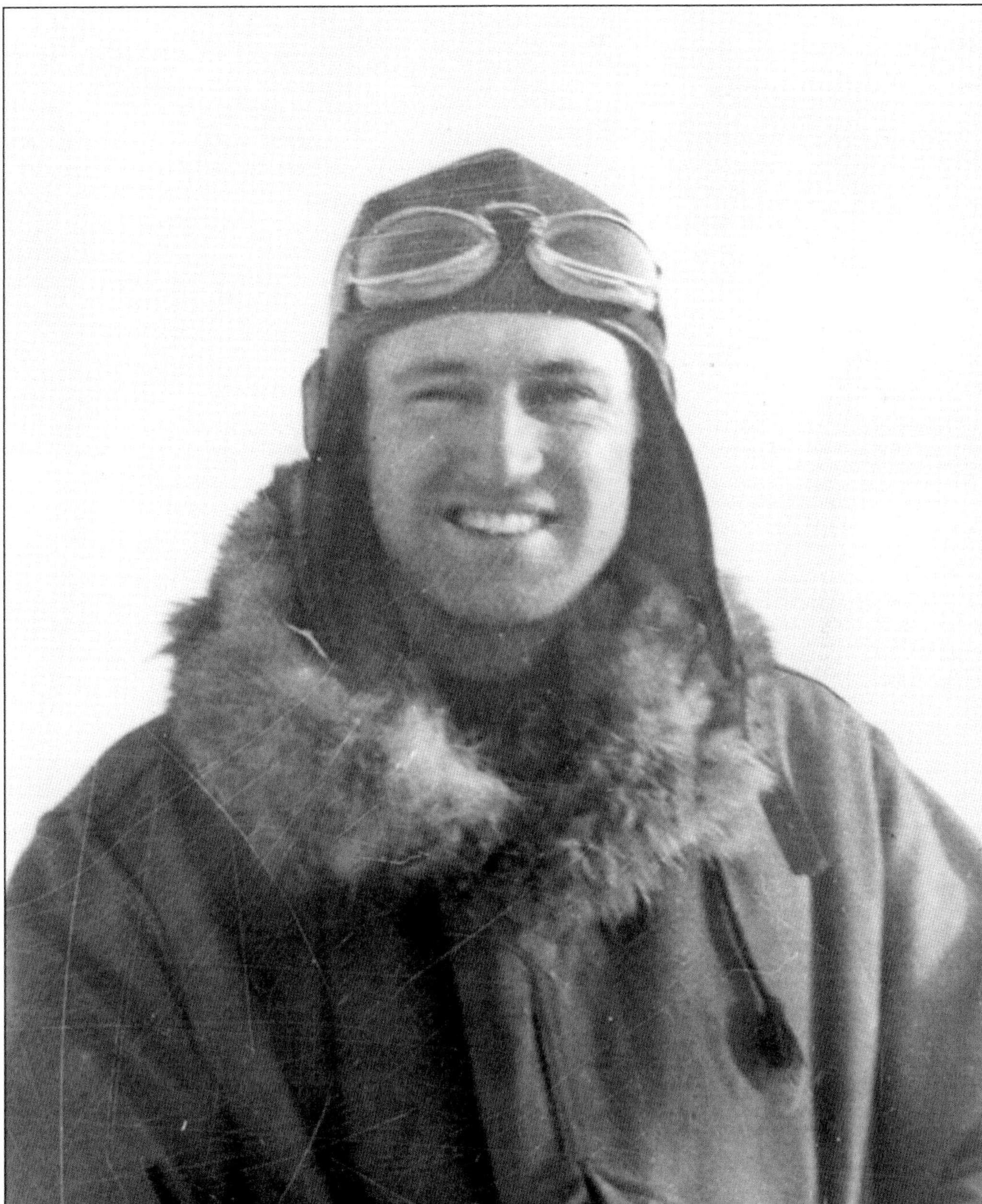

Joe E. Crosson was born on June 29, 1903, at Minneapolis, Kansas. He and his sister, Marvel (1904–1939), learned to fly in San Diego, California, and barnstormed together before moving to Fairbanks Aircraft Co. in March 1926. Crosson and Ben Eielson were pilots on the 1928 Wilkins-Hearst Antarctic expedition. Crosson was one of the pilots who found the site of the Eielson crash in Siberia in 1929. He also flew the bodies of Will Rogers and Wiley Post out of Barrow in 1935. Later, Crosson led Pacific Alaska Airways, a Pan Am subsidiary. Crosson later started a parts and maintenance business at Boeing Field in Seattle. He died suddenly in Seattle in 1949 at age 45. He was inducted into the Alaska Aviation Museum Hall of Fame in 2002. (Courtesy of the Alaska Aviation Museum.)

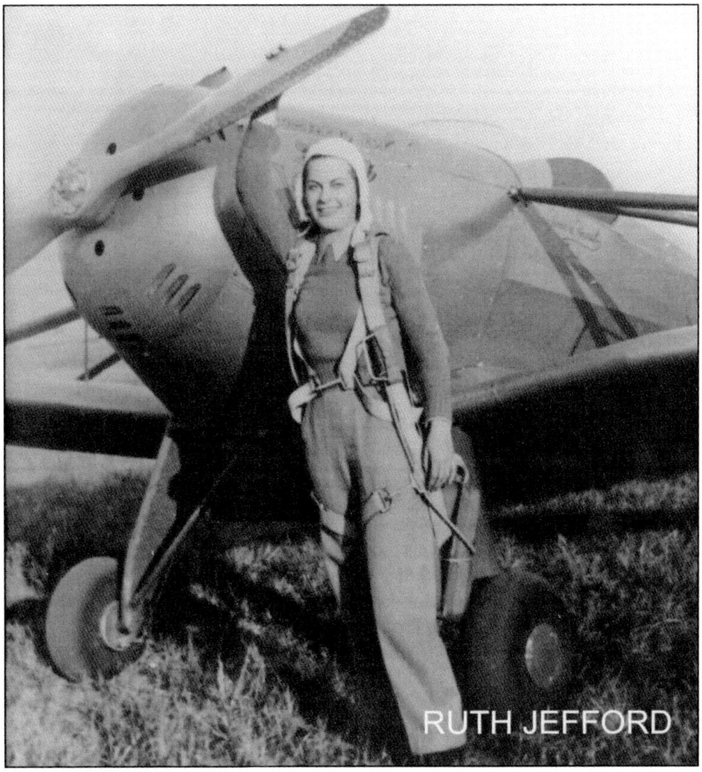

Ruth Jefford was born in Des Moines, Iowa, in 1914. Jefford learned to fly in Nebraska with Jim Hurst and earned her pilot's license in 1938 in an Aero Sport with a Ford V-8 engine. Jefford and Hurst moved north to Alaska in December 1941. In her early years in Alaska, she worked with the Red Cross Motor Corps during World War II, and she later founded the Anchorage Symphony in 1946. After a divorce from Hurst, Ruth married Jack Jefford in 1970. The couple formed Valley Air Transit in 1971. Ruth Jefford was the first woman flight instructor at Merrill Field in Anchorage. (Courtesy of the Alaska Aviation Museum.)

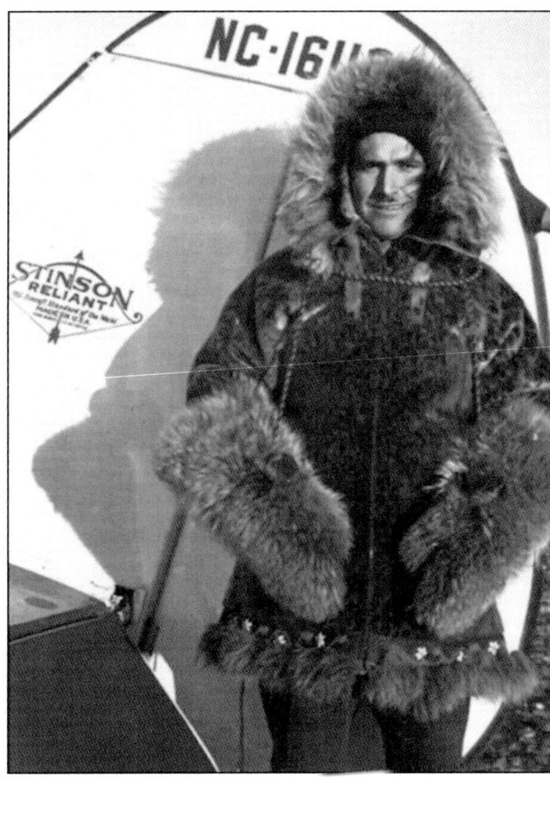

Jack Jefford was born in Nebraska on September 6, 1910. He earned his private pilot's license in 1931 and flew in Nebraska before coming to Alaska. Jefford first flew for Mirow Air Service, then joined the Civil Aeronautics Administration when it established a flight division. He was chief pilot for the Alaska region from 1940 to 1972. He was the first to fly instruments over new range routes. Jefford died at his home in Wasilla on August 12, 1979. (Courtesy of the Alaska Aviation Museum.)

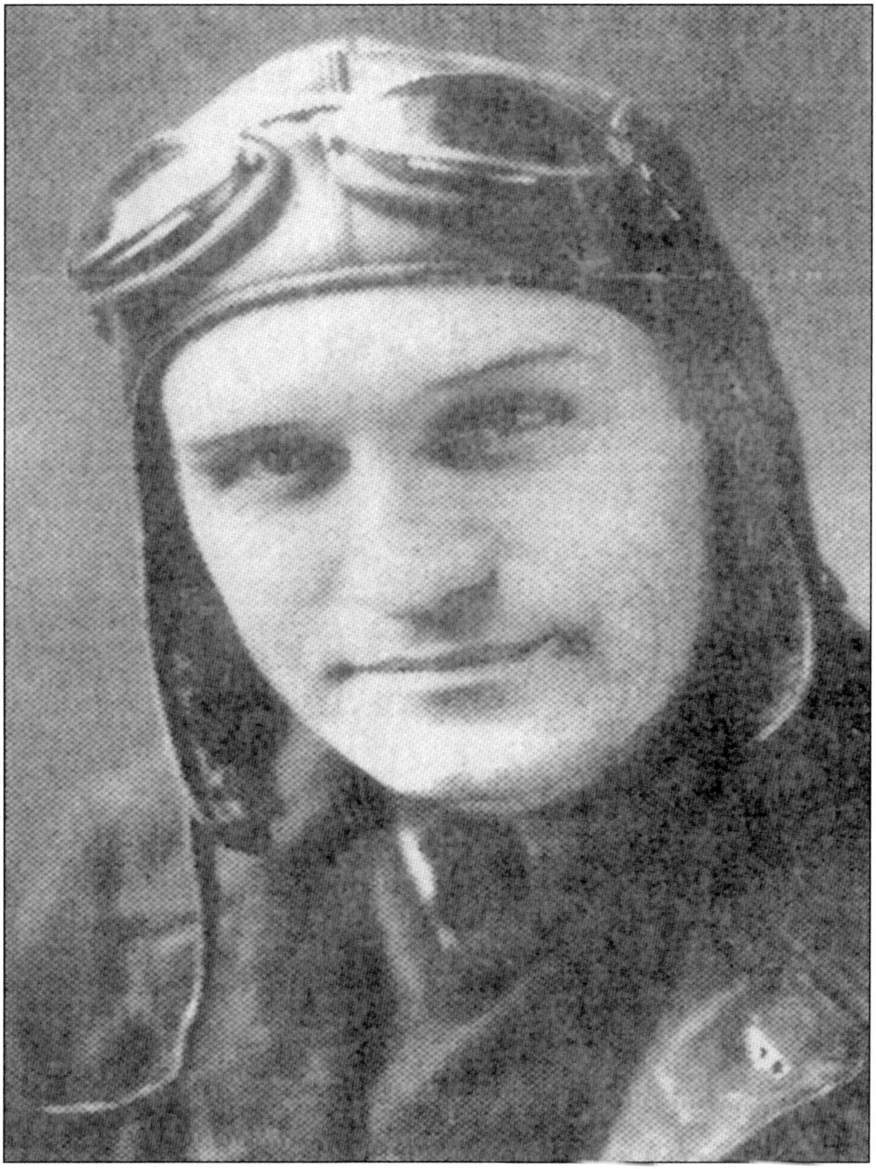

Carl Benjamin Eielson was born in Hatton, North Dakota, in 1897. Eielson is known as one of the most influential pilots in aviation history. He arrived in Fairbanks in 1922 as a schoolteacher. He pioneered airmail service in Alaska, flying twice a month from Fairbanks to McGrath in a de Havilland biplane. Eielson and Joe Crosson flew on the Wilkins-Hearst Antarctic expedition in 1928. The same year, Eielson received the Distinguished Flying Cross for the first flight across the North Pole, taking Sir Hubert Wilkins from Point Barrow to Spitsbergen, Norway, in a Lockheed Vega. He purchased Anchorage Air Transport in 1929 and changed the name to Alaska Airways. Eielson obtained a contract to fly 15 stranded passengers and six tons of furs from the trading ship *Nanuk*, which was stranded in the ice off Siberia. Eielson and his mechanic, Earl Borland, were killed in their Hamilton Metalplane in Siberia (Chukotka) on November 9, 1929, on their second flight to the ship. Eielson was inducted into the National Aviation Hall of Fame in 1985 and the Alaska Aviation Museum Hall of Fame in 2003. Eielson Air Force Base east of Fairbanks was named in his honor. (Courtesy Alaska Aviation Museum.)

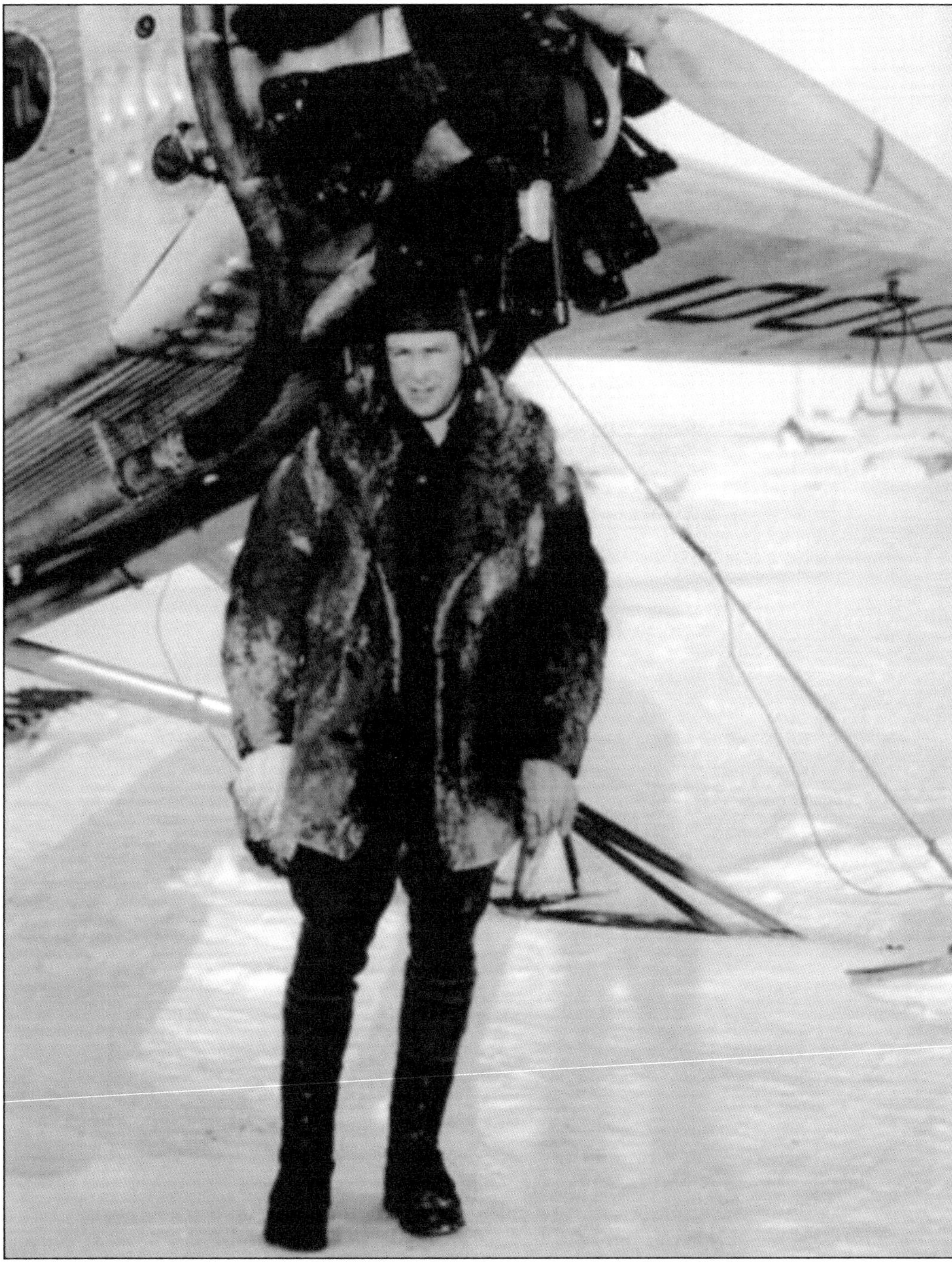

Considered the leading bush pilot of Alaska, Noel Wien is the "Dean of the Alaska Bush Pilots." He was born on June 8, 1899, at Lake Nebagamon, Wisconsin, where he learned to fly. After arriving in Alaska in 1924, he flew a Hisso J-1 Standard biplane for Rodebaugh's Alaska Aerial Transport Co. in Fairbanks. Wien is credited with the first flight between Anchorage and Fairbanks in the Hisso Standard. (Courtesy of the Alaska Aviation Museum.)

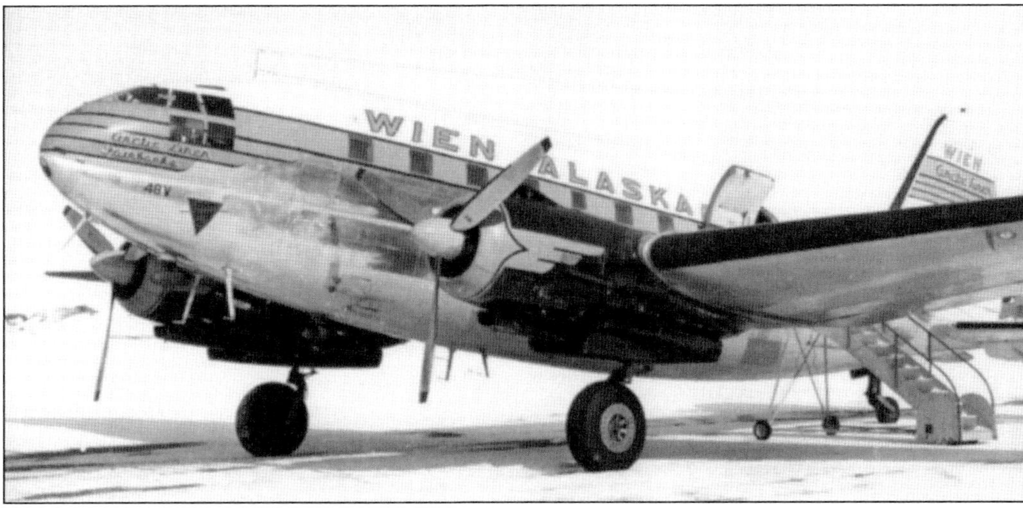

Wien Alaska Airways was the first company to offer scheduled service between Nome and Fairbanks, in 1927. Wien Alaska Airways was sold in 1929 as part of an acquisition that formed Alaskan Airways, operated by Joe Crosson and Charles Thompson and funded by the Aviation Corporation of America. Noel Wien delivered the first photographs and film of the Rogers/Post wreck in 1935 to Seattle. In 1940, Wien, who was responsible for starting several airlines, sold his interest in Wien Alaska Airlines to his brother Sigurd "Sig" Wien. Noel was inducted into the OX-5 Club Hall of Fame in 1973, the Minnesota Aviation Hall of Fame in 1989, and the Alaska Aviation Museum Hall of Fame in 2000. The library in downtown Fairbanks is named the Noel Wien Public Library. He died on July 19, 1977, in Bellevue, Washington. (Both, courtesy of the Alaska Aviation Museum.)

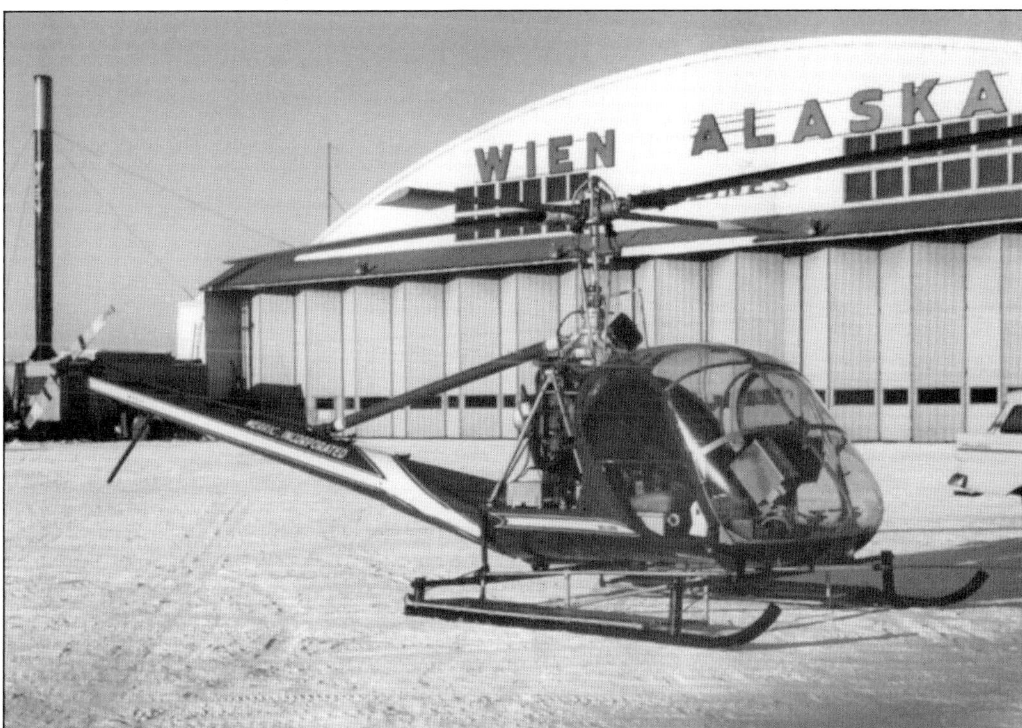

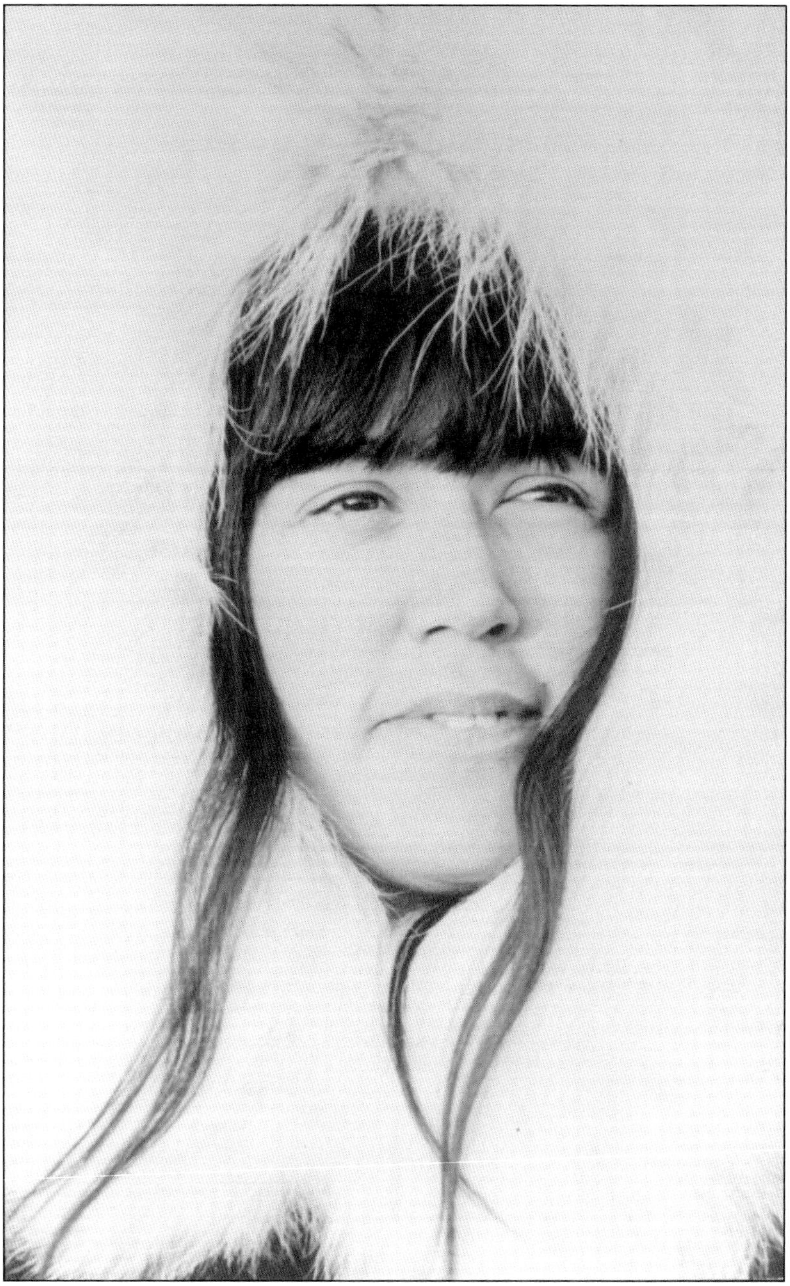

Many Alaska Native pilots fly for regional and major airlines today. Historically, one pilot stands out above them all, Ellen Paneok. She was the first Alaska Native female pilot to become commercially rated. She transported everything from dynamite to mail, passengers, and medical patients, and she even flew live wolverines. Paneok's passion for flying stemmed from reading an article about aviation in a magazine when she was only 15 years old. Using dividends from her regional corporation, she started taking flying lessons. When those funds were depleted, she worked as an artist and used the money she earned to complete her training. At the age of 20, Paneok earned a GED and a private pilot's license. By the age of 23, she had obtained her commercial and flight-instructor certificates. (Courtesy of the Alaska Aviation Museum.)

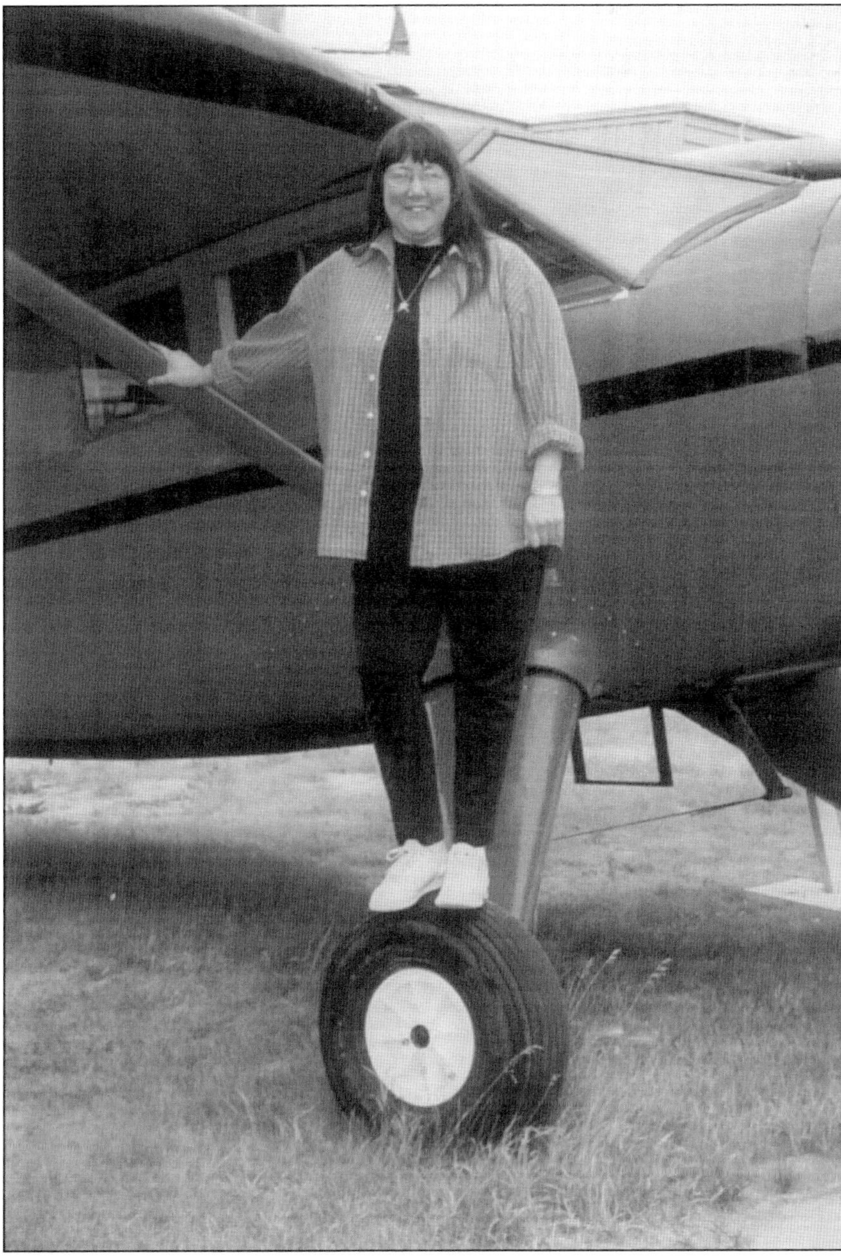

Ellen Paneok's first commercial piloting job was flying a Piper Cherokee Six from Kiana, Alaska. After flying for commercial air-taxi operations around Bush, Alaska, she took a job with the Federal Aviation Administration. She also worked for the Alaska Aviation Foundation as a statewide aviation safety coordinator. Eventually, Paneok became one of a handful of pilots able to fly vintage aircraft owned by the Alaska Aviation Museum. She was a supporter of the Alaska Ninety-Nines and served on the board of the Alaska Heritage Museum, the Alaska Airmen's Association, Big Brothers Big Sisters, the Alaska Historical Commission, and Challenge Alaska. Ellen Paneok was honored by being inducted into the Alaska Women's Hall of Fame. Paneok passed away in 2008, but shortly after her death, she was honored by US senator Lisa Murkowski in the *Congressional Record*. (Courtesy of the Alaska Aviation Museum.)

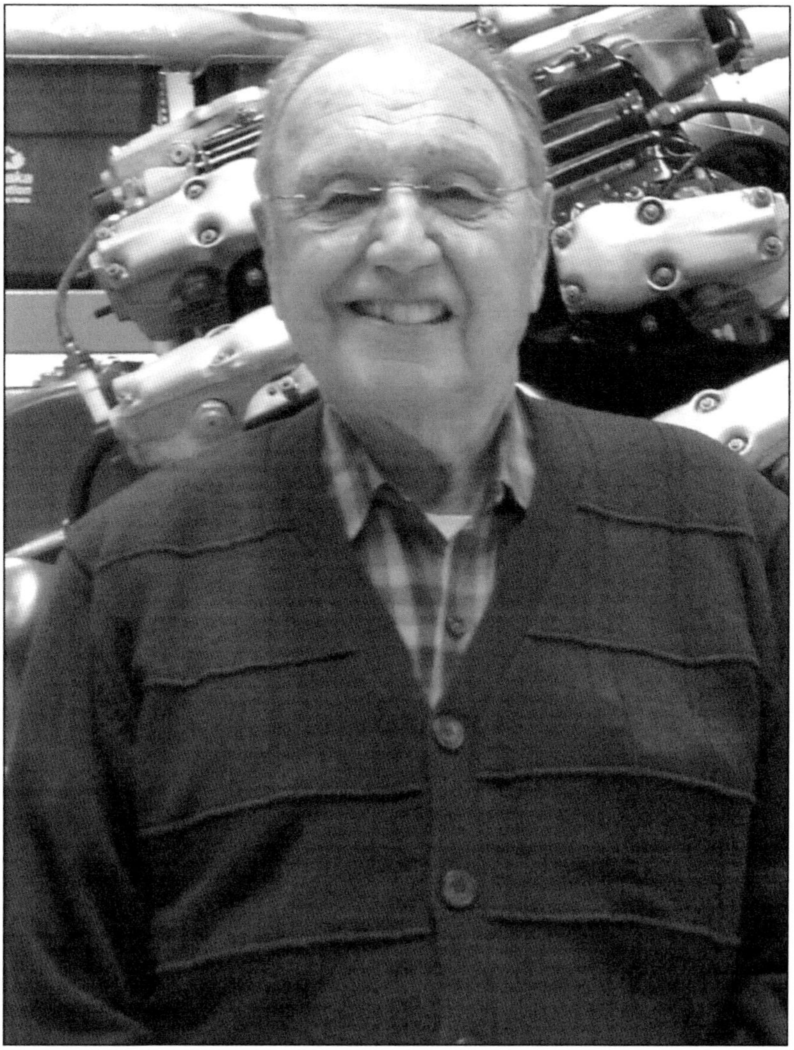

Cliff Everts started flying when he was 15 years old, before receiving his driver's permit. Everts rode his bicycle to the Valhalla airport in Westchester County, New York, where he learned to fly a 1939 Taylorcraft. He became an airline pilot for Wien Airlines and retired in 1980, accumulating 30,000 hours carrying passengers, cargo, and mail to villages all over the territory and, later, the state of Alaska. Everts purchased his first Curtiss C-46 (N92853) from Wien Airlines when it was upgrading its fleet. He leased the plane to Jack Coghill, owner of Nenana Fuel Company. Everts eventually purchased a second aircraft, a DC-6, again leasing it to Coghill, who used the aircraft to haul fuel and freight. When Everts acquired his own operating certificate in the early 1980s, he took over the two aircraft from Coghill and began operating under Everts Air Fuel. By January 1985, Everts was able to purchase the Wien hangar at Fairbanks International Airport. The 1990s proved to be a transitional period for Everts, when his son Robert purchased several DC-6 aircraft from him and developed an all-cargo business. Everts Air Fuel was dedicated to the carriage of bulk fuel and petroleum product transportation, while Everts Air Cargo focused on the transportation of cargo. With the air fuel and cargo airlines, in addition to Robert's Tatonduk Outfitters Limited, the Everts duo owned 21 airplanes. During this era, Everts became the largest owner of large-piston engine aircraft in North America. He was inducted into the Alaska Aviation Museum Hall of Fame in 2013. (Courtesy of the Alaska Aviation Museum.)

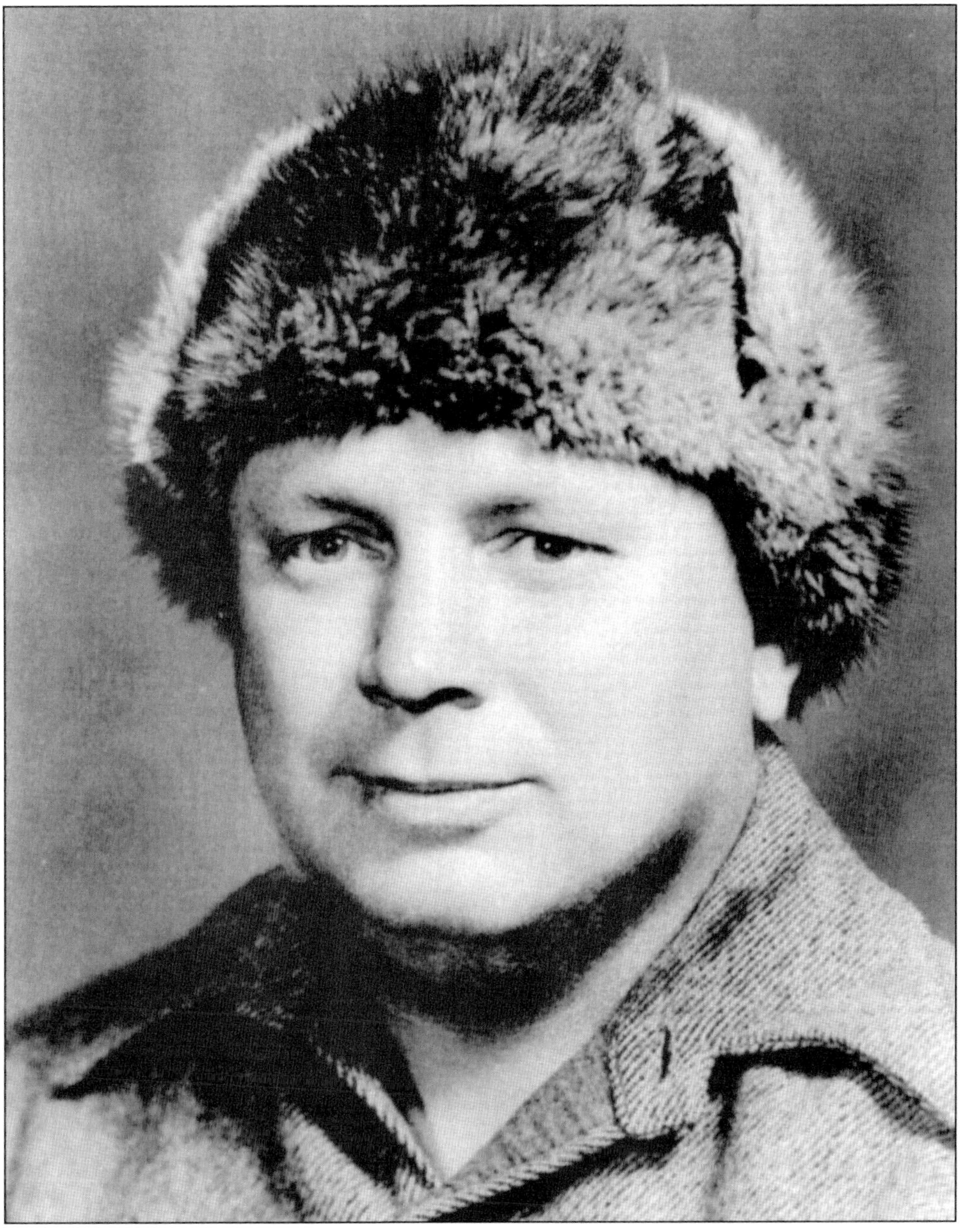

Merle K. "Mudhole" Smith learned to fly in 1928 and barnstormed all over the Midwest. "Kirk" Kirkpatrick brought him to Alaska in 1937 to fly for Cordova Air Service. Smith got his nickname from Bob Reeve, who according to some accounts observed his plane nosed over in a mud hole. Smith later became president of Cordova Air Service after owner Kirkpatrick was killed in a 1939 crash. In 1952, it merged with Christensen Air Service to become Cordova Airlines, which merged with Alaska Airlines in 1968. Smith was a vice president and director of Alaska Airlines until 1973. He was inducted into the OX-5 Aviation Pioneers Hall of Fame and the Alaska Aviation Museum Hall of Fame. Born on September 22, 1907, in Kansas, Smith died on June 16, 1981, at Cordova. The Cordova Airport is named Merle K. (Mudhole) Smith Airport. Smith was inducted into the Alaska Aviation Museum Hall of Fame in 2006. (Courtesy of the Alaska Aviation Museum.)

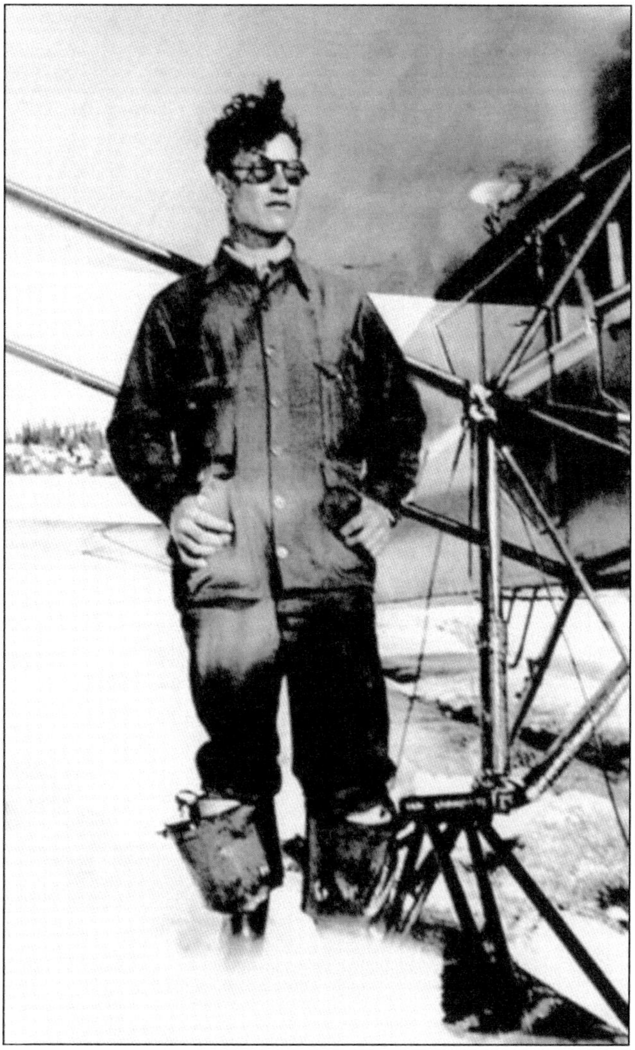

Ray Petersen, who came to Alaska in 1934, is credited with bringing turboprop service to Alaska villages in 1958. He is also thought to be the first to implement an aviation industry retirement plan. Petersen's career began in the 1930s, when he and Noel Wien flew from Seattle back to Alaska in separate airplanes. In 1943, Ray Petersen Flying Service purchased Jim Dodson Air Service and Bristol Bay Air Service. In 1945, it added Northern Airways and two other uncertified operations that further expanded equipment and personnel. After a two-year period waiting for the Civil Aeronautics Board to approve the merger, Northern Consolidated was created. In 1968, it merged with Wien Air Alaska, which offered jet service to Alaska with Boeing 737s and turboprop Fairchild F-27s. Wien Air Alaska was phased out of business in the late 1980s after it was sold to the Household Finance Corp. Petersen last flew the Stinson Tri Motor and the Lockheed 10A. "We had to solve the curse of the mountain passes, so we bought the IFR [instrument flight rules] equipped DC-3 to take care of that challenge," he said. The National Park Service read a letter written by Rob Armburger, regional director of the national parks in Alaska, recognizing Petersen for the preservation of Brooks Camp and the Katmai National Monument. Petersen took the concession for Katmai in the 1950s, but only after he suggested that they only allow fly fishing in the Brooks River. Petersen was inducted into the Alaska Aviation Museum Hall of Fame in 2001. (Courtesy of the Alaska Aviation Museum.)

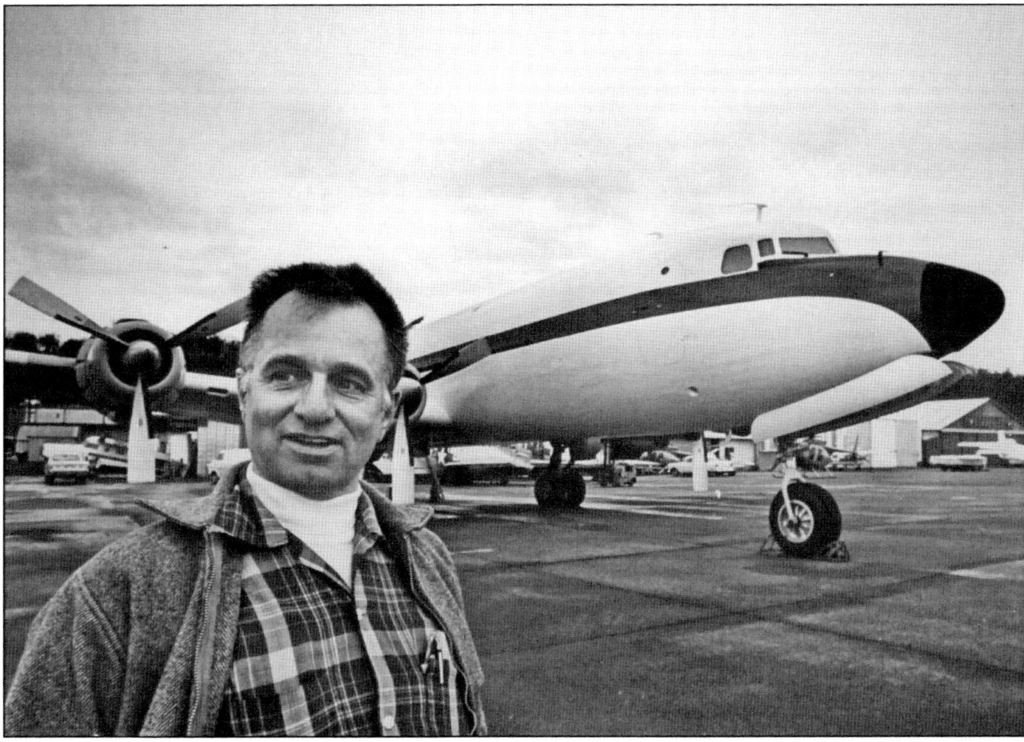

Bobby Sholton (above) and Morrie Carlson are credited with starting the first all-cargo airline, Northern Air Cargo (NAC), in 1956. Air cargo shipments rapidly became a lifeline for rural Alaskan residents and, as Alaska grew, so did Northern Air Cargo. In 1969, Sholton added a DC-6 to the fleet. By the end of the 1970s, NAC had 14 DC-6s delivering critical cargo to villages statewide. Sholton passed away just 24 hours before the first scheduled cargo flight, on December 17, 1982. His pioneering role in Alaska aviation was recognized by the state legislature in 1983. (Courtesy of the Sholton family.)

Rita Sholton, known as the first and only woman president and chief executive officer of an all-freight airline operating above the Arctic Circle, was a pioneer in bringing the Alaska air cargo industry from propeller-driven aircraft into the jet age. Rita and Bobby were inducted into the Alaska Aviation Museum Hall of Fame in 2011. Rita Sholton sits in the front seat of her de Havilland Gypsy Moth, piloted by her son Adam Sholton. (Courtesy of the Sholton family.)

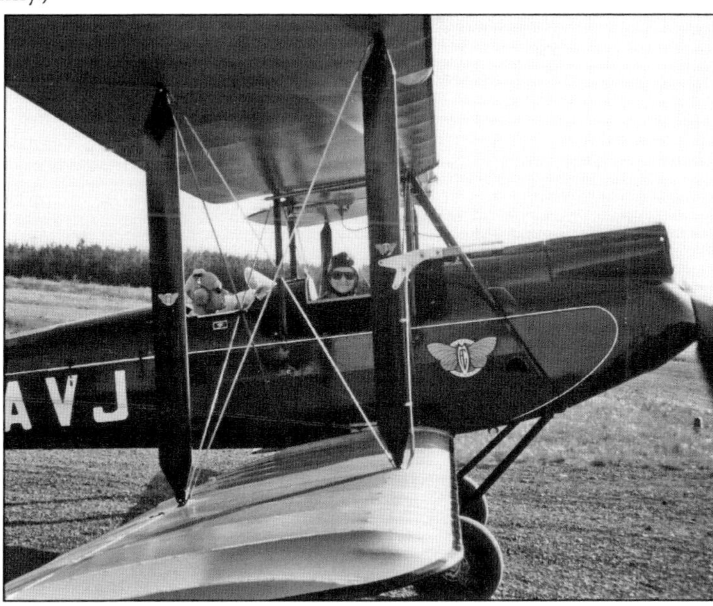

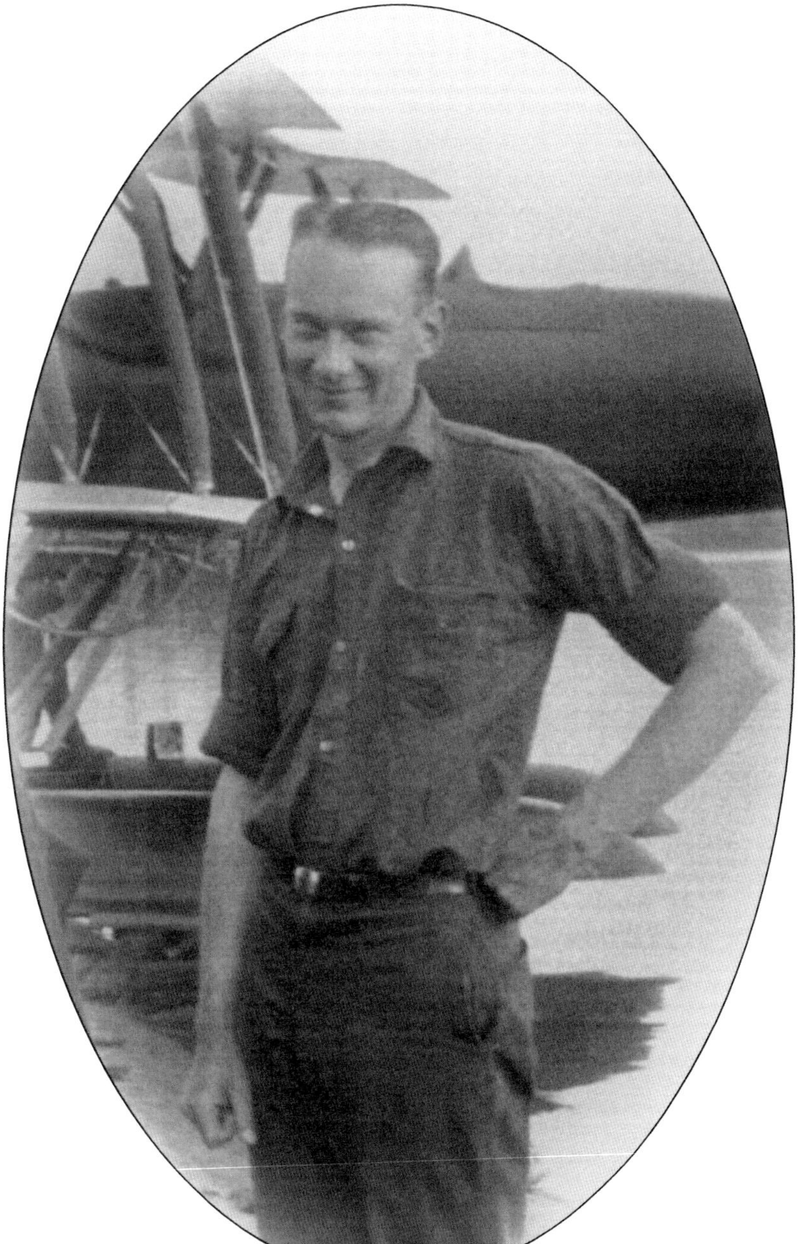

Russel Merrill received his flight instruction while enlisted in the US Navy Reserve. He was in the Naval Flying Corps from 1917 to 1921. After receiving a bachelor's of science in chemistry from Cornell University, he rejoined the corps from 1922 to 1925. Merrill and Roy J. Davis piloted Davis's Curtiss flying boat on the first flight across the Gulf of Alaska. The craft became the first airplane to arrive in Anchorage. Local investors formed Anchorage Air Transport in 1927, and Merrill was hired as chief pilot. He is credited with the discovery of what is now known as Merrill Pass. He left Anchorage alone on September 16, 1929, in a Whirlwind Travel Air bound for Akiak village and was never heard from again. Merrill was inducted into the Alaska Aviation Museum Hall of Fame in 2007. (Courtesy of the Alaska Aviation Museum.)

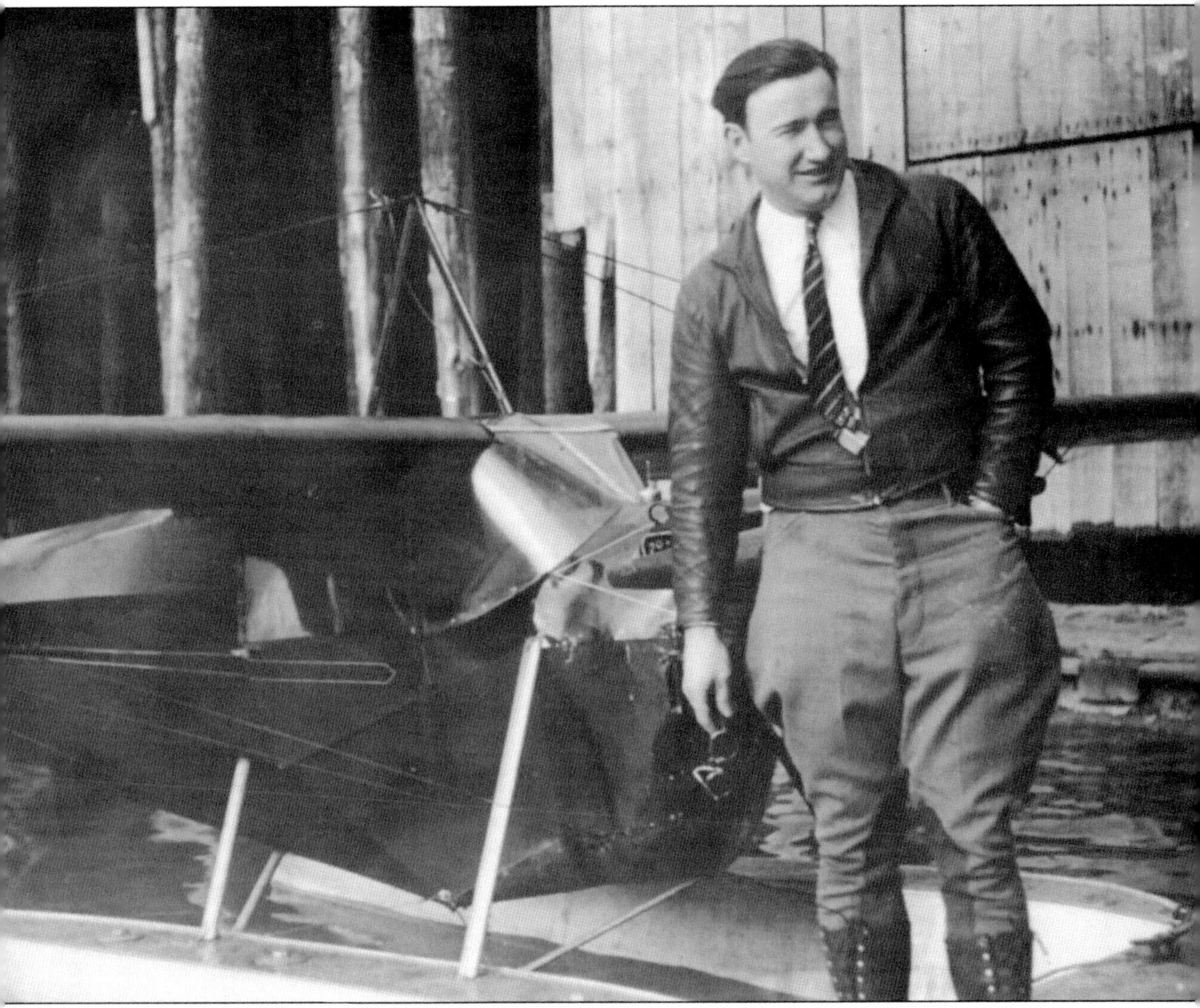

In 1929, Sheldon Simmons went to Yakima, Washington, and learned to fly at a school run by John L. Seawall, a World War I pilot. Simmons returned to southeast Alaska and, after several failed attempts at air service involving the only Curtiss Jenny on floats and an open-cockpit Aero-Marine Klem, started Alaska Air Transport in 1935. Simmons joined Alex Holden's Marine Airways in 1939 to form Alaska Coastal Airlines, which joined with Ellis Airlines in 1965 to form Alaska Coastal–Ellis Airlines. This company became part of Alaska Airlines in 1968. Simmons became a director emeritus of Alaska Airlines in 1981. Born on October 8, 1908, in Clearwater County, Idaho, he grew up in Grandview, Washington. Simmons died on November 16, 1994, in Juneau. He was inducted into the Alaska Hall of Fame on February 18, 2010, and the Alaska Aviation Museum Hall of Fame in 2010. (Courtesy of the Alaska Aviation Museum.)

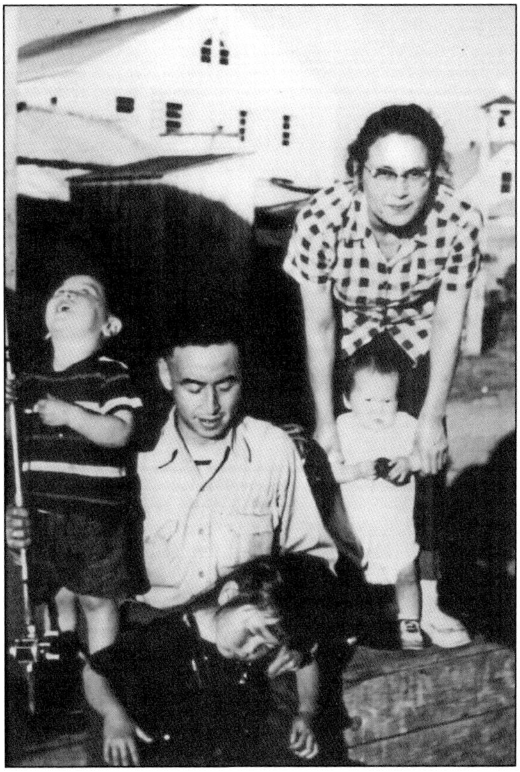

Operating one of the first Alaska Native–owned aviation businesses from Unalakleet, Wilfred Ryan Sr. and his wife, Eva, prospered by servicing the villages of the Bering Straits. Unalakleet Air Taxi was founded in 1953, when Wilfred Ryan Sr. begins regular charter flights across Alaska. He flew all the flights for his popular air service with assistance from Eva. In 1960, Unalakleet Air hired its first pilot and began handling Alaska mail delivery between Unalakleet, St. Michael, Stebbins, and other communities along the lower Yukon River. In 1977, Wilfred Ryan Sr. died of cancer. His son, Wilfred P. Ryan Jr., known to friends and associates as "Boyuck," took over the family business, which operates to this day as Ryan Air. Eva Ryan continues to live in Unalakleet where she enjoys hunting and fishing in nearby spots. The Ryans were inducted into the Alaska Aviation Museum Hall of Fame on March 22, 2012.(Both, courtesy of the Alaska Aviation Museum.)

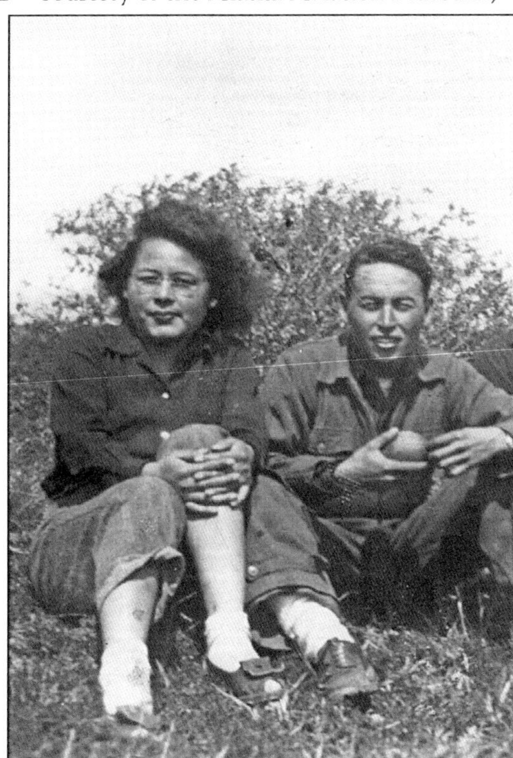

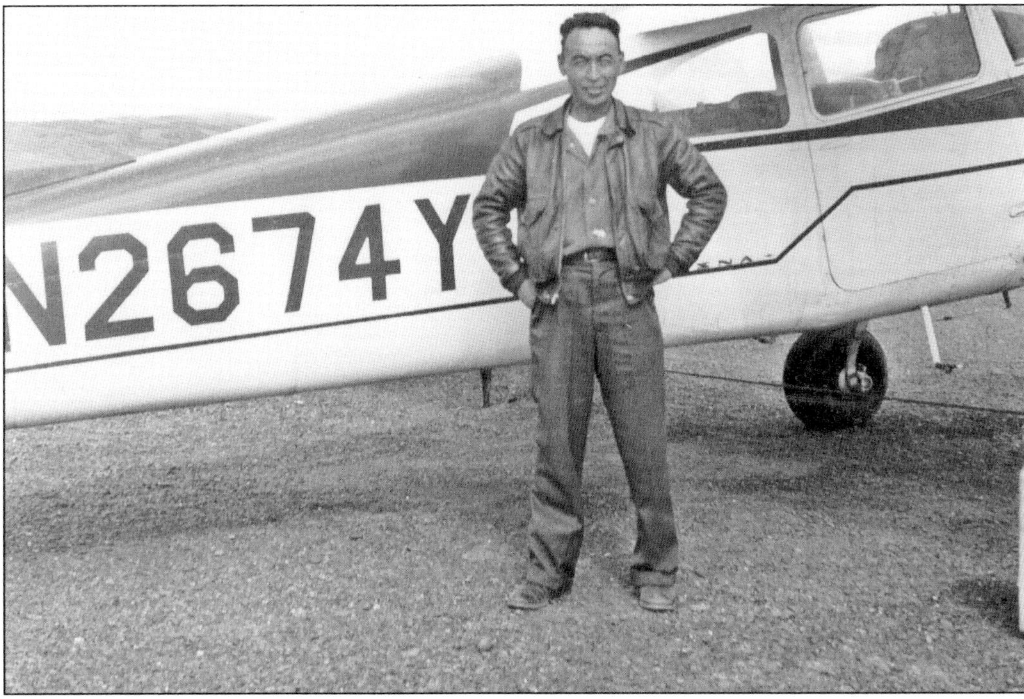

Pictured here is Wilfred Ryan Sr. in his piloting days. (Courtesy of the Alaska Aviation Museum.)

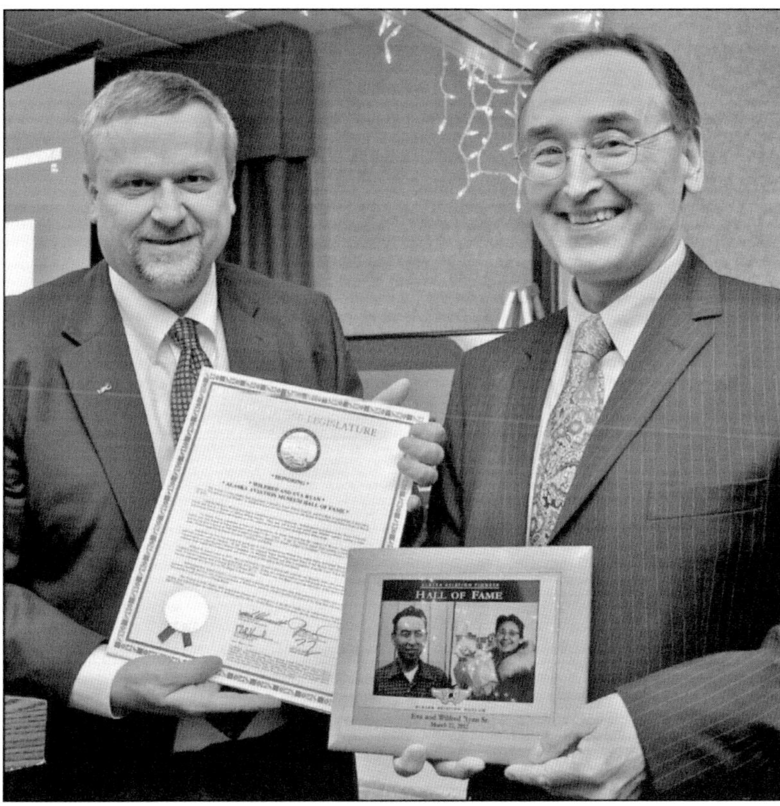

Pictured is Dave Karp (left), former board president of the Alaska Aviation Museum and chief executive officer of NAC with Wilfred "Boyuck" Ryan (right) when Eva and Wilfred Ryan Sr. were inducted into the Alaska Aviation Museum Hall of Fame. (Photograph by Rob Stapleton.)

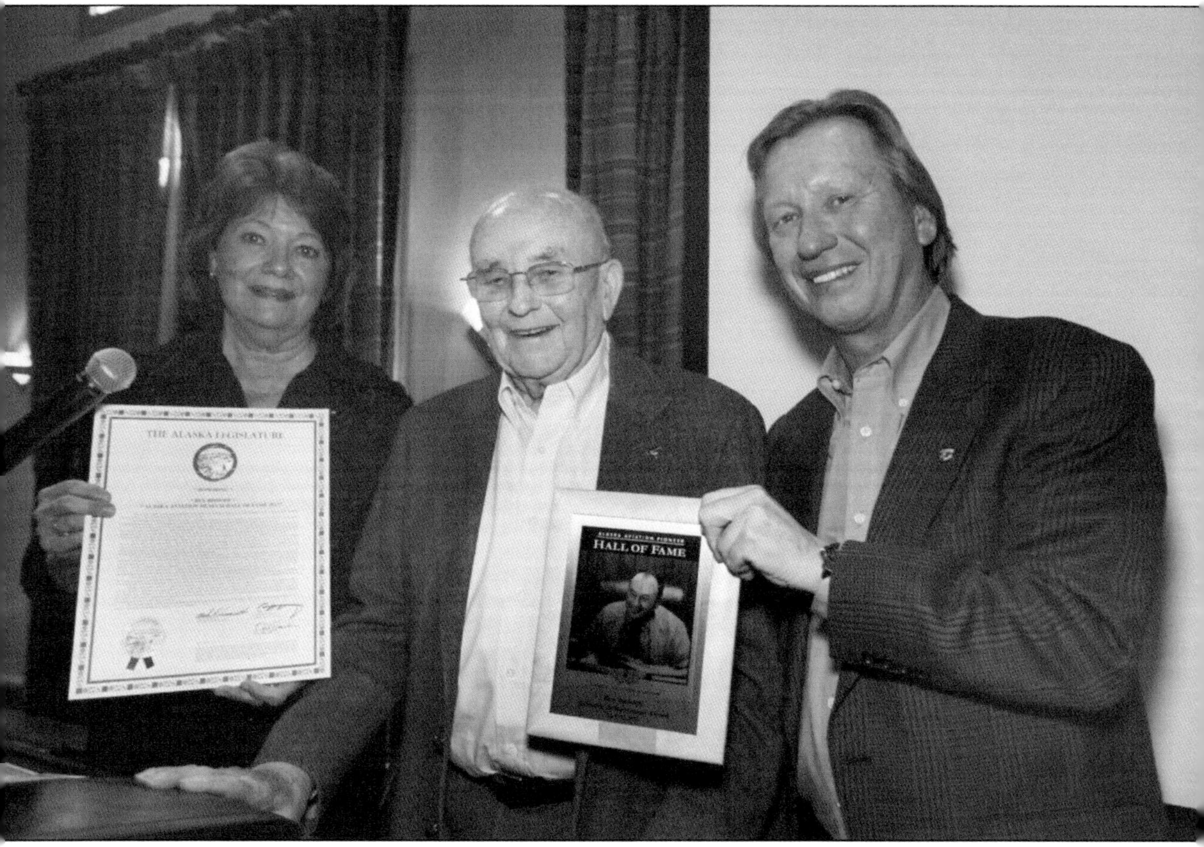

Rex Bishopp was instrumental in starting rotor wing operations in Alaska in the late 1950s, and he eventually purchased Alaska Helicopters. He was also instrumental in creating the Alaska Air Carriers Association in 1966 and a founding member of the Alaska Aviation Safety Foundation. In 1987, in recognition of his selfless leadership in aviation safety and his formation of the Alaska Air Carriers Association, Bishopp was awarded the Arlo Livingston Award by the Alaska Air Carriers Association, which represents over 300 aviation companies. Rex and his wife, Ruth, sold the business in 1995 and retired. He was inducted into the Alaska Aviation Museum Hall of Fame in 2013. (Courtesy of the Alaska Aviation Museum.)

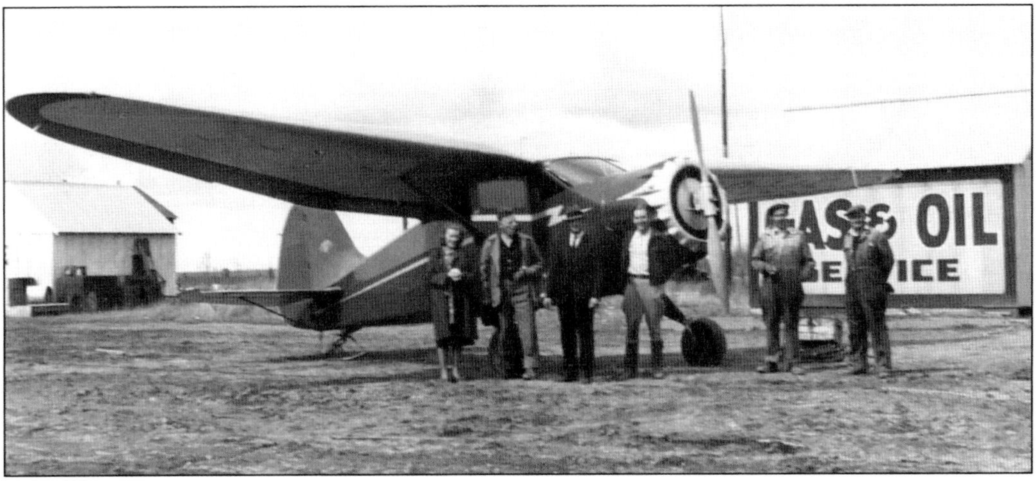

Used in interior and western Alaska, the Stinson SR-9 came to Alaska directly from the manufacturer. This Reliant was initially owned by Bill Lavery of Lavery Airways, based in Fairbanks, and was eventually owned by Albert Ball and Alaska Airlines. The Reliant was also used by Munz Airways in Nome, where it was in service until the late 1940s. (Courtesy of the Alaska Aviation Museum.)

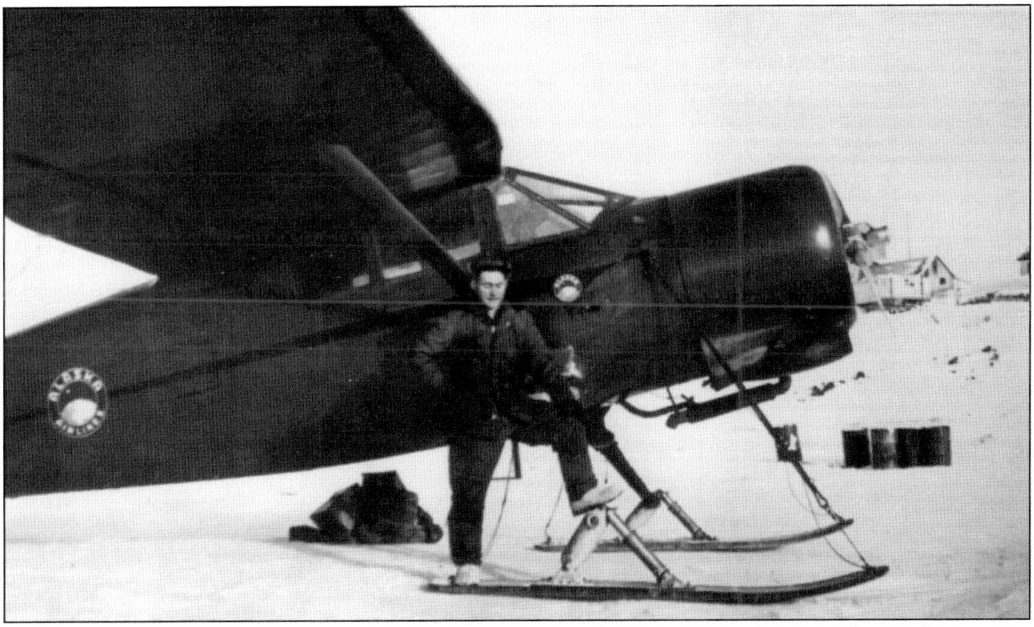

Many of this Stinson aircraft model were used by postwar bush carriers. The aircraft was also used by Alaska Airlines for early Alaska passenger service. (Courtesy of the Alaska Aviation Museum.)

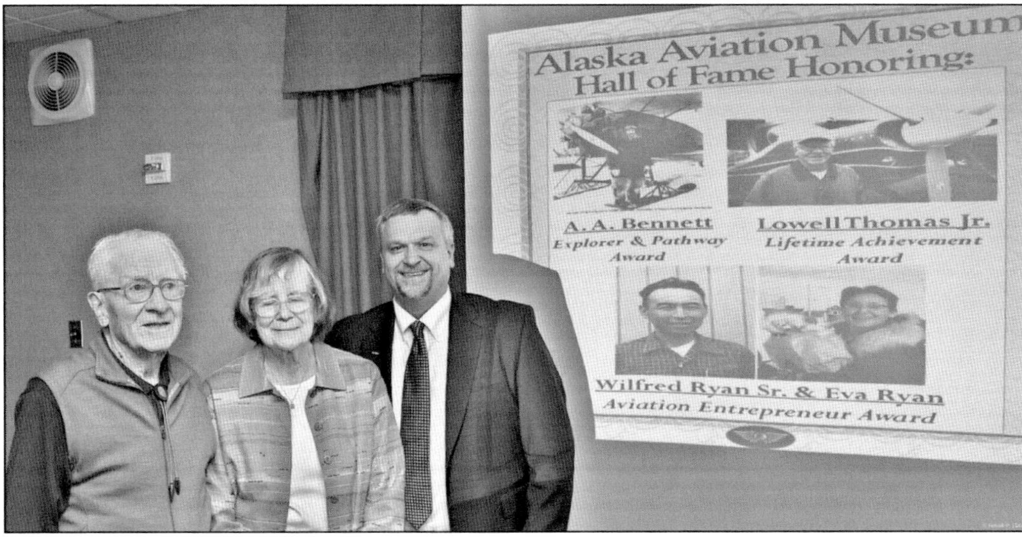

Every year, the Alaska Aviation Museum Hall of Fame honors aviators who have been key to developing and growing aviation in Alaska. The event, a sit-down dinner, honors each aviator entering the hall of fame that year and tells his or her aviation story. To attend this event, reservations must be made in advance with the museum. Commonly, this event has been held in Anchorage, although in 2013, the museum did host the event in Fairbanks, as pictured here. Shown here is the inductee ceremony honoring Lowell Thomas Jr. He is a bush and glacier pilot, a mountaineer, a film producer, and author of several books. A former Alaskan state senator, Thomas became the fifth lieutenant governor of Alaska (1974–1978). He owned and operated Talkeetna Air Taxi in the 1980s. He is an active conservationist and recipient of the Alaska Conservation Foundation's Award for Outstanding Civil Service. Thomas donated his Helio Courier aircraft, used for many of his mountain flights and ski adventures, to the Alaska Aviation Museum, where it is on display. *Flight to Adventure: Alaska and Beyond*, a book of Thomas's adventures, was published in 2013. (Both, courtesy of the Alaska Aviation Museum.)

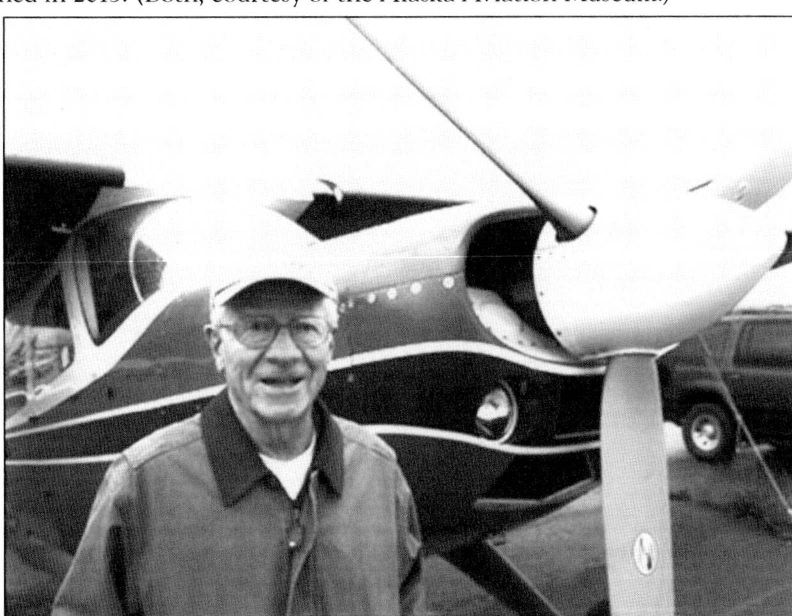

* HONORING *

* EDWARD B. "ED" RASMUSON *
* ALASKA AVIATION MUSEUM HALL OF FAME *

The Twenty-seventh Alaska State Legislature is proud to honor philanthropist Ed Rasmuson who will be inducted into the Alaska Aviation Museum's Hall of Fame on March 10, 2011, in recognition of his support and dedication with a "Lifetime Achievement Award for Outstanding Contribution to Aviation".

Ed Rasmuson is a third generation Alaskan whose roots go back to 1901 when his grandparents came to Alaska to serve as missionaries with the Swedish Covenant Church in Yakutat. From a young age, he was involved in the family banking business, National Bank of Alaska (NBA), working his way up from assistant cashier to chairman of the board. In 2001, NBA was sold to Wells Fargo Bank and Ed remains chairman of the Statewide Advisory Board. He also chairs the Rasmuson Foundation, which focuses on sustainable giving that promotes a better life for Alaskans throughout the state.

Early in his life, Ed became interested in aviation. He started flying at age 16 and got his pilot's license at age 17. When he was a young boy visiting the Museum of Flight in Seattle, he noticed that many of the great old airplanes that he had seen flying around Alaska were now being displayed in Seattle. He didn't think that was right and vowed at that time to do his part to help preserve Alaska's aviation heritage within Alaska.

The Rasmuson family became involved in the Alaska Aviation Museum shortly after its creation in 1986. They donated personal and corporate wealth to assist in the development and growth of the Museum and Ed donated considerable personal time. He also leveraged his influence with other private, corporate and government sector entities to bring support to the Museum.

Several major aircraft have been donated to the Museum by the Rasmusons and, over the years, major donations by them have been used to acquire and renovate hangar exhibit space and restore vintage aircraft. Without question, Ed's promise to help preserve Alaska's unique aviation history can be credited with helping to keep the Alaska Aviation Museum afloat and progressing. In recognition of his support, the Museum dedicated one of their major exhibit halls in his honor in 1994.

Contributions from Ed and the Rasmuson Foundation have enabled the Museum to completely restore the historic 1932 "American Pilgrim 100B" aircraft which came to Alaska in 1936 and is noted on the National Register as an American historic structure. This project is anticipated to be completed in April 2011.

Mr. Rasmuson is an active, involved philanthropist and community supporter. He continues to participate with a wide variety of organizations and educational entities, providing incredible resources throughout Alaska. The Aviation Museum greatly appreciates a young boy's dream to make sure that those great old airplanes that were responsible for opening up Alaska, had a place in Alaska to be preserved and available for future generations to see, experience and build their own dreams upon. This award and recognition is truly well-earned and well-deserved.

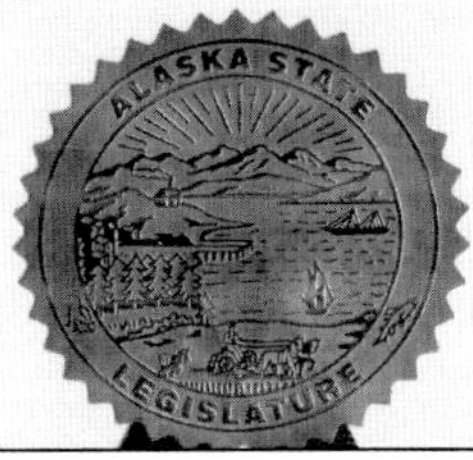

MIKE CHENAULT
SPEAKER OF THE HOUSE

GARY STEVENS
PRESIDENT OF THE SENATE

REP. MIKE HAWKER
PRIME SPONSOR

Date: February 18, 2011

This is the Alaska Aviation Museum Hall of Fame Certificate awarded to inductee Ed Rasmuson. It tells quite a story of a lifetime and a family devoted to aviation in Alaska. (Courtesy of the Alaska Aviation Museum.)

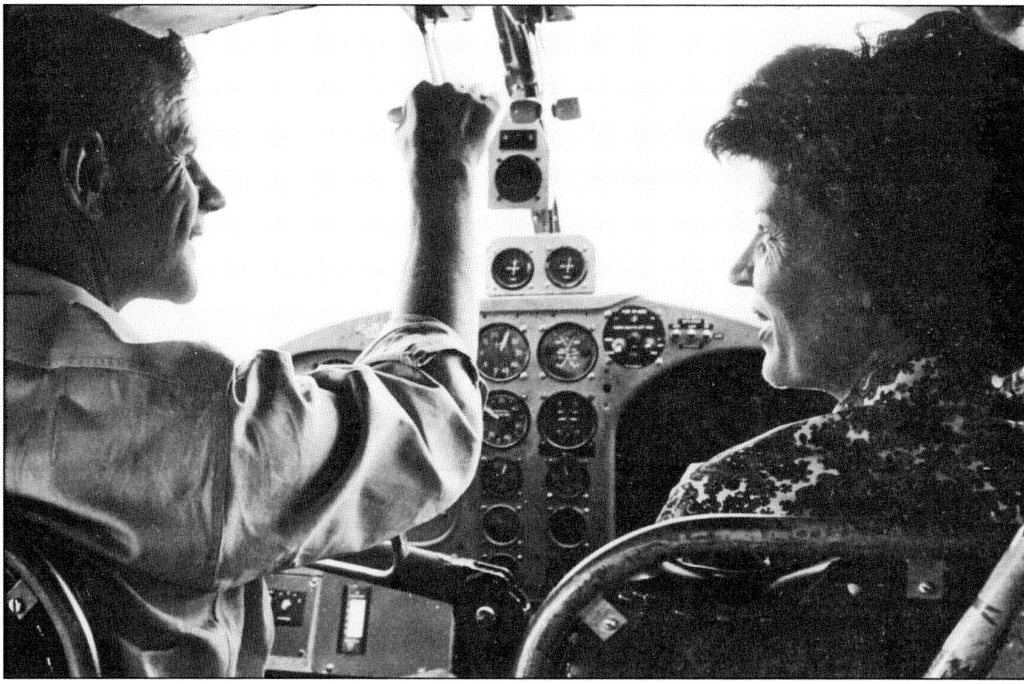

In 1946, Jim, who was working as an instructor for the Air Corps at Maxwell Field in Alabama, and Dottie, who was working as a secretary at the base, met and were married. Immediately after the wedding, the Magoffins headed north, driving the new Alaska Highway to Ester. Jim soon found work as a flight instructor for Fairbanks Air Service. Both Jim and Dottie dreamed of having their own aviation business, cashing in their World War II bonds to buy their first airplane—a Taylorcraft BC-12D. They founded Interior Airways and for decades provided service to the interior regions of Alaska. The Magoffins donated two of their aircraft to the Alaska Aviation Museum—a 1944 Noorduyn Norseman (used as a troop transport during World War II) and a 1943 Grumman Super Widgeon, which was their personal and favorite aircraft. The Magoffins were inducted in the Alaska Aviation Museum Hall of Fame in 2013. (Courtesy of the Alaska Aviation Museum.)

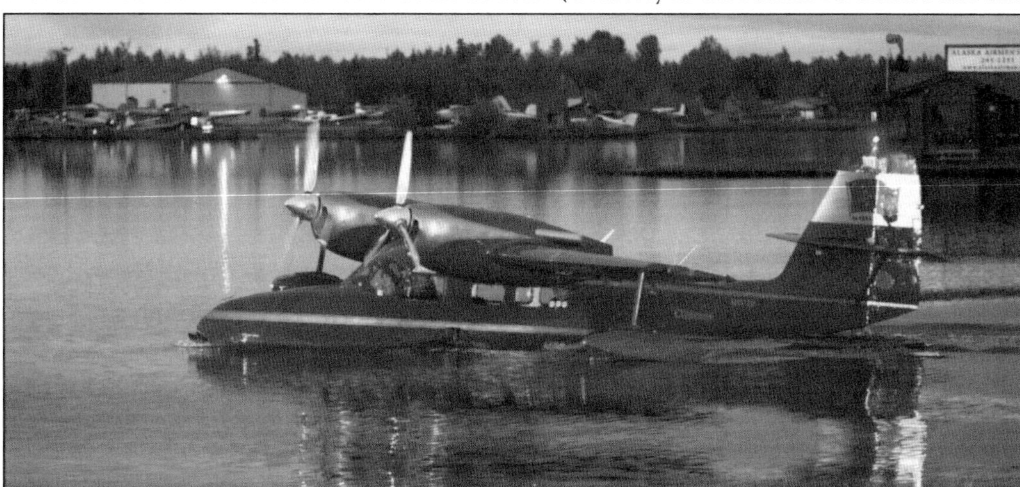

The Alaska Aviation Museum's Grumman Widgeon taxis back to the ramp after an evening flight. (Photograph by Rob Stapleton.)

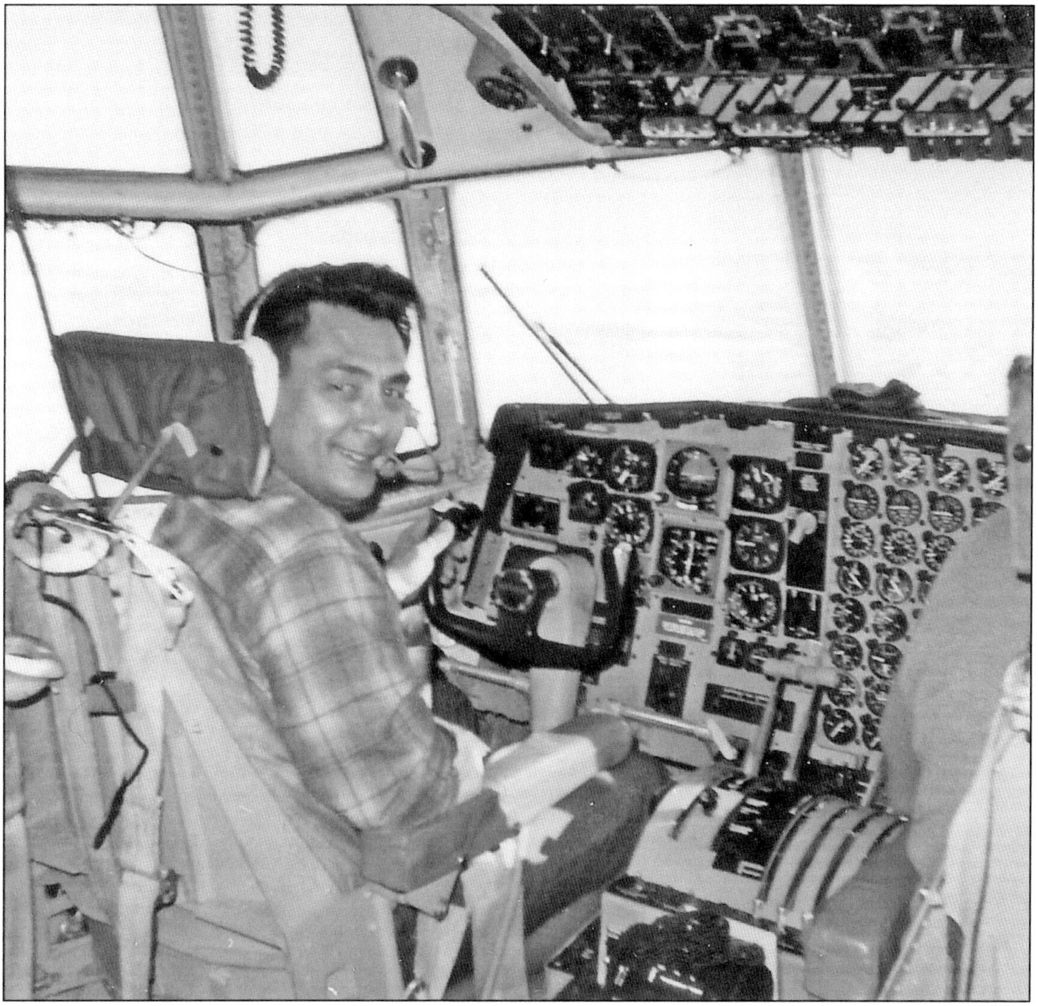

Jorgy Jorgensen was one of the first Alaska Natives to obtain an air transport rating. He is seen here at the controls of a Hercules cargo aircraft used for hauling equipment to build the Trans-Alaska Pipeline. Jorgensen, born in Haycock on Dime Creek on the Seward Peninsula on January 26, 1927, recalled first seeing an airplane when he was six years old. "It was a sight to behold," said Jorgy. "Noel Wien arrived and the whole place came to see the plane land. At the time I didn't know what was more exciting the airplane or the way ole Noel was dressed, leather helmet, coat, pants and gloves and the goggles too. But I'll tell you this: I wanted to dress just like him." Jorgy would indeed one day fly for Wien Air Alaska, as well as Alaska International Air, Frontier Interior Airways, and others, as well as serving in the Alaska Territorial Guard with the Eskimo Scouts, made up of Alaska Natives during World War II. He later served as director of aviation for the State of Alaska Division of Aviation under Gov. Bill Egan. (Courtesy of the Jorgensen family collection.)

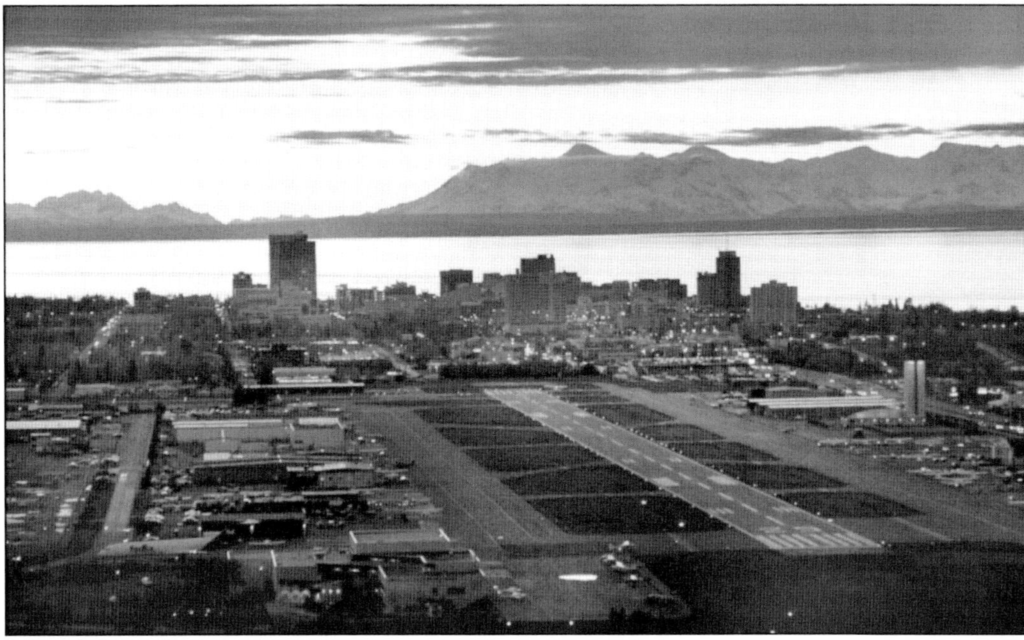

This aerial photograph, taken after sunset, shows the landing strip at Merrill Field in downtown Anchorage, Alaska. (Photograph by Rob Stapleton.)

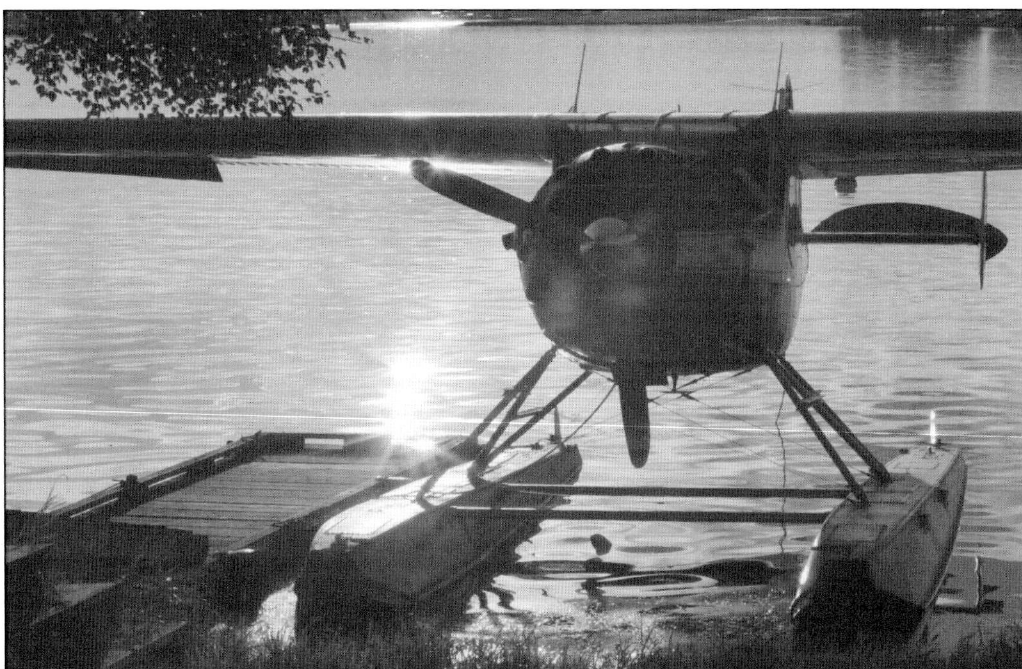

A Cessna 195 sits moored at Lake Hood Seaplane Base in Anchorage, Alaska. This Cessna Businessliner is owned by Kirk Garautte of Susitna Energy Systems. The aircraft is a conversation piece that sits outside the Millennium Hotel in Anchorage, where it can be seen in front of the outdoor patio and restaurant. (Photograph by Rob Stapleton.)

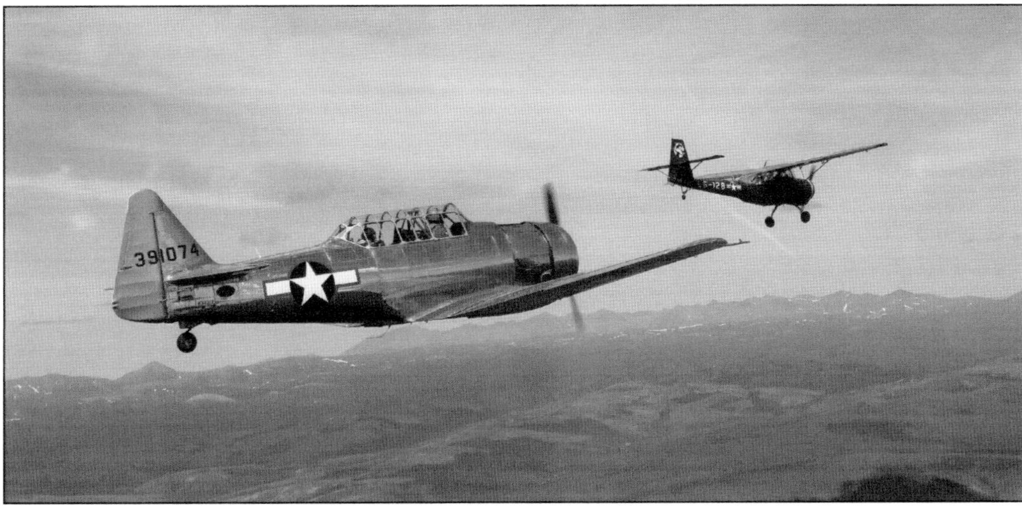

Chuck and Patti Miller, in the AT-6, gain on Ed Kornfield and Jane Dale, flying the L-13 Grasshopper, over the Kuskokwim Valley on the way to McGrath. These aircraft were only some of the rare planes that participated in the Alaska Aviation Centennial Celebration in the summer of 2013. This flight went from Bethel to Aniak and then to McGrath, where the aviators spent the night. The AT-6 and L-13, based at Merrill Field, can be seen flying just about anywhere in Alaska when the weather agrees. This photograph was shot from another North American AT-6 in formation, flown by Crickett Renner. (Photograph by Rob Stapleton.)

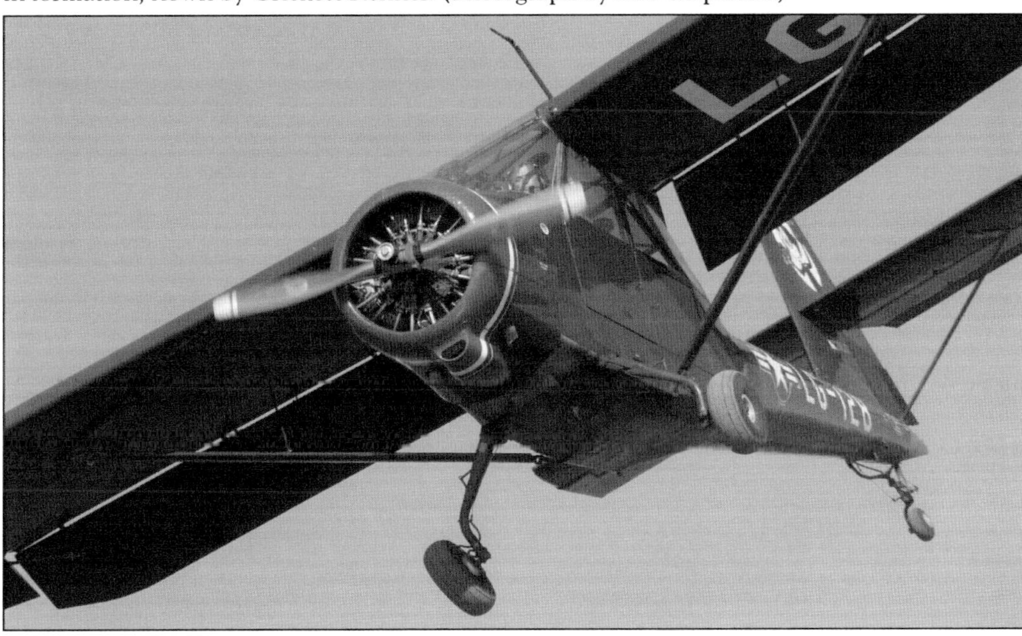

Chuck Miller pilots his Stinson L-13 in a slow turn over Lake Hood to demonstrate the slow-flight characteristics of this post–World War II military aircraft. Miller, owner of Chaz, Ltd., in Alaska, is the owner/operator of this aircraft and has used it to access hard-to-reach areas in Alaska, thanks to the plane's short-field takeoff and landing and slow-flight characteristics. Called the Grasshopper, the L-13 was designed by Stinson, then a subsidiary of Consolidated Vultee. It was mass-produced by Convair. This aircraft also participated in the Alaska Aviation Centennial Celebration, which visited locations statewide in 2013. (Photograph by Rob Stapleton.)

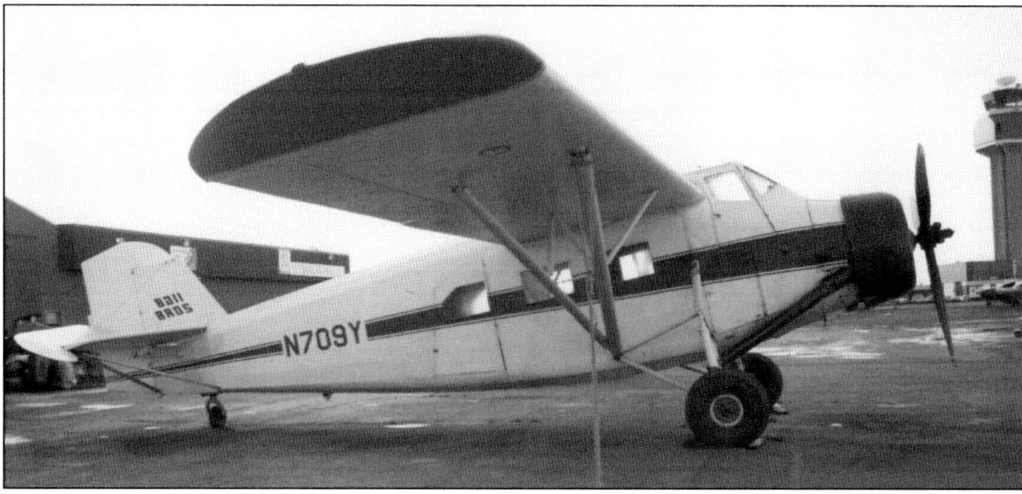

This Alaska Pilgrim was used by Ball Brothers to haul over one million pounds of salmon off of beaches at Bristol Bay and western Alaska. The 1931 Fairchild Pilgrim as it looked when owned by the Ball brothers is shown here in the 1980s at Ted Stevens Anchorage International Airport before being refurbished by the Alaska Aviation Museum. (Courtesy of the Alaska Aviation Museum.)

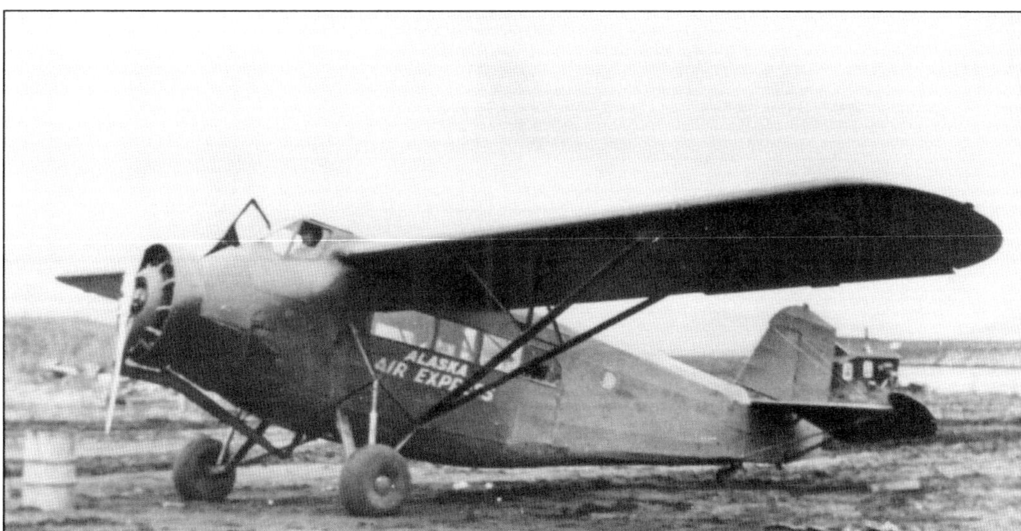

N709Y saw many different uses in its tenure as a bush aircraft. It is shown here during its time with Alaska Air Express. (Courtesy of the Alaska Aviation Museum.)

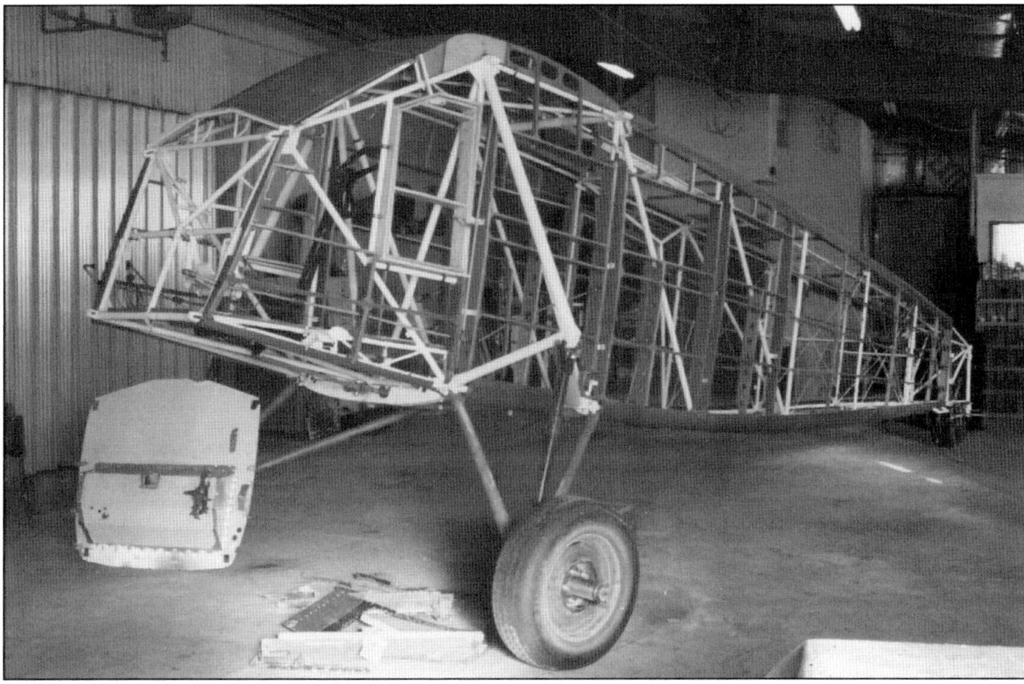

Pictured here is the Pilgrim very early in the refurbishing process. The aircraft fell out of airworthiness and was retired in 1985 due to fish slime and seawater corrosion that ate away at the floorboard and belly stringers. (Courtesy of the Alaska Aviation Museum.)

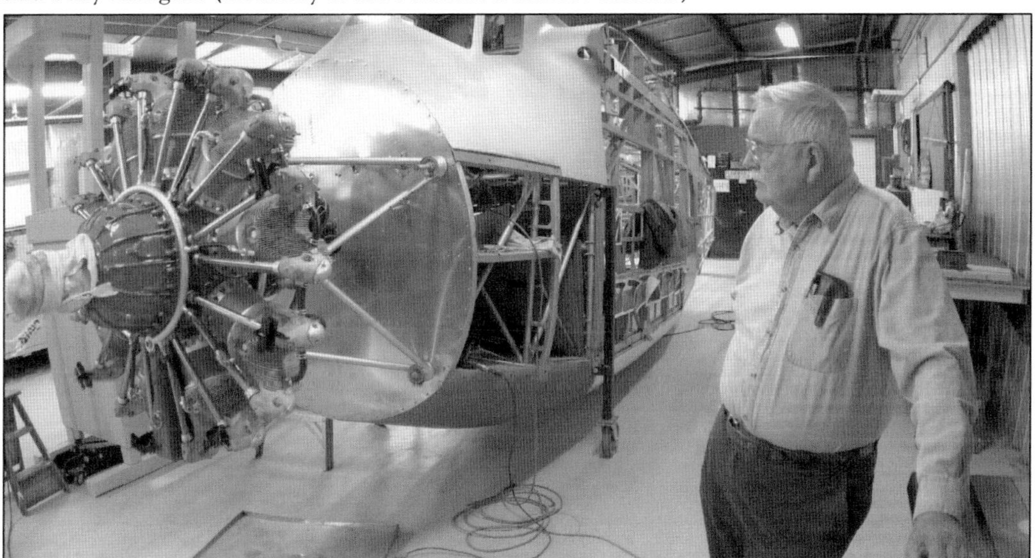

Museum volunteer George Dorman right, reflects on the rebuilding of the Pilgrim after nearly 10 years from when the project started. The Fairchild-built tube, wood, and fabric aircraft has been meticulously restored to as near its original condition as possible. "With the exception of the engine, this aircraft is as it was intended to be; a nine-passenger carrying aircraft in the main enclosed cabin with the pilot sitting behind the engine in a separate cockpit compartment," said Chuck Miller, who acted as the project manager for the finishing of the project. (Photograph by Rob Stapleton.)

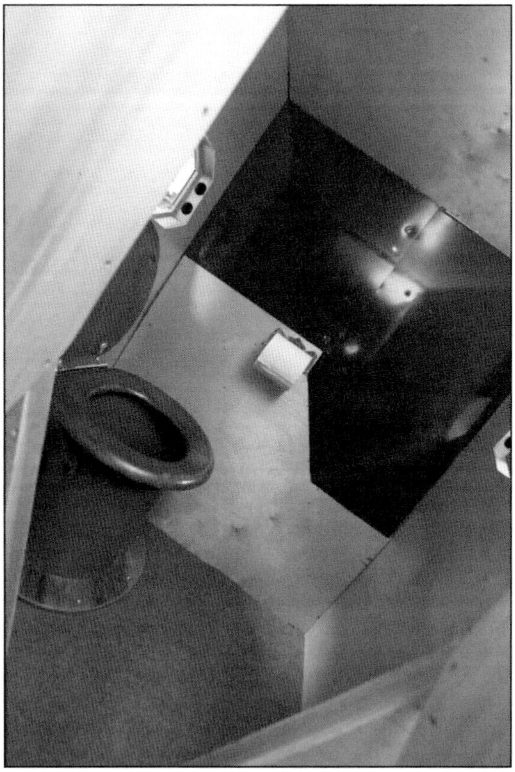

The Alaska Aviation Museum initially received a grant from the State of Alaska in 2002 to start the refurbishing project. Every detail, including even the toilet bucket, conforms to its original state. (Photograph by Rob Stapleton.)

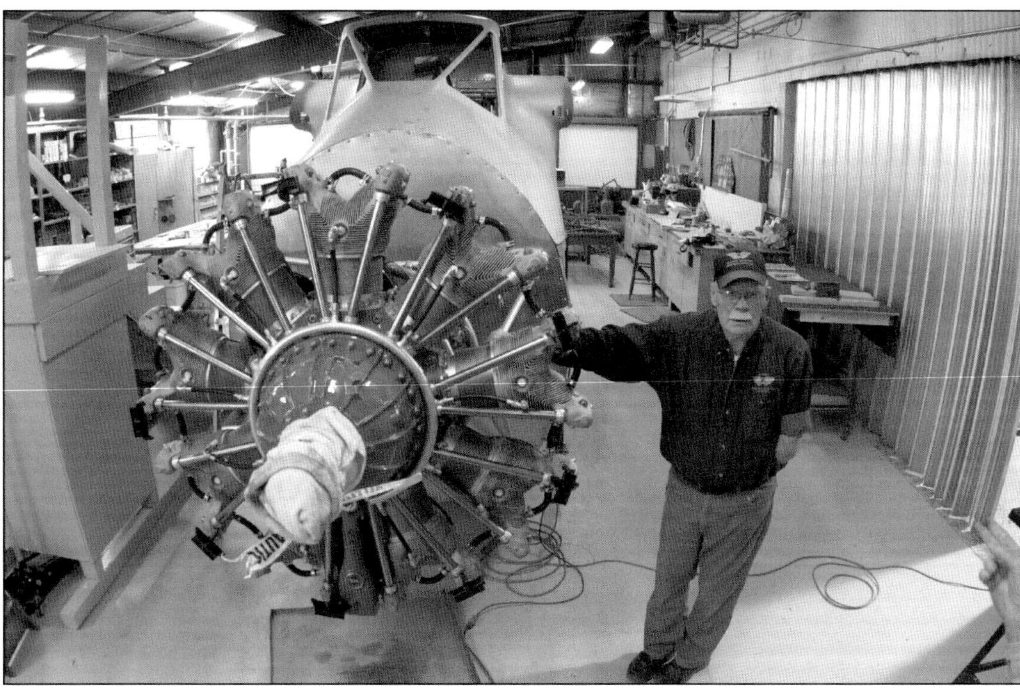

The refurbishing of the 1931 Fairchild Pilgrim at the Alaska Aviation Museum is now finished. Al Fleener is seen here with the massive Pratt & Whitney powerplant during the final years of the project. (Photograph by Rob Stapleton.)

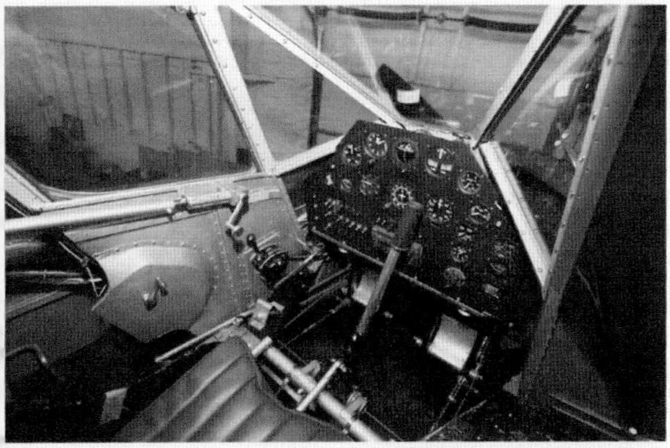

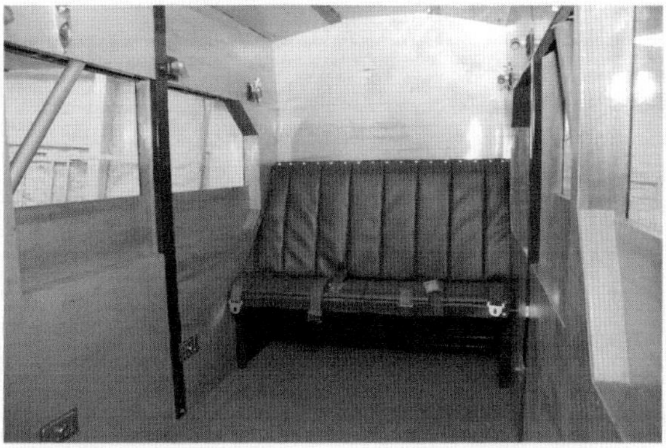

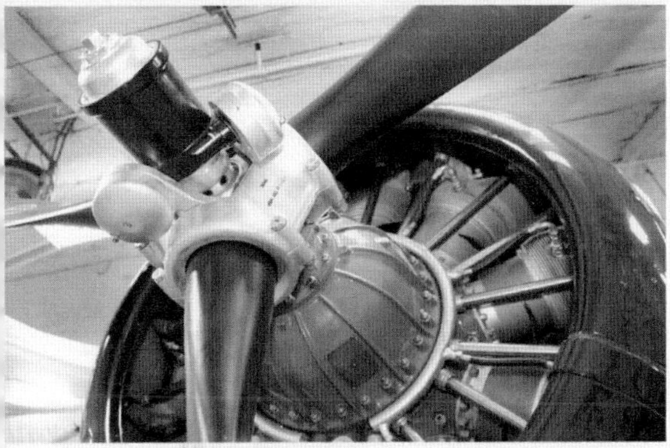

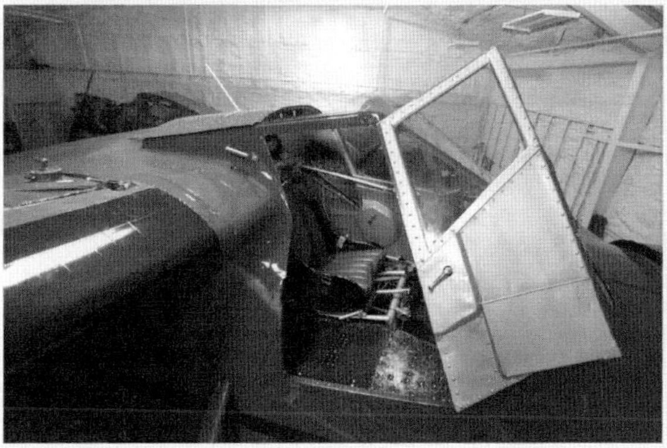

The 10-year restoration project was an on-and-off process. It received an infusion of capital from Ed Rasmuson. During this period, the museum has seen two different executive directors and major changes to its board of directors. "We are especially grateful to the Rasmuson Foundation for its support of this ongoing project over the past years," said Shari Hart. "This aircraft is key to the museum's mission statement and to the history of Alaska Aviation." The interior of the aircraft, seen in this series of photographs, is finished with special birch plywood, which was supported by a donation from Experimental Aircraft Association's Chapter 42. (Photographs by Rob Stapleton.)

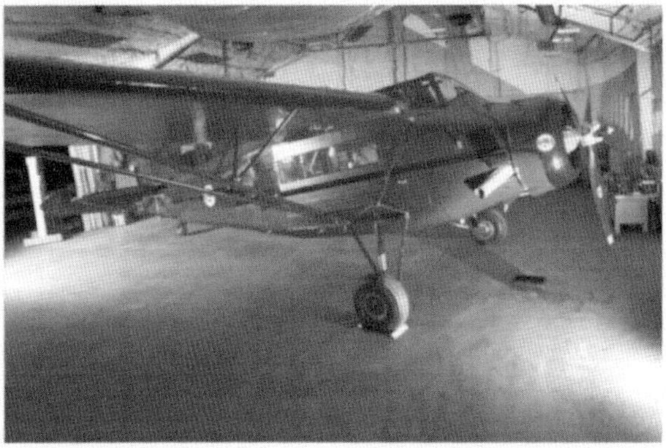

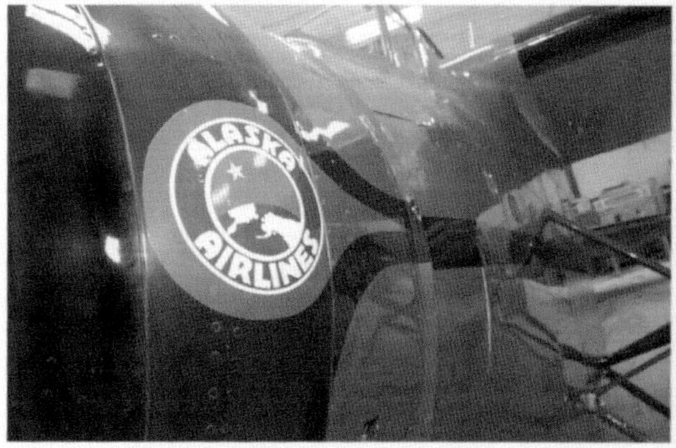

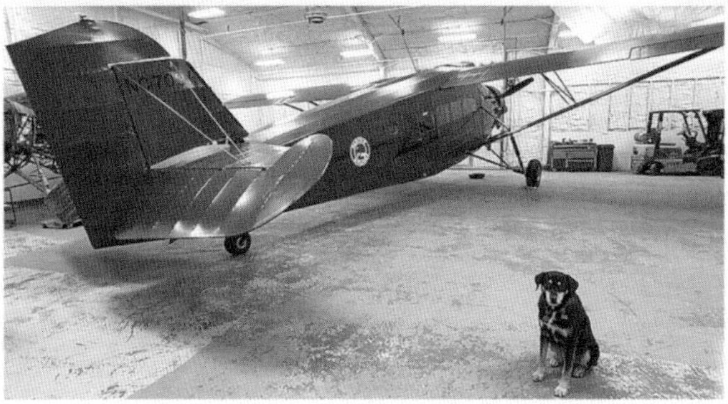

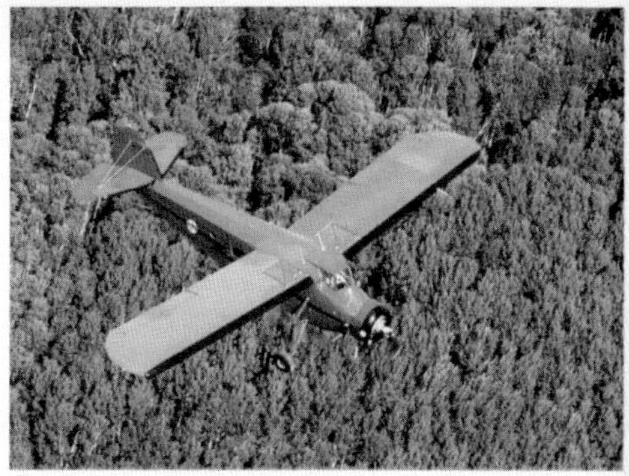

The Pilgrim project moved along more rapidly after Chuck Miller of Chaz, Ltd., came to the rescue as its project manager. "It just needed some leadership, the people working on it were all volunteers and were doing a fine job. They just needed someone to help organize what was left to do, and when it needed to get done," said Miller. Employees of Chaz, Ltd., an auto-repair corporation, gave the Fairchild's metal parts several coats of a red paint matching the fabric color. A key to accomplishing the final steps came when Terry Holliday of Holiday Air at Birchwood Airport came to the rescue and offered to help with completing the fabric covering of the fuselage. (Photographs by Rob Stapleton.)

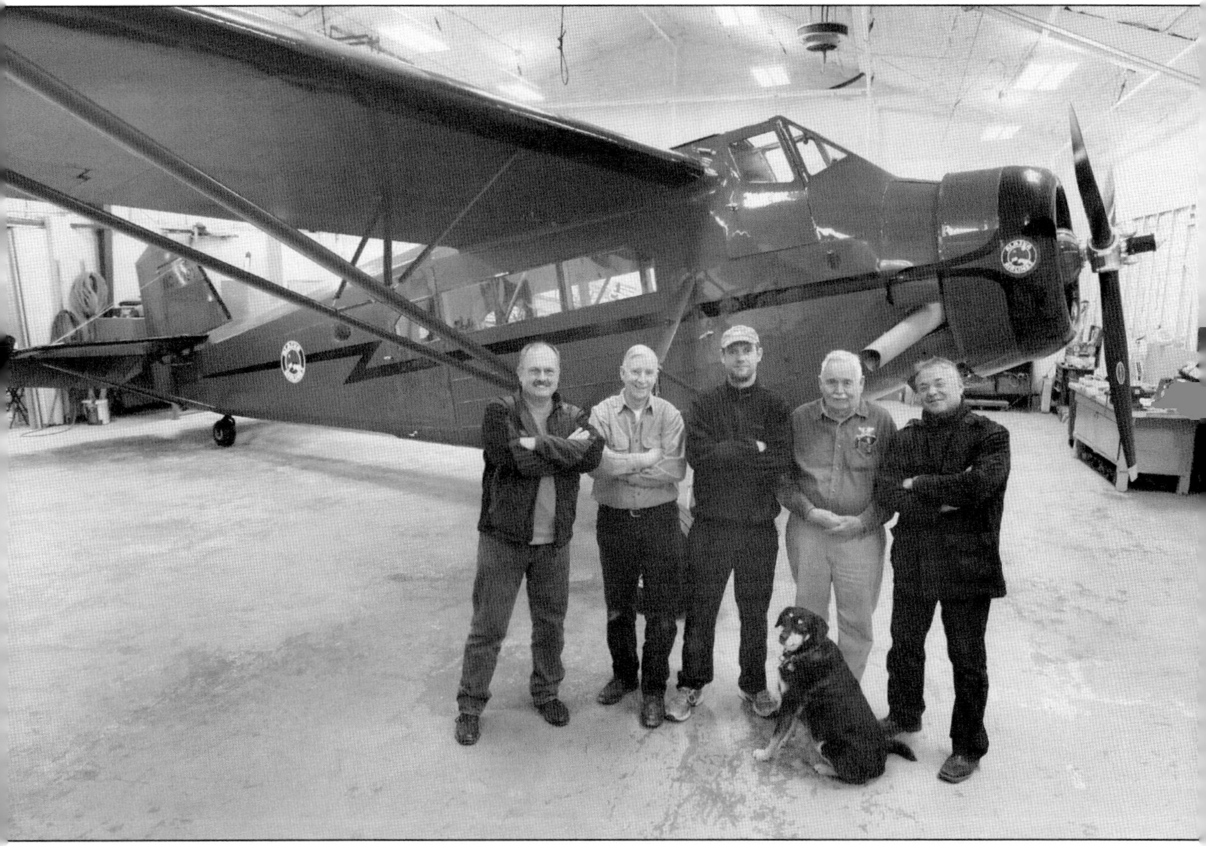

This 1931 Fairchild American Pilgrim 100B NC709Y is one of only four aircraft listed in the National Register of Historic Places. Today, the red-and-black aircraft is reminiscent of the golden era of aviation, with its three-bladed Hamilton Standard propeller mounted on a Pratt & Whitney R1340 Wasp, a 550-horsepower radial engine. It was originally fitted with the less-reliable Wright Cyclone R-1820F-31 engine. Shown here is the final crew that assembled the renovation of the Pilgrim; from left to right are Terry Symonds, Lee Clausen, Dick Benner, George Dorman, Chuck Miller, and the hangar dog Tucker. (Photograph by Rob Stapleton.)

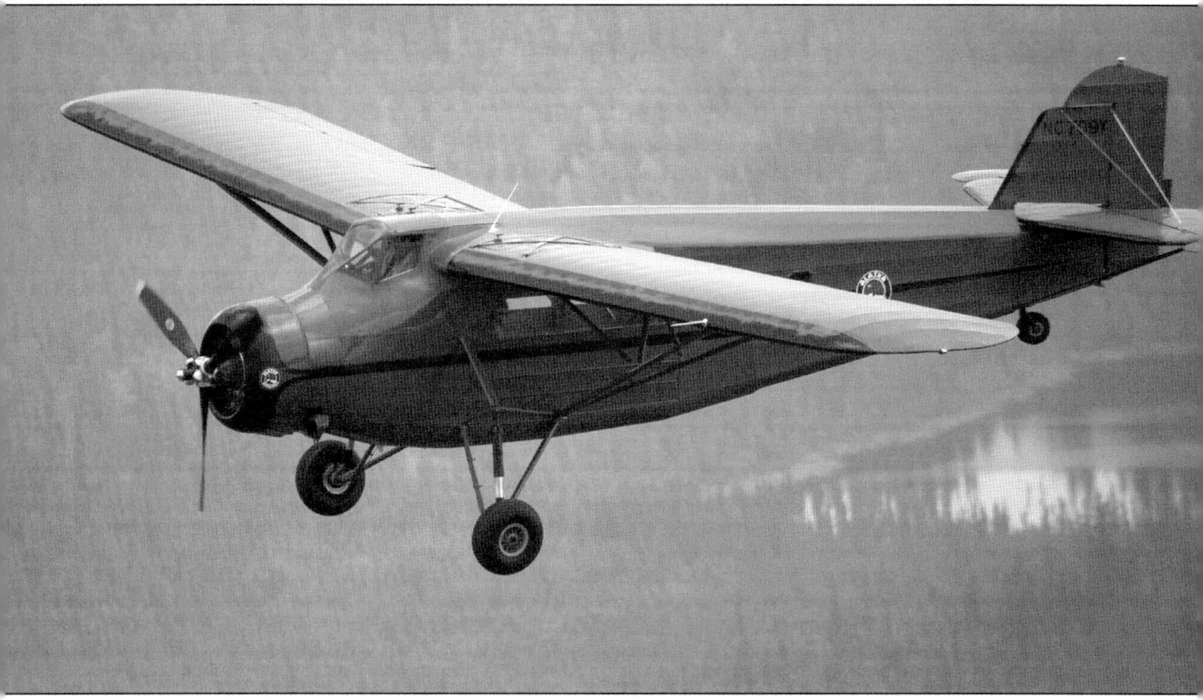

Features of the aircraft include a movable horizontal stabilizer, used to trim the aircraft, allowing the plane to lift its 7,700 pounds into the skies above Alaska. With a cockpit above and behind the engine, separate from the passenger compartment, the pilot used a longer than standard control stick for the ailerons and elevators. The aircraft's sturdy main landing gear and tail wheel allowed landings on rough airfields and at off-airport locations. While many Fairchild Americans were flown by American Airways in the Lower 48, this aircraft was also used for Alaska Air Express by Herb Nicholson and Murrell Sasseen to deliver mail to the McGrath and Lower Kuskokwim areas in the 1930s. It was purchased by Star Airlines in 1940 for passenger service by Alaska Airlines and other air services. The aircraft was then purchased by Ball Brothers for fish hauling. (Photograph by Rob Stapleton.)

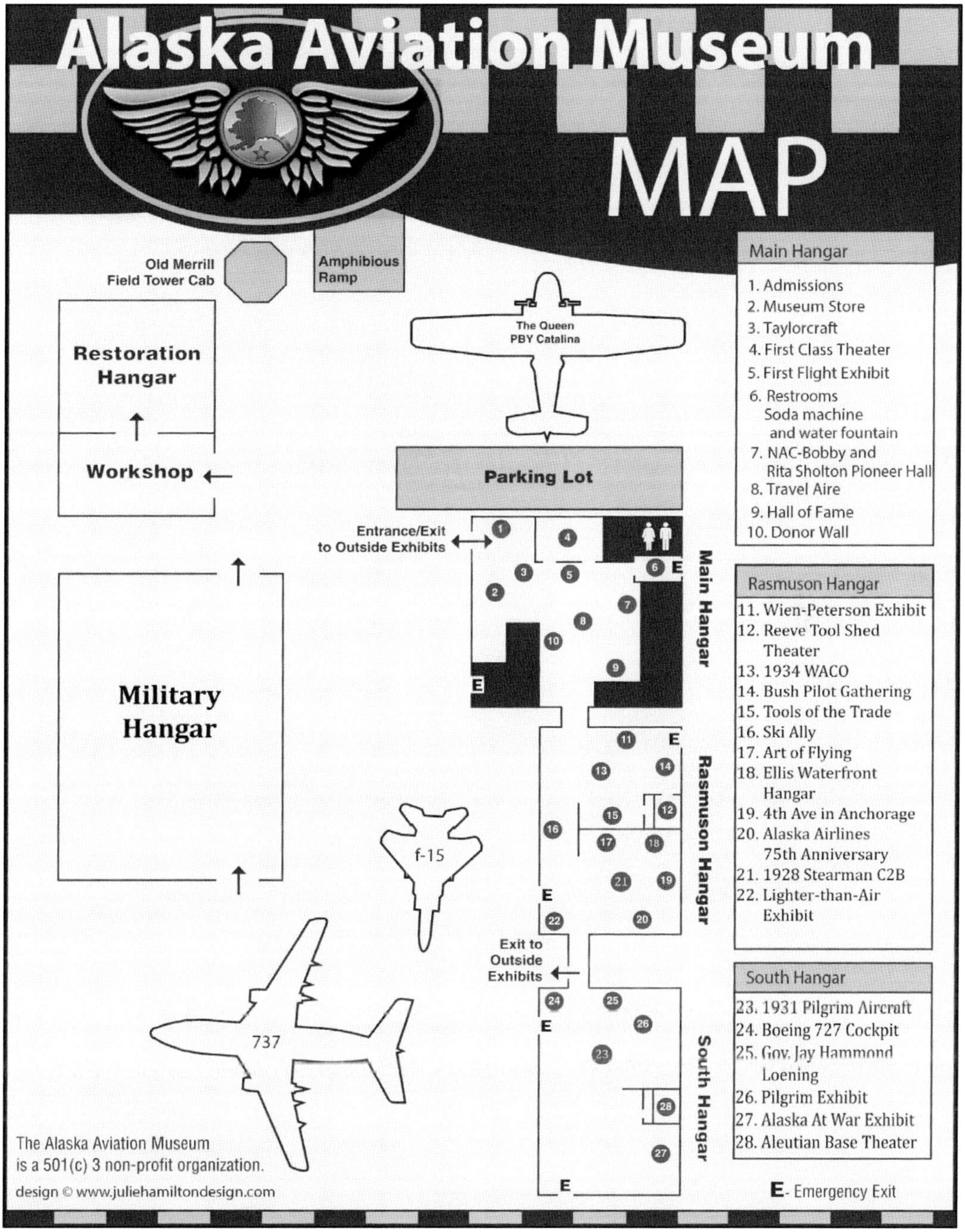

This is a detailed map of the Alaska Aviation Museum. As a small nonprofit institution, the museum relies on volunteers to help the museum grow and improve. The museum staff greatly appreciates all of the volunteers and is always excited to have more volunteers around to help out. Anyone interested in helping out at the museum can either stop by the museum and pick up a volunteer form to fill out or print out the form and either email it to director@alaskaairmuseum.org or bring it by! (Courtesy of the Alaska Aviation Museum.)

Discover Thousands of Local History Books Featuring Millions of Vintage Images

Arcadia Publishing, the leading local history publisher in the United States, is committed to making history accessible and meaningful through publishing books that celebrate and preserve the heritage of America's people and places.

Find more books like this at
www.arcadiapublishing.com

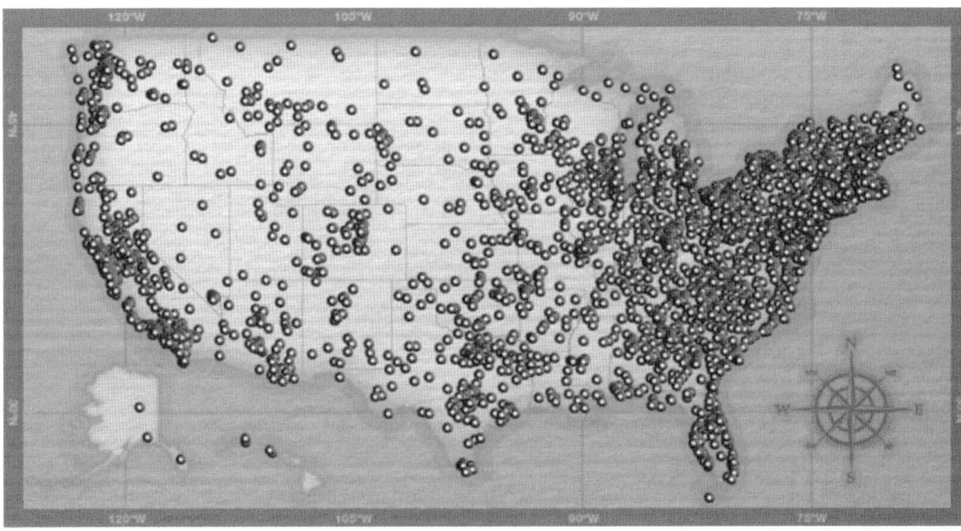

Search for your hometown history, your old stomping grounds, and even your favorite sports team.

Consistent with our mission to preserve history on a local level, this book was printed in South Carolina on American-made paper and manufactured entirely in the United States. Products carrying the accredited Forest Stewardship Council (FSC) label are printed on 100 percent FSC-certified paper.

MADE IN THE USA